CONTENTS

ACKNOWLEDGMENTS

Many thanks to everyone at Peace News Press, especially Milan Rai and Gabriel Carlyle, for considering my book proposal, deciding to publish it and working hard to finalise the book you now hold in your hands. The Lipman-Miliband Trust kindly provided a grant to assist with publication. Several people have provided me with much needed encouragement and counsel during the more than three years I worked on the book including Denise, Emilie, Hannah, Jamie, Lindesay and Russ. Andrew, Harry, John and Phil at Lincoln were inspirational and knowledgeable teachers who continue to influence my thinking long after university. I would also like to thank my parents for helping to fund my higher education – which gave me time to think and read outside the formal curriculum I was there to study, and also for doing some much needed checking of the text. Finally, I would like to thank all the interviewees who generously gave their time to speak to me. – *Ian Sinclair*

Peace News Press acknowledges the generous support of the Lipman-Miliband Trust, and of our noble Kickstarter backers: David Alan Baker, Veronica R Ball, Katy Beinart, Ian Dixon, Fay Dowker, James Eagle, John Gardner, David Gribble, James Heaver, Tony Hodgson, John Horne, Huw, Helen Innes, Chris Jury, Thomas Kearney, Viv Kendon, Jonangus Mackay, Derek John Miller, Peter Offord, Luke Parks, David Pybus, Nigel Sinclair, Helen Sinclair, Robert Stuart, Vijay Varman, Martha Worsching and Peter Worth.

ACRONYMS

9/11	The terrorist attacks on the United States on 11 September 2001
ANL	Anti-Nazi League
ARROW	Active Resistance to the Roots of War
ASLEF	Associated Society of Locomotive Engineers and Firemen
BBC	British Broadcasting Corporation
CAAT	Campaign Against Arms Trade
CIA	Central Intelligence Agency
CND	Campaign for Nuclear Disarmament
CCTV	Closed Circuit Television
CWU	Communications Workers Union
EDO	EDO Corporation
ESF	European Social Forum
EU	European Union
FBU	Fire Brigades Union
G8	Group of Eight
GMB	General Municipal, Boilermakers and Allied Trade Union
IRA	Irish Republican Army
ITN	Independent Television News
LSE	London School of Economics and Political Science

MAB	Muslim Association of Britain
MCB	Muslim Council of Britain
MMR	Measles, Mumps and Rubella immunization shot
MoD	Ministry of Defence
MP	Member of Parliament
MTV	Music Television
NATFHE	National Association of Teachers in Further and Higher Education (in 2006 it merged with the Association of University Teachers to form the University and College Union)
NCCL	National Council for Civil Liberties (now known as Liberty)
NME	New Musical Express
NUJ	National Union of Journalists
NUM	National Union of Miners
NVDA	Nonviolent Direct Action
PCS	Public and Commercial Services Union
PPU	Peace Pledge Union
RAF	Royal Air Force
RMT	National Union of Rail, Maritime and Transport Workers
SWP	Socialist Workers Party
STW/STWC	Stop the War Coalition
UN	United Nations
UN SCR	United Nations Security Council Resolution
UNISON	Public sector trade union
USSR	Union of Soviet Socialist Republics
T&G/TGWU	Transport and General Workers' Union (in 2007 it merged with Amicus to form Unite)
TUC	Trades Union Congress
WMD	Weapons of Mass Destruction

PROLOGUE

"IT CHANGED ABSOLUTELY NOTHING" VS. "WE ACHIEVED A LOT, AND A HELL OF A LOT MORE THAN WE REALISE"

Carol Naughton, Campaign for Nuclear Disarmament Chair 2001–3: It took me about three days to come down from the march. Sunday, Monday and then bam! My adrenaline level just stopped. When it stops you get very, very down. And I did get down when the war actually started. We did other demos, but it was hard to do them. I found it very hard once the war had started to pick myself and say "You've still got a job to do. You've failed."

Ellie Mae O'Hagan, UK Uncut activist: The Stop the War march in 2003 was so huge and monumental and it did absolutely nothing.[1]

Michael Goldfarb, Author, on the *BBC News* website: Political marching, protest marching, call it what you will, has become in the new millennium a way of exercising one's ego... Political leaders tolerate marching but don't fear it. When more than a million and a half people marched through London in February 2003 to protest the impending war with Iraq, it changed absolutely nothing.[2]

Clive Bloom, Professor Emeritus, Middlesex University: I think it was a failure. I've had lots of arguments about this... [Tony] Blair's model as prime minister was Margaret Thatcher, not someone in the Labour Party. And I think that he was a conviction politician and he thought, even though he was elected, he was elected to make his own moral decisions: not elected to follow anyone else. And that's the traditional idea of parliament and politics – that you are elected but you make your own moral decisions. So in that respect, having taken that decision, nothing was going to sway him, absolutely nothing... So it wouldn't have mattered if everybody had got on the street. It wouldn't have changed his mind.

Greg Dyke, *BBC* Chairman 2000–4: It had no chance of success. Blair had decided long before the march he was going to war. He committed himself to war. And the only chance of success was whether he was defeated in the House of Commons. I don't think another million people on the march would have meant he was defeated. That's not to say it was wrong to march. It's just that it didn't have a chance of success.

Gabriel Carlyle, Peace Activist: There is a range of evidence to suggest that, whilst we didn't generate sufficient pressure to stop the war, we came much closer than we actually realised. So it wasn't that policymakers were completely impervious to what was going on outside: quite the opposite. I think that is important to recognise. I've heard countless people say "It had no effect at all, but we've got to keep on plugging away". But I don't think it was true.

Milan Rai, Activist, Author and Co-Editor of *Peace News*: The truth is rather different, though it is not transmitted through the mass media or recorded in the triumphalist instant history books. We were not ignored. The astonishing truth is that the combined efforts of anti-war movements around the world very nearly succeeded in detaching the British Government, and British military forces, from the US invasion of Iraq.[3]

Mike Marqusee, Press Officer, Stop the War Coalition: It is too early to assess the impact of not just that demonstration, but the whole wave of mass action and protest that led up to the war. Although we don't know the inner workings of the Government – we don't know the calculations they made – we do know that they did begin to take the anti-war movement quite seriously from September 2002 onwards. That is why they issued the dodgy dossier – it came three or four days before the [28] September [2003] demo. That was a response to the perceptible growth of the anti-war movement.

Milan Rai: If you look at the evidence you can see that the British Government was forced into a series of retreats. First of all the scale of the anti-war mobilisation was such – inside and outside the Labour Party – that Tony Blair had to make every effort to get a second resolution at the UN Security

Council. I don't think that was his natural inclination, but politically it became essential for him to try to do that. I'm sure that delayed the war. The US would rather not have waited for that process. So the fight came down to the Security Council in the first place.

Chris Nineham, Chief Steward, Stop the War Coalition: I don't think there was any doubt there were moments it was very, very knife edge. And obviously the protests and public opinion were the crucial elements in that.

Tony Blair, Prime Minister 1997–2006: At home in Downing Street, I was a bit of a zombie; eating meals distractedly; not hearing questions the kids asked; trying to keep family life normal but with all of them acutely aware it was all very abnormal, not least because of how I was behaving. I forced myself on occasions to relax and stop working, but the issue was like an incessant throbbing ache that wouldn't go away, wouldn't let you forget it for an instant, and didn't stop reminding you of the necessity of dealing with it.[4]

Cherie Blair, Barrister and wife of Tony Blair: Sometime in 2006, I was on *Radio 4*'s A Good Read, and for my book I chose *Saturday* by Ian McEwan, which takes place over twenty-four hours on 15 February 2003, the day of the big anti-war demonstration. The atmosphere he describes is very evocative to me… I remember so well being in the centre of a storm. Tony was now the pariah and there were anti-Blair slogans everywhere. The kids were badly affected. To see their father portrayed as 'B-LIAR' everytime they left the house was upsetting, to say the least.

We shielded them as much as we could but it was difficult. They couldn't be wrapped in cotton wool.[5]

Andrew Rawnsley, Journalist: Blair appeared wrecked. The official line was that he had a bad bout of the flu which he couldn't shake off. The reason he couldn't beat the flu was because he was so utterly shattered by anxiety over Iraq. "He wasn't sleeping," says [Blair's director of political and government relations] Sally Morgan. "He looked terrible."... A Cabinet minister noted: "He lost weight and became quite gaunt. You could see that he was under great strain. He was throwing all his authority at it and desperately trying to hold the thing together."[6]

Mark Thomas, Comedian and Activist, 20 March 2003 stand up show: He [Tony Blair] is the fucking point man for barbarity and murder. That fucking man is an evil pig dog. He opens his mouth and fucking words come out like Milli Vanilli never fucking went away. [Putting on a pompous questioner's voice] "Yes Mark, but what do you think the peace movement has achieved?" We've put ten years on that fucker, and that's enough. Ten years. Somewhere in Downing Street there is a portrait getting younger and that fucking suits me just fine.[7]

***Guardian*, 18 April 2003:** Tony Blair was ready to quit his job as prime minister if he had lost a crucial Commons vote [on 18 March 2003] over the war with Iraq, he revealed today. He said he had been ready to resign if he had been defeated in last month's vote authorising military action and disclosed that he had instructed officials to prepare for his resignation. "In the end, it is a decision you put the whole of the premiership on the line for," Mr Blair said in an interview with the *Sun* newspaper. In his first interview since the outbreak of war, the prime minister said that he had prepared his family for the possibility he could lose his job.[8]

Ken Livingstone, Mayor of London 2000–8: It [the march] put massive pressure on Blair. At that stage he was fighting for his life. If you read [Labour MP] Chris Mullin's diaries *The view from the foothills*, you read that Blair spent twenty minutes speaking to Mullin – he was fighting for every vote.[9] The march was a huge counterweight to all of that. The pressure on Blair translated to pressure on the Americans... By making Blair fight for his life, I suspect the Americans were alerted to the fact there was a real global problem.

***Guardian*, 19 April 2004:** Eleven days before the invasion of Iraq, Tony Blair was given three chances by President George Bush to keep British troops out of the war at no political cost, but refused, according to a book published today. An impressively sourced account of the run-up to the war – *Plan of Attack* by Watergate journalist Bob Woodward – depicts a president acutely conscious of the political cost to Mr Blair of tying his fortunes so closely to Washington's policy on Iraq. On the day of Mr Bush's offer – March 9, 2003 – Tony Blair faced a rebellion by Labour MP's opposed to the war, and it was becoming increasingly clear that the United Nations would not produce the international sanction for the war that was so important to Mr Blair's credibility at home.[i] Mr Blair's government and his political career were in peril.... In a telephone conversation, Mr Blair was asked three times if he wanted to keep Britain out of the war – and was offered a face-saving alternative of sending British forces only as part of a second wave of attack. He refused.[10]

Milan Rai: Blair never wanted to go to a vote in the House of Commons, but because of the strength of the anti-war movement he had to. You look at the two weeks before that vote and what you find in the *Daily Telegraph*, the *Sunday Telegraph* and I think the *Sunday Mirror* are reports that Geoff Hoon, the Defence Secretary, had to ring up [US Defense Secretary] Donald Rumsfeld and say "I'm not sure we are going to win this vote, I'm not sure we are going to be able to join the invasion. We may have be part of the post-invasion occupation forces". That's why Donald Rumsfeld said on that day – "Wobbly Tuesday" – "we don't need the British for this".

***Sunday Telegraph*, 16 March 2003:** By Tuesday [11 March 2003] there were serious worries in the White House that Mr Blair, its staunchest ally, might not survive the political crisis at home. Geoff Hoon, the Defence Secretary, tried to explain the problems to Donald Rumsfeld, the US defence secretary, in a telephone call which had meant to be devoted to the fine detail of the war plan.[11]

***Sunday Mirror*, 16 March 2003:** During the transatlantic telephone conversation on Tuesday, Mr Hoon stressed the

---

i According to the *Times*, on 9 March 2003 Blair was facing "a rebellion by up to 200 Labour MPs and the resignation of as many as 10 members of his government if he proceeds with military action against Saddam Hussein." Eben Black, Adam Nathan and Tony Allen-Mills, '200 Labour MPs revolt over war', *Times*, 9 March 2003, www.mail-archive.com/antinato@topica.com/msg08184.html [Accessed 8 August 2012].

political problems the Government was having with both MPs and the public.[12]

***Sunday Telegraph*, 16 March 2003:** As we reveal today, Mr Hoon's department was frantically preparing contingency plans to "disconnect" British troops entirely from the military invasion of Iraq, demoting their role to subsequent phases of the campaign and peacekeeping... Mr Rumsfeld confided to one friend: "I am learning to hate the British." However, he decided to give them a way out. Later that day, at a press conference in Washington, Mr Rumsfeld suggested that US troops could go to war without the British, if necessary. One Cabinet Minister said, in tones of desperation: "It is just Rumsfeld being Rumsfeld." The British media was encouraged to believe that the US Defence Secretary had been speaking hypothetically. The trouble was that he hadn't been doing any such thing. As a senior Number 10 official said: "Rumsfeld was telling the truth." The cat was out of the bag: Mr Hoon stormed into the whips' office at the Commons, grim-faced and appalled. This, of course, was exactly what the Labour rebels wanted to hear: that British troops were not needed and that Mr Blair could withdraw forthwith. In a second call on his secure telephone, Mr Hoon told Mr Rumsfeld in blunt terms that his remarks were causing pandemonium. "Wobbly Tuesday" was the lowest point of the crisis for Mr Blair.[13]

Milan Rai: Everybody, including me, thought that was just Rumsfeld being wild and crazy. But he was saying that because he had been told by Hoon that Britain may not be in the invasion force. So the anti-war mobilisation was such that we pushed back the schedule, we had forced a vote in Parliament – that set a constitutional precedent. That caused a lot of fear at the top reaches of the US and UK governments.

***Guardian*, 17 February 2003:** Ministers and officials insisted the protests – which saw more than 1 million people march in London on Saturday – would not delay military preparations for the war next month... In spite of their bullishness, there were signs that the scale of the protests, combined with the report by the UN chief weapons inspector, Hans Blix, on Friday [14 February 2003], has disrupted US and British diplomatic plans. A joint US-UK resolution authorising war that was to have been circulated at the UN security council at the weekend has been put on hold while Washington and London rethink their tactics.[14]

Milan Rai: If someone was to say the anti-war movement achieved nothing, I think that is plain, flat wrong. If you are saying we didn't succeed from extracting Britain from the invasion, which was what we were trying to do, that's clearly the case. But I think it is just like the [1984-5] Miners' Strike. At the time [Prime Minister Margaret] Thatcher and her cabinet had an air of invincibility, which was one of their weapons fighting the Miners' Strike. Years later we find out they were within weeks of running out of coal and being defeated. But they gave no sign of it at the time. And I think it is exactly the same with the 2003 invasion.

Seamus Milne, Journalist, in his book *The enemy within. The secret war against the miners*: Thatcher's hand was, however, nothing like as strong as has generally been supposed. It only gradually became apparent during the 1990s, as memoirs were published and participants felt able to speak more freely, how near the government came to defeat at the hands of the striking miners in 1984. Norman Tebbit, Thatcher ally and member of the Cabinet committee charged with beating the NUM [National Union of Miners], remarked in the wake of the 1992 pit-closures crisis that the strike had been a "close-run thing" – and eighteen months earlier the NUM would have almost certainly triumphed. The period during which the miners came closest to victory and the Thatcher government to falling was in fact in the autumn of 1984, when most pundits had already written the strike off.[15]

Johann Hari, Journalist: Let's look at a group of protesters who thought they had failed. The protests within the United States against the Vietnam War couldn't prevent it killing three million Vietnamese and 80,000 Americans. But even in the years it was "failing", it was achieving more than the protesters could possibly have known. In 1966, the specialists at the Pentagon went to US President Lyndon Johnson – a thug prone to threatening to "crush" entire elected governments – with a plan to end the Vietnam War: nuke the country. They "proved", using computer modeling, that a nuclear attack would "save lives." It was a plan that might well have appealed to him. But Johnson pointed out the window, towards hordes of protesters, and said: "I have one more problem for your computer. Will you feed into it how long it will take 500,000 angry Americans to climb the White House wall out there and lynch the President? He knew that there would be a cost – in protest and democratic revolt – that made that cruelty too great.[16]

Noam Chomsky, American dissident, citing the Pentagon Papers, a US Department of Defense history of the Vietnam War, leaked in 1971: The Joint Chiefs of Staff, considering additional U.S. troop deployments to Vietnam after the Tet Offensive in 1968, noted that they had to make sure that "sufficient forces would still be available for civil disorder control". Similarly, a Pentagon Working Group warned in a top secret Defense Department memorandum in March 1968 that increased force levels in Vietnam would lead to "growing disaffection accompanied, as it certainly will be, by increased defiance of the draft and growing unrest in the cities," and ran "great risks of provoking a domestic crisis of unprecedented proportions".[17]

Milan Rai: The way Blair, the cabinet and the political establishment present it is that all of these ants run around on the streets, but it doesn't affect what they are doing. But actually the ants running around on the streets very nearly brought the British part of the invasion to a halt and very nearly toppled Tony Blair as he himself acknowledged at the time – he said, I may have to resign over this. We achieved a lot, and a hell of a lot more than we realise...

INTRODUCTION

Waking up in Edinburgh on 15 February 2003, Tony Blair told his Communications Director and confidant Alastair Campbell he had not slept well. "Even I am a bit worried about this one", admitted the Prime Minister.[1] He had good reason to be worried. A few hours later more than one million people marched through the centre of London in an attempt to stop British involvement in the looming invasion of Iraq – the biggest demonstration in British history, about the most controversial political issue of recent times. "There had never been a larger demonstration, reminding me of my isolation and the responsibility of the decision I was about to take", Blair noted in his autobiography about the policy that he had staked his political career on and which would come to define his premiership.[2]

The enormous Chartist public meetings in the 1840s, the Suffragette marches to Hyde Park in the early 20th century, the violent anti-Vietnam War disturbances outside the American Embassy in 1968, the anti-cruise missile marches organised by CND in the 1980s – in terms of numbers 15 February 2003 dwarfed them all.[3] Of course, there was the usual controversy over the precise number of participants but a *Guardian*/ICM poll found that at least one person from 1.25 million households in Britain marched in London on that bitterly cold Saturday in February.[4] Ken Livingstone told me that he had calculated the number of people on the march was the equivalent of the entire population of England circa 1200. The sheer size of the march meant that "for most of those who marched against the Iraq war on February 15 2003 it was the first time they had ever demonstrated for or against anything in their lives", noted the Chairman of Stop the War Coalition.[5] The demonstration was part of a vast worldwide mobilisation. Between six and ten million people in up to 400 cities in 60 countries around the globe demonstrated against the war in Iraq on 15 February 2003, from perhaps three million people in Rome to tiny demonstrations in such remote places as Antarctica and the Pacific Islands.[6]

To take just one of the many contemporary journalistic commentaries on the London demonstration, an upbeat Madeleine Bunting described how the march "brought the entire business of a capital city to a glorious full-stop. Not a car or bus moved in central London, the frenetic activities of shopping and spending halted across a wide swathe of the city; the streets became one vast vibrant civic space". It was "a defining moment in contemporary political culture", she argued. Why? Firstly because "it shifted the tone of what Britain believes itself to be... we showed ourselves to be a nation that is at ease with itself, compassionate, multicultural and tolerant". Secondly because it "proved that the decline in democracy has been overstated." Turnouts at general elections and membership of political parties may have been at an all time low, Bunting noted, but the fact we had just experienced the largest demonstration in British history was "a conundrum to keep hundreds of political scientists busy."[7]

Was 15 February 2003 a "defining moment" in British history? An example of a vibrant civic culture? Proof that the decline in democracy had been overstated? Something to celebrate and remember like The Battle of Cable Street and the now mythic anti-Vietnam War protests? Or should we be more sombre and critical in our analysis of something that continues to be widely viewed as an "absolute failure", as one UK Uncut activist said in 2011?[8] Did the march simply lead to widespread disillusionment with protest as an effective political tool for change? It certainly didn't achieve its immediate aim – to stop British participation in the invasion of Iraq in 2003 – but does this mean it had no verifiable short or long-term influence on the Iraq War, progressive social movements or the British political and social landscape? Before the book attempts to answer these questions I need to put 15 February 2003 into its historical context.

The road to war and the importance of public opinion

The British anti-Iraq War movement was a direct response to the increasingly loud drumbeats for war with Iraq which had started up after 11 September 2001. According to CBS News "barely five hours after American Airlines Flight 77 ploughed into the Pentagon, Defense Secretary Donald H. Rumsfeld was telling his aides to come up with plans for striking Iraq – even though there was no evidence linking Saddam Hussein to the attacks."[9] It soon became clear the US Administration would attempt to use the terrorist atrocities to gain support for an attack on Iraq. In London a huge meeting was quickly convened on 21 September 2001.

The gathering at Friends Meeting House was the beginning of Stop the War Coalition, the group that would play the central role in 15 February 2003 and the wider anti-war movement.

However, citing 9/11 as the turning point in American efforts to topple Hussein is something of a red herring. As early as January 1998 a lobby group dedicated to US "global leadership" called the Project for the New American Century sent an open letter to President Clinton urging him to remove Hussein's regime from power. If Hussein continued as the President of Iraq "the safety of American troops in the region, of our friends and allies like Israel and the moderate Arab states, and a significant portion of the world's supply of oil will be put at risk". Among the letter's signatories were prominent neo-conservatives such as Rumsfeld, Paul Wolfowitz, Richard Perle, John Bolton and Zalmay Khalilzad – all names that would become very familiar over the next few years as architects of post-9/11 US foreign policy.[10] With many in the US Government believing Hussein should have been toppled in 1991, regime change in Iraq became official US policy with the passing of the Iraq Liberation Act in October 1998. The neo-conservatives position was further strengthened by the election of George Bush in 2000. According to Paul O'Neill, US Treasury Secretary from 2000–2, "From the very beginning" of the Bush Administration "there was a conviction that Saddam Hussein was a bad person and he needed to go".[11]

Following the perceived success of the bombing and invasion of Afghanistan in October 2001, President Bush's belligerent January 2002 State of the Union address pointed the way forward for US foreign policy. Iraq, Iran and North

Korea "constitute an axis of evil, arming to threaten the peace of the world. By seeking weapons of mass destruction, these regimes pose a grave and growing danger", he warned. "They could provide these arms to terrorists, giving them the means to match their hatred. They could attack our allies or attempt to blackmail the United States. In any of these cases, the price of indifference would be catastrophic."[12]

Like Bush, Blair said he believed the world fundamentally changed on 9/11, with Saddam Hussein's Iraq a threat that could no longer be ignored.[13] Keen to stand shoulder to shoulder with the American President, Blair travelled to Crawford, Texas in April 2002 for a summit with Bush. With Iraq high on the agenda, senior UK officials sounded out their American counterparts in Washington prior to the meeting. David Manning, Blair's chief foreign policy advisor, dined with Condoleeza Rice, then US National Security Advisor. British Ambassador Christopher Meyer spoke with US Deputy of Defense Wolfowitz. In his subsequently leaked "strictly personal" memo to the Prime Minister, Manning wrote: "I said that you would not budge in your support for regime change but you had to manage a press, a Parliament and a public opinion".[14] Meyer's memo to Downing Street echoed Manning's report. "We backed regime change", he said, with the caveat that "if the UK were to join with the US in any operation against Saddam, we would have to be able to take a critical mass of parliamentary and public opinion with us."[15] During his private meeting with Bush in Crawford, Blair reaffirmed that the UK would back regime change, despite repeatedly stating in public no decision had been made on British involvement and not having consulted the cabinet, parliament or the British public.[16]

With the UK military beginning to make detailed plans for the invasion a "Secret UK Eyes Only" Cabinet Office paper was published on 21 July 2002. "Time will be required to prepare public opinion in the UK that it is necessary to take military action against Saddam Hussein", the paper noted. "An information campaign will be needed...This will need to give full coverage to the threat posed by Saddam Hussein, including his WMD, and the legal justification for action".[17] The problem was, as Foreign Secretary Jack Straw explained to Blair in a top secret meeting at Downing Street two days later, "the case [for war] was thin. Saddam was not threatening his neighbours, and his WMD capability was less than that of Libya, North Korea or Iran". Nevertheless, the Head of MI6 noted that "military action was now seen as inevitable" in Washington, with "the intelligence and facts... being fixed around the policy". With Defence Secretary Geoff Hoon, the Head of the Joint Intelligence Committee John Scarlett, the Attorney-General, Blair's Director of Political and Government Relations Sally Morgan, and Campbell also in attendance, the meeting concluded by agreeing they "should work on the assumption that the UK would take part in any military action."[18]

It should already be clear the British Government was extremely concerned and fearful of domestic public opinion, making significant efforts to influence the debate over Iraq. As the historian Mark Curtis argues, from 2002 onwards the British public was "subject to a government propaganda campaign of perhaps unprecedented heights in the post-war world."[19] The Government's concern is confirmed by a Ministry of Defence strategy document from the time, which noted "public support will be vital to the conduct of military interventions", and complaints by the Spanish UN Ambassador in March 2003 that the British Government was "nervous" and "exclusively obsessed" with domestic public opinion.[20]

So what was the public's mood in the late summer of 2002? Anti-war sentiment had been steadily growing, with an August 2002 YouGov/*Telegraph* poll showing that more than two-thirds of the public believed a potential attack on Iraq was not justified at the present time.[21] It was in response to this hostile political climate that the UK Government released the 'Iraq's Weapons of Mass Destruction: The Assessment of the British Government' report – aka the infamous September Dossier – on 24 September 2002. "I am in no doubt that the threat is serious and current, that he has made progress on WMD, and that he has to be stopped", wrote Blair in the report's foreword. His further claim that "The document discloses that his [Hussein's] military planning allows for some of the WMD to be ready within 45 minutes of an order to use them" was duly and hysterically amplified by much of the British press the next day.[22] Speaking to the Chilcot Inquiry in 2011, Campbell maintained the dossier was not written to make the case for war. Major General Michael Laurie, the director general in the Defence Intelligence Staff when the dossier was being compiled, remembers things differently: "We knew at the time that the purpose of the dossier was precisely to make a case for war, rather than setting out the available intelligence, and that to make the best out of sparse and inconclusive intelligence, the wording was developed with care."[23]

The Saturday after the dossier was published approximately 400,000 people marched in London against the war – the biggest demonstration against the impending war so far. The demonstration was organised by Stop the

War Coalition and the Muslim Association of Britain, a historic partnership between secular and Muslim organisations. On 30 September 2002 the Archbishop of Canterbury stated he could see no reason for attacking Iraq at the current time.[24] Despite the dossier's publication and favourable media coverage, public opinion continued to side with the growing anti-war movement, with an early November 2002 *Guardian*/ICM tracker poll showing "support for military action against Iraq has slumped to its lowest". Approval for a military attack stood at 38 percent, with opposition at 41 percent.[25]

Within Whitehall it was keenly understood that the support of the United Nations was crucial to gaining public support for the war. At this point, according to the generally accepted narrative, Blair, with the help of US Secretary of State Colin Powell, successfully persuaded the Bush Administration to work through the United Nations, something many neo-conservatives were very hostile to. However, this somewhat self-serving account omits the UK Government's own, far from sincere, position on the UN process. As Meyer wrote in his memo to Manning in March 2002, the plan was "to wrongfoot Saddam on the inspectors and UN SCRs [Security Council resolutions]".[26] How? The July 2002 Cabinet paper explains: "It is just possible that an ultimatum could be cast in terms which Saddam would reject (because he is unwilling to accept unfettered access) and which would not be regarded as unreasonable by the international community".[27] The goal then, was to use the weapons inspectors and the UN as a tool for triggering war, not, as Blair publicly stated at the time, to negotiate a peaceful solution to the crisis.

Thus, on 8 November 2002, after intense diplomacy, the

US and UK managed to secure the passage of UN Security Council Resolution 1441. The resolution gave Hussein "a final opportunity to comply with its disarmament obligations". Later that month UN weapons inspectors returned to Iraq, under the leadership of Dr Hans Blix. It should be noted that, contrary to US and UK statements in the months that followed, UNSCR 1441 was only passed by Russia, China and France on the understanding a second resolution would be required to authorise military action. As the UK Ambassador explained at the time:

> "We heard loud and clear during the negotiations the concerns about 'automaticity' and 'hidden triggers' – the concern that on a decision so crucial we should not rush into military action; that on a decision so crucial any Iraqi violations should be discussed by the Council. Let me be equally clear in response, as a co-sponsor with the United States of the text we have just adopted. There is no 'automaticity' in this resolution. If there is a further Iraqi breach of its disarmament obligations, the matter will return to the Council for discussion as required in paragraph 12. We would expect the Security Council then to meet its responsibilities."[28]

From late 2002 onwards Blair was fighting for his political life. "The political pressure was just enormous in December, January, February 2002/2003", he noted at the Chilcot Inquiry.[29] "The anti-war mood was definitely growing", noted Campbell in his diary on 22 January 2003. "Sally [Morgan] said to TB [Tony Blair] if we didn't take real care, this was the end of him".[30] Perhaps buoyed by Blix's criticisms of Iraqi compliance in his 27 January 2002 report to the Security Council, on 31 January 2003 Blair told Bush he was "solidly behind" US plans to invade Iraq, with or without a second UN resolution.[31] A day earlier Nelson Mandela had condemned the US/UK push for war as an attempt to take control of Iraq's oil supplies, calling Blair the "US foreign minister".[32]

By this time preparations for the 15 February 2003 anti-war march in London, coordinated by Stop the War Coalition, the Muslim Association of Britain and the Campaign for Nuclear Disarmament, were in full swing. So too, it seems, was the Government propaganda machine. On New Year's Day Simon Jenkins, the former editor of the *Times*, scolded the Government for summoning the press to Downing Street for what he called "the Sunday scare story". Jenkins goes on to list the alleged planned terrorist plots including "the sarin-on-the-tube scare, the smallpox scare, the 'threat to public transport' scare, the Christmas shopping scare and last Sunday's 'London quarantine' scare." These were, noted Jenkins, "pure heebiejeebie."[33] On 3 February 2003 the Government released a second dossier titled 'Iraq: It's Infrastructure of Concealment, Deception and Intimidation', which quickly backfired when it was discovered it had been plagiarised from a postgraduate student's thesis.[34] On 6 February 2003 Blair appeared on a special edition of *BBC*'s *Newsnight* to make the case for war to a sceptical audience in Gateshead, arguing that he would consider going to war without UN authorisation if a member of the Security Council used what he called "an unreasonable veto".[35] On 9 February 2003 the *Sunday Times* reported that the Government was preparing to introduce a national network of air pollution detectors to provide early warning of a biological attack.[36] Supposedly in response to an imminent threat from al-Qaida-linked terrorists, tanks and 1,500 troops and police were deployed at Heathrow airport on 11 February 2003.[37] A couple of days later a grenade scare at Gatwick airport made the front pages of the newspapers. "This atmosphere of near hysteria" constituted "a campaign to win round a sceptical public", according to former head of the Joint Intelligence Committee Sir Rodric Braithwaite. Or, as he also eloquently put it: "Fishmongers sell fish; warmongers sell war".[38]

Meanwhile, at a much trailed presentation to the Security Council, Powell used satellite images, transcripts of telephone calls and other intelligence data as proof that Iraq had still not disarmed.[39] "When I saw all that", the *BBC*'s prize attack dog Jeremy Paxman admitted a few years later, "I thought, 'Well, we know that Colin Powell is an intelligent, thoughtful man, and a sceptical man. If he believes all this to be the case, then, you know, he's seen the evidence; I haven't'".[40] This naïveté was not shared by the general public, with a *BBC* online poll of just over 21,000 people finding 60 percent of respondents were not convinced by Powell's evidence.[41] Neither was Tony Benn, who in an attempt to avert war, had just travelled to Baghdad to speak to Hussein. Broadcast by *Channel Four News* on 4 February 2003, during the interview Hussein clearly tells Benn: "Iraq has no weapons of mass destruction whatsoever".[42]

Public opinion was still stubbornly against the war. According to a *Times* newspaper poll 86 percent of respondents wanted more time for the weapons inspectors. Asked by a YouGov/*Channel Four* poll which nation was "the greatest threat to world peace", 25 percent of respondents said Iraq. The problem for Blair and co. was that 32 percent of respondents answered "the United States" to the same question.[43] On 11 February 2003 the *BBC*'s

European Affairs analyst reported "From Portugal to Russia, opinion surveys suggest that without a further UN resolution, most Europeans are overwhelmingly against war – and even a second resolution would not convince many of them". Furthermore, despite strong support for the US and UK from eastern European Governments – 'New Europe' according to Rumsfeld – "public opinion in eastern Europe is even more hostile to war than in the west".[44] Blix reported back to the Security Council on 14 February 2003. According to the *BBC*, he "took a more positive line than... his report two weeks ago, saying Baghdad had made progress in a number of areas". Blix had found no evidence of WMDs and, much to the annoyance of Washington, cast doubt on the intelligence Powell used in his presentation days before. Blix noted inspections were continuing and that the number of inspectors would be increased. In response, Jack Straw implored the members of the Security Council to "hold our nerve" while the French foreign minister said "The use of military force is not justified today."[45]

It was in this heightened atmosphere of continuous tension and crisis, with the Government making extraordinary efforts to manipulate public opinion, that over one million people gathered on the morning of 15 February 2003 to march against war in Iraq.

15 February 2003 in the history books

Critiquing what he sees as the insularity and neurotic obsession of Ian McEwan's *Saturday*, a novel set entirely on 15 February 2003, science fiction author China Mieville argued the march was "the most extraordinary political event that has happened in Britain for however many years".[46] Of course, the protest's record size and overarching historical significance are self-evident to the author. However, a quick survey of the history section of any decent-sized bookshop shows that contemporary mainstream historians have largely ignored or downplayed the events of 15 February 2003. In the 736 pages of his *A History of the English-Speaking Peoples Since 1900* Andrew Roberts quickly dismisses the march as giving comfort to Saddam Hussein. After making the extraordinary claim the demonstration "made war even more likely than it already was", Roberts goes on to give more space to an admiring account of George Bush's stage-managed May 2003 'Mission Accomplished' speech than the largest protest in British history. "The president had taken a turn at the controls during the flight", Roberts breathlessly recounts. "The aircraft made a 'tailhook' landing at 150 mph, coming to a complete stop in less than 400 feet".[47] A staunchly conservative historian who mourns the loss of the British Empire, Roberts' disdain for popular protest is perhaps not surprising. But what about the more liberal chroniclers of our national story? In his bestselling 629-page tome *A History of Modern Britain BBC* grandee Andrew Marr dedicates fully two sentences to the demonstration.[48] CND's protests since the 1950s receive more than two pages.[49] Former Liberal MP David Marquand bests Marr in *Britain Since 1918. The Strange Career of British Democracy*, giving the march a generous seven lines of his 477 pages.[50] Published by the Museum of London, the 352-page *London. The Illustrated History* fails to even mention the march.[51] And what to make of Clive Bloom's *Violent London. 2000 Years of Riots, Rebels and Revolt*, a 575-page book "intended as a synoptic record of the history of political protest, riot and disorder" of the capital? Bloom, Professor Emeritus at Middlesex University, gives the march – the largest protest in the 2000 years covered in his book! – the briefest of brief mentions, only referring to it in passing when discussing the much smaller Countryside Alliance march of September 2002.[52]

Why this gaping hole in the historical record? Perhaps the events are not quite "history" yet, are too close for comfort for objective and disinterested historical study? Or is the historical black hole a political one? Marxist historian Eric Hobsbawn argues "Most history in the past was written for the glorification of, and perhaps for the practical use of, rulers".[53] This may explain large chunks of Roberts' hagiographical musings, but it seems an inadequate explanation for the more modern-thinking, liberal commentators. Rather it seems Marr, Marquand et al, who not unimportantly are nearly always from the same social strata as our rulers, continue to work within the traditional historical narrative framework – that of elevating descriptions and analyses of the behaviour of the decision makers in the political elite – what might be called 'high politics' – at the expense of grassroots social movements and the lives of those not directly involved in formal politics. But what about Bloom? His book is explicitly about the history of political protest in London, yet he felt there was no need to look at the largest protest that has ever occurred in this country. "I didn't mention it for a very simple reason", he told me when I interviewed him. "All the marches and all the protests I've got in the book had some element of action. And it [15 February 2003] didn't have any element of action so it doesn't count... I spent some time writing about Otis Ferry [who broke in to the House of Commons chamber on 15 September 2004 to protest anti-hunting legislation] because it makes a narrative, to be blunt."[i]

Writing in the late 1960s, American dissident Noam Chomsky noted that "antagonism to mass movements and to social change that escapes the control of privileged elites is... a prominent feature of contemporary liberal ideology."[54] For example, writing in the *Guardian* on the eve of the 26 March 2011 TUC-organised march against the Coalition Government's cuts agenda, Simon Jenkins told readers that demonstrations "are mostly boosts to group morale, childish song festivals, obsessions with the media and desperate attempts to cause a genteel nuisance without breaching the law". His contempt virtually oozing off the page, Jenkins went on to explain that "Britain has long been a poor venue for crowd power", arguing that the machinations of formal politics have been the enabler of progress: "It was in parliament that the great debates of 1831–32 took place".[55] That the "great debates" preceding the Great Reform Act of 1832 (which, as every student of history knows, actually changed very little) may have been in response to popular protest and pressure from below seems to have eluded Jenkins. Not ex-slave Frederick Douglass though, who once famously remarked: "Power concedes nothing without a demand; it never did and it never will."[56] On 15 February 2003 itself *BBC Newsnight* provided an excellent example of liberal "antagonism" towards mass movements, asking:

---

i More worryingly for me and this book, Bloom went on to say about the march "If you think about it, what's the story? A lot of people marched, heard speeches and went home. There is no story there. There is nothing you can write about. I couldn't get a handle on what I was going to say that would interest people sufficiently. I could have said 'so and so was on the march and he was very annoyed' – it doesn't make anything... The difficulty is making a story out of what is essentially a non-story."

"The people have spoken, or have they? What about the millions who didn't march? Was going to the DIY store or watching the football on Saturday a demonstration of support for the government?"[57]

If they are not ignoring or downplaying the largest protest in British history, historians and commentators have largely marked it down as a failure. Writing in the Labour-Left *Tribune* magazine Ian Hernon, author of *Riot! Civil Insurrection from Peterloo to the Present Day*, describes the march as a "qualified [failure]" because "Tony Blair ignored it and was re-elected at the subsequent general election."[58] Echoing Jenkins' contemptuous approach, writing on the *BBC*'s website author Michael Goldfarb argues "political marching, protest marching, call it what you will, has become in the new millennium a way of exercising one's ego… a retro activity, an act of political nostalgia more than a tactic to bring about specific change". His conclusion? "Political leaders tolerate marching but don't fear it. When more than one million and a half people marched through London in February 2003 to protest the impending war with Iraq, it changed absolutely nothing."[59] [My emphasis added]

In writing *The march that shook Blair* my intention is to address and refute these two popular arguments – that the march was an unimportant and inconsequential historical event and that it achieved "absolutely nothing". My aim is to document, celebrate, investigate and critically analyse the largest political march in British history and the wider anti-war movement. In addition I hope the testimonies that follow show that although the march did not stop British participation in the invasion of Iraq, it has "cast a long shadow over British politics since then", from playing a central role in Tony Blair's plummeting popularity and his early exit from office to influencing the nature of subsequent British protest movements such as the environmental direct action groups and the varied activism in response to the Coalition Government's austerity measures.[60] It was the Iraq War, or more precisely the vibrant resistance to it and the Government's ignoring of that resistance, that led to a huge dip in the public's trust in our governing institutions – a downward spiral that has continued with the MPs' expenses scandal, the financial crisis and Hackgate. There is also substantial evidence that the march and the anti-war movement has had a positive effect on community relations in the UK and, as several interviewees note, has done more to reduce the threat of terrorism in this country than any Government policies have ever achieved. Moreover, contrary to the naysayers, the book will present testimony that suggests the anti-war movement actually came very close to derailing Blair's drive to war in early 2003 and constrained the style and content of the British involvement too. All of these achievements and influences should be part of general consciousness – well known to those who marched on 15 February 2003, the general public, and future generations and historians. As Chomsky has noted:

> Part of the whole technique of disempowering people is to make sure that the real agents of change fall out of history, and are never recognised in the culture for what they are. So it's necessary to distort history and make it look as if Great Men did everything – that's part of how you teach people they can't do anything, they're helpless, they just have to wait for some Great Man to come along and do it for them.[61]

"We have believed too long in our own helplessness", notes Chomsky's friend, the late historian Howard Zinn. "The new history [history from below] tells us how, sometimes, movements of people who don't seem to have much power can shake the rich and the powerful."[62] However, as the march failed to stop the slaughter of perhaps one million Iraqis since the 2003 invasion it would be churlish for this book to be a simple celebration. I have therefore included lengthy discussion about the failure of the march to achieve its short-term objective and the limitations of, and conflicts within, the wider anti-war movement – Stop the War Coalition in particular.

Why an oral history?

This book is an oral history – that is a book based on "the interviewing of eye-witness participants in the events of the past for the purposes of historical reconstruction."[63] While oral history has had a significant impact on the study of history for over 50 years, there are still many professional historians who view it with distrust and even disdain. Niall Fergusson has dismissed it as "a recipe for complete misrepresentation because almost no one tells the truth, even when they intend to", while a book reviewer in the *Washington Post* once noted: "[A]nything calling itself oral history probably ought to be approached with deep suspicion." The sceptic elaborated: "People who present interviews as history are farther from the mark than a cook who insists that a loose collection of eggs, sugar, milk, vanilla, flour and a few squares of butter chocolate are in fact a chocolate cake."[64]

Despite these criticisms, when I was initially contemplating writing a book about 15 February 2003, an oral history presented itself as the natural format. As historian Paul Thomson notes "Oral history is a history built around people. It thrusts life into history itself and widens its scope."[65] Its ability to collate and mix a plethora of voices means it is well suited to an event which was organised by hundreds of people and attended by more than a million. Well suited to presenting both complimentary and conflicting testimony. More importantly, I've always found oral histories very readable, accessible and exciting to read. Peter Manso's *Mailer. His life and times*, Jonathon Green's seminal oral history of the 1960s, Peter Grafton's *You, you & you! The people out of step with World War II and The other Hollywood. The uncensored oral history of the porn film industry* by Legs McNeil and Jennifer Osborne have been some of the most memorable reading experiences of my life.[66] In addition, with its focus on oral testimony of eyewitnesses, an oral history allows the historian to gather important information that is not written down. Soon after beginning the research for the book it became apparent there were very few written records to study about the 15 February 2003 anti-war march and the wider anti-war movement. Perhaps due to the fast-evolving nature of the growing resistance to the US and UK's rush to war, decisions and discussions within the leadership of the anti-war movement were often taken on an informal basis and evidently not recorded. The Stop the War Coalition did have regular management meetings but no records of these meetings seem to exist. In fact, according to some interviewees, some decisions were consciously taken by a small number of people, with other people involved in the supposed leadership deliberately excluded from this decision-making process. One interviewee suggested I visit the Stop the War archive at the Bishopsgate Institute in London. However, a subsequent visit, though interesting, did not turn up any useful documents over and above some inchoate Stop the War Coalition paraphernalia such as posters, fliers and generic mailouts. Whether the written record is incomplete or not, a key strength of oral history is its ability to move beyond insights informed solely by an analysis of official or unofficial written documents to reveal "unknown events or unknown aspects of known events".[67] For example, oral evidence is often better at illuminating the emotional and personal experience people have of a particular historical event – what it actually felt to be there on the day – compared to other historical sources.

In the standard oral history academic textbook Rob Perks and Alistair Thomson note:

> the most distinctive contribution of oral history has been to include within the historical record the experiences and perspectives of groups of people who might otherwise have been 'hidden from history', perhaps written about by social observers or in official documents, but only rarely preserved in personal papers or scraps of autobiographical writing. Through oral history interviews, working-class men and women, indigenous peoples or members of cultural minorities, amongst others, have inscribed their experiences on the historical record, and offered their own interpretations of history.[68]

I see *The march that shook Blair* as a hybrid oral history. By focussing on the workings and activities of grassroots social movements, activists and non-activists it certainly seeks to document the experiences of those who have been 'hidden from history'. However, the majority of interviews undertaken were with the leadership of the anti-war movement, along with politicians and privileged commentators. Mostly the people I interviewed were highly-educated and articulate people, many of whom have reached the top of their chosen profession or activist organisation. Because of this focus, I believe this book should also be seen as what Anthony Seldon and Joanna Pappworth call "elite oral history".[69]

My methodology

The majority of the book is made up of testimony from face-to-face interviews. I completed 71 face-to-face interviews and collected 51 written testimonies, largely by email. The first face-to-face interview, with Tony Benn, was conducted in January 2009, with the last completed in September 2012. Interviews were generally chosen using what sociologists call the snowballing method – with each interviewee suggesting other people for me to contact. However, as each person naturally tends to recommend friends or colleagues who support their position or political beliefs I was careful to regularly break this cycle and choose who to interview based on independent research I had conducted. Most people I contacted were more than happy to be interviewed. A number of people (Oliver Kamm, Jack Straw, John Pilger and Anjem Choudary among them) declined to be interviewed, usually because of their busy schedules, they said. To make the interviewee as comfortable with the process as possible I always travelled to the interviewees preferred meeting point – generally a public place such as a café or their workplace, occasionally their home. Most interviews were conducted in London, as this is where most people were located, although I also made trips to Liverpool, Birmingham and Bristol on occasion. Interviews generally lasted between 30 minutes and two hours in length depending on the interviewee's role in events, what they had to say and the time they had to spare. For each interview I prepared a set of questions to structure the interview. This was informed by the interviewee's background, experience on 15 February 2003, role in the anti-war movement and research I had already carried out. Of course the interviews rarely followed my planned question order – either because the interviewee was difficult to control in a conversational sense (the more famous people, presumably experienced with interviews, especially) or because an interesting topic came up that was not included in my questions that I felt was important to pursue. As Studs Terkel, arguably the most important oral historian to have ever picked up a tape recorder, once advised, "stay loose, stay flexible" because interviewing is "like jazz, you've got to improvise".[70] Each interview was recorded on an electronic voice recorder, which I then transcribed within a few days of the interview. When requested and where possible the content of the transcript was sent to the interviewee for their records and for them to make any factual corrections.

While an oral history seemed to be the best format for the book, some discussion about the problems associated with oral histories is useful, I think. Firstly, it is important to remember that oral histories, and the interviews that inform them, are in no way a definitive, objective or final account of events. "Personal memory", said Hobsbawn, "is a remarkably slippery medium for preserving facts... not so much a recording as a selective mechanism, and the selection is, within limits, constantly changing."[71] Should I or someone else interview the same people today about the same events, even using the same questions I did, we would receive very different answers than I did during the original interview, and would no doubt write a very different book. With the interviews carried out six, seven and eight years after the march all the interviewees (and the author) were thinking about the events of 2003 with the increased clarity of hindsight, their testimony influenced by already published accounts (newspapers, books etc) of the events in question. In addition to unwanted forgetfulness there is the deliberate falsification and distorting of events by those being interviewed. As one of the largest political campaigns of recent history headed and run by some very big egos, there was and continues to be intense rivalries and political arguments within the UK anti-war movement and the broad Left. As such it would be wise to read the testimonies that follow with a critical and sceptical eye, always mindful of the political and personal allegiances of the speaker.

Like my favourite oral histories mentioned above, *The march that shook Blair* is an oral history with little direct authorial intervention. The plan was always for the interviewee's testimonies to speak for themselves rather than to include summarising or introductory text written by me. Where context or explanation is needed I have used contemporary news reports or other published sources such as books or short commentaries. However, my attempt to exclude any direct authorial intervention in the actual text is something of a red herring. On the narrow issue of the interview process itself, it is important to remember the interview is not simply the formal record of the memories and thoughts of the interviewee but rather the product of the complex, transitory and infinitely variable relationship between the interviewee and the interviewer. More broadly, E.H. Carr notes: "The historian is necessarily selective. The belief in a hard core of historical facts existing objectively and independently of the interpretation of the historian is a preposterous fallacy, but one which it is very hard to eradicate."[72] As the author I have chosen the topic of study, the themes of inquiry, the general layout of the text, who to interview and who not to interview, what questions to ask and what part of their testimony to ask for clarification on or not, among other assorted biases. Alessandro Portelli believes that historians may "ventriloquise" their own bias and prejudices through the interviewees testimony: "Instead of discovering sources, oral historians partly create them. Far from becoming mere mouthpieces for the working class, oral historians may be using other people's words, but are still responsible for the overall discourse."[73]

Ever the radical, Zinn takes this line of thought a step further, arguing objectivity is neither possible or desirable: "The world is already moving in certain directions. And to be neutral, to be passive, in a situation like that, is to collaborate with what is going on."[74] In this spirit of moral responsibility, human fallibility and openness I am happy to set out my own bias. In the middle of a masters degree in American Studies, I attended the rally in Hyde Park on 15 February 2003 in opposition to the war. Looking back at my time studying, I am reminded of Neil Young's comment that his song *Ohio*, written immediately after four American students were shot dead by the National Guard at Kent State University in 1970, was "probably the biggest lesson ever learned at an American place of learning". For me, the march and subsequent invasion of Iraq were arguably a greater lesson in the machinations of Western power and issues of war and peace than any textbook I read for my masters degree. Though I didn't fully comprehend the make-up of the anti-war movement at the time, I was, and continue to be, broadly in agreement with its aims. And, of course, a line could certainly be drawn from my personal experience of 15 February 2003 and my wider interest in the war to the writing of the book you hold in your hand. However, with all this in mind I have tried to treat individual interviewees and the wider historical events as fairly as possible. So while I have not included probably more than five percent of the total testimony I collected, I have attempted to allocate space to people and arguments and events based on the relative importance of historical events and testimony that I gathered. No doubt some will be frustrated, possibly angry, about the representation of themselves or how I have treated a specific individual, organisation, argument or event. I can only apologise in advance to them.

Housekeeping

The book is split into three main sections. The first chapter looks at the establishment and growth of the anti-war movement after 9/11 and the preparations for 15 February 2003. The second chapter concerns the day of the march, looking at the experiences of the organisers and "ordinary" people who marched through London. The final chapter looks at the immediate events following the march and its wider historical influence. At the back of the book are a number of lists and tools to assist in the reading and understanding of the narrative, including a timeline, a map of the march route, short biographies of all the interviewees and an extensive bibliography for those who wish to research the topic in more depth.

At the start of my research I myself was under a couple of small, but important, misapprehensions about the subject, which I would like to clarify here. Firstly, although they are often used interchangeably, it is important to remember Stop the War Coalition is not the anti-war movement. As I have already mentioned 15 February 2003 itself was organised by a tripartite coalition – Stop the War Coalition, the Muslim Association of Britain and the Campaign for Nuclear Disarmament. However, there were a plethora of other groups who opposed the war independently of these three groups – War Resisters International, Voices UK, Sussex Action for Peace and ARROW among them. Secondly, while 15 February 2003 was the biggest march in British history, the anti-war movement in Scotland had a different composition to the anti-war movement in England and Wales. So while Stop the War Coalition was dominant south of the border, they were not a strong force in Scotland, where CND played a central role. Finally, while 15 February 2003 may have been the high point for Stop the War Coalition and the broader anti-war movement, it was just one of thousands of public events and meetings organised to oppose the invasion and occupation of Iraq. So a book on 15 February 2003 will necessarily also be a book about the wider anti-war movement. For example, when looking into the influence of the demonstration it is of course near impossible to separate the influence of the march with the influence of the anti-war movement.

SECTION ONE

BUILDING THE ANTI-WAR MOVEMENT

9/11: "It's impossible now to recapture the hysteria"

Andrew Murray, Stop the War Coalition Chair 2001–11 and Lindsey German, Stop the War Coalition Convenor: The Stop the War Coalition was born out of one of the most remarkable historical events any of us has witnessed. The twin towers of New York's World Trade Centre were hit on 11 September 2001 in the early afternoon, British time... It is easy to forget the pressure which resulted from 11 September... any challenge to the war consensus was greeted with amazement if not outright hostility.[1]

Tariq Ali, Author and political campaigner: It's impossible now to recapture the hysteria. You should go and look at the newspapers from that time. It was horrendous. When the *London Review of Books* published short comments by various of its writers, a classical historian called Mary Beard, who is Professor of Ancient History at Cambridge –

she isn't even a political person – she said "I don't know but everyone I talk to said they had it coming". And all hell broke loose. This literary magazine was attacked by so-called liberal journalists like Ian Jack in the *Guardian* and numerous others in the papers saying it was outrageous that the LRB published this comment by Mary Beard. That was the degree of hysteria around and that's the context in which we organised that [21 September 2001] meeting, which laid the basis for the anti-war movement.

***Observer*, 14 July 2002:** A year ago at the Siege of Genoa, a quarter of a million protesters surrounded the annual meeting of G8 political leaders and many fought running battles with the Italian police. It was the peak of the anti-globalisation movement. Anti-globalisation seemed unstoppable, as the defining agenda of the new century and "the most sweeping rebellion since the Sixties". Where is it now? What changed after 11 September? Now the movement has all but vanished from the bulletins and the headlines, has it been dumped in the dustbin of history along with other failed slogans such as Solidarity with the Striking Miners or All Power to the Soviets? Was its brief stretch in the spotlight – two years from surfacing in Seattle to its apotheosis at Genoa – simply a passing fad, and its youthful, mainly middle-class army of protesters yesterday's children? Or is it all the fault of the media? Have we turned our backs on a still-vibrant radical movement and a key issue in the modern world – distracted by the World Trade Centre attacks and war on terror?[2]

Hilary Wainwright, Editor, *Red Pepper*, November 2001: Only the day before 11 September we thought we'd got the Prime Minister on the run over privatisation. And after

Genoa, the institutions of global capitalism, led by the United States, were definitely looking shaky, losing some of their legitimacy. 11 September has dramatically changed the balance of forces. In addition to the human misery – now mainly compounded by the bombing and the violent repression of resistance to the war – it created an opportunity for the US to re-establish its political dominance.[3]

Tariq Ali, January 2002: Anglo-Saxon capitalism was in a state. Bush was virtually on the floor. Now they've been able to cover it up. From every progressive point of view, September 11 has been a disaster.[4]

Chris Nineham, Stop the War Coalition Chief Steward: Immediately prior to Stop the War I was one of the organisers of a network called Globalise Resistance, which was a network of anti-capitalist activists. It was involved in a whole number of things including the international mobilisations like Genoa in 2001, like European Social Forums, and I continued with some of that work after Stop the War was set up. I'm a member of the SWP [Socialist Workers Party], and had been prior to that for quite some time... One of the things I was involved in was making sure what happened in America didn't happen in Britain, in terms of the movement. 9/11 destabilised and disorientated the anti-capitalist movement, which was actually quite strong in the States at the time. There was a fear that was generated much more effectively in America than in Britain in the aftermath of 9/11. And because of the more difficult political questions it raised, the anti-capitalist movement in the States didn't respond very well and actually became de-mobilised. We put an argument to people who had been involved in organising a lot of the May Day protests and so on that we had to respond in a very clear, principled way to what had happened. However much 9/11 was a tragedy and a terribly regrettable incident, nevertheless it was clearly a product of US and Western policies generally in the Middle East, and that it was liable to lead to policies that would make the situation worse, and that we had to do everything we could, everything possible, to stop that happening. And that was quite a serious argument for several weeks. It was a question of making sure people got on board and the anti-war message permeated from the various networks that had been created.

Kevin Gillan, Jenny Pickerill and Frank Webster, co-authors of Anti-war activism. New media and protest in the information age: Immediately after 9/11... many individuals and organizations switched their focus from contesting globalization to contesting the expected military response.[5]

The creation of the Stop the War Coalition: The 21 September 2001 meeting at Friends Meeting House in London.

Mike Marqusee, Press Officer, Stop the War Coalition: I was very active against the Vietnam War when I was a teenager in the '60s and '70s. I've been politically active on the Left, in the labour movement and the Labour Party. I left the Labour Party in 2000 for reasons which are probably obvious. I've been a trade unionist and a campaigner against unjust wars. Also, I have a particular interest in South Asia as I have been there a lot and worked there. I've got close links with the peace movement there and I've been to Pakistan quite a bit.

Kevin Gillan, Jenny Pickerill and Frank Webster: From the outset one major driving force behind StWC has been the Trotskyite Socialist Workers Party. With a 30-year presence on the British Marxist Left and a fluid membership of around 3000, the SWP was well organised, conscious of the enormity of the terrorist attack and alert to the likelihood of a military reaction from the United States. This made it possible for the SWP to respond quickly and to seize the reins of opposition, though a great deal of this remained inchoate and uncertain in those opening weeks.[6]

Mike Marqusee: The SWP had a very quick but interesting meeting... And because I was in the network, and we worked closely with the Socialist Alliance, I went to that meeting. What was interesting was that all it was, was a straight up SWP meeting, so it wasn't exactly something that, in ordinary circumstances, anyone would have been interested in. But the hunger for alternative points of view, and frankly also for some community – that you weren't sitting alone in front of this insanity – meant it was packed out, including obviously with SWP members, and people like myself who had been working with them. I spoke a bit, and different people spoke, and it's interesting because it's still very confused at that point exactly what the perspective was, except we knew we didn't want a war. But people were just, you know, "What is Islam?" That was not even remotely dealt with at that meeting, and the question of Islamophobia wasn't particularly significant at that point, although everyone knew the backlash danger.[7]

John Rees, Stop the War Coalition National Officer: We had all been active against the Kosovo War in the late 90s and against the first Gulf war in the early 90s. In the first Gulf War I had been working with Paul Foot and John Pilger and we launched the Media Workers Against the War... We had been active on the Left, and previous anti-war movements... We had a sensation already that people's reaction to George Bush and what he might do in reaction to 9/11 would be at least as strong as their feelings about the event itself. That meeting very strongly confirmed that. A lot of people who spoke from the floor had been in their workplaces, colleges, talking to their friends and family ever since the attack on the twin towers had taken place, and were saying this – that people were scared about what the Americans were going to do next. So that was the immediate trigger to then call the 21 September meeting [at Friends Meeting House in London] the following week... And I think I wrote the leaflet for that meeting, which was called "Stop the war before it starts." That's where the name came from. I think the first leaflet mentioned Iraq as well as Afghanistan because anybody who had looked at the neo-conservatives in the States and seen the 1998 letter to [President Bill] Clinton knew that an absolute prime objective was Iraq. So I'm fairly certain the leaflet mentioned both Afghanistan and Iraq, even at that stage. Chris [Nineham] booked Friends Meeting House, I wrote the leaflet and phoned round some of the speakers – Tariq [Ali], Jeremy Corbyn. Lindsey [German] chaired it and I spoke at it.[i]

Mike Marqusee: In the initial development after 9/11, we were all surprised to find there were a lot of people from different backgrounds coming out and there was a common hunger for deeper understanding for all these issues. What is terrorism? What is imperialism? Why is the United Stated doing this? Why did Al-Qaeda do this? What do the people of Afghanistan want and what is their history? It was beautiful at those early meetings seeing people – including the SWP – working together trying to forge a deeper understanding of all this, so we would get off the back foot as it were, which we were on because of the whole way the media had handled 9/11. I think that period was genuinely participatory and exciting because the SWP had not at that time determined a single, all embracing line for it. It was a period of exceptional intellectual honesty in the movement, which having been in the movement a long time I was very impressed by.

John Rees: It [the 21 September 2001 meeting in Friends Meeting House] was absolutely huge. When you really ram Friends Meeting House, and have people upstairs along the long benches, I think you have around 1400 people in the main hall. And then we had the upstairs hall as an overflow hall as well with another 250 people in it and the hall down on the ground floor we also had 150 in. And then I think there was another 4–500 stood in that well of a garden. And all of us spoke in all the halls – we went round and repeated the speeches in all the halls, including on the megaphone to the people stood outside. It was an absolutely massive meeting. There must have been 2,500 people in Friends on that night. And that was the biggest indoor political rally in

---

i According to the official Stop the War Coalition history "Tariq Ali, Jeremy Corbyn MP, Liz Davies from the Socialist Alliance, George Monbiot, John Rees from the Socialist Workers Party (SWP) and Helen John from CND were speakers" at the meeting. Andrew Murray and Lindsey German, *Stop the war. The story of Britain's biggest mass movement* (London: Bookmarks, 2005), p. 47.

London for I should think ten years. It had a huge impact on us. There was a tremendous energy and excitement in the room. I remember Tariq [Ali] spoke very well. I think Helen John spoke from CND [Campaign for Nuclear Disarmament], so it was very good that CND were there from the beginning.

Tariq Ali: Essentially the atmosphere in the whole of Britain was how to react to this because there was a huge wave of hysteria. So what we did in that meeting was to treat the event rationally and try and pose questions as to why 9/11 had happened, who had carried it out and what was going on in the Arab world. Of course the tactics were completely wrong but they were terrorist tactics which had been used by anarchists in the past, by the IRA. They weren't new – it was very dramatic. It was a very large crowd at Friends Meeting House. I hope that meeting played some part in orientating people to think rationally and not to just accept the huge hysterical campaign that was mounted – that America is great and anyone who attacks it is evil.

Andrew Murray and Lindsey German: Although the [Stop the War] Coalition's main aim was to stop an attack on Iraq, further demands were added at its founding meeting – against any racist backlash and in defence of civil liberties. These were of greater or lesser mobilising significance at different times, but they were one element in building major support among ethnic minority communities – especially the Muslim community, which felt particularly under attack and which has borne the brunt of the assault on civil liberties since 9/11.[8]

Asad Rehman, Steering Committee member, Stop the War Coalition: My main area of political activity is anti-racist work. Anti-racist policing work. But I'm one of those people who crosses over on a lot of Left political issues. The [1984–5] Miners' Strike, [the 1986–7] Wapping print workers strike – I was very active around these. I come from a working-class town – Burnley – so a lot of issues around racist violence. So that is what politicised me. Then I got into Left politics when I was young like Militant. I went to Essex University and was very active in the Labour Club and Black Student's Alliance. I was Student President on a very left-wing platform. I then became a community activist. Lots of grassroots community work on issues around racist violence in east London, but also international work, such as the anti-apartheid movement, and Palestine. I used to take human rights delegations to Palestine. I was on the Intifada Committee. I was also very much involved in the Social Forum movement as well. I was one of the UK reps for the first ESF [European Social Forum] in Florence [in November 2002]. Basically social movement, progressive Left politics... So when the first public meeting happened at Friends Meeting House on 21 September I was the Chair of the Newham Monitoring Project – a grassroots, anti-racist organisation based in east London. A very well known community organisation. It did the [Stephen] Lawrence campaign. It had an authenticity. At the meeting we very much raised the issue that the building of the anti-war movement shouldn't just be about 'No War', it should also be about defending civil liberties and the rise of racism and islamophobia. Otherwise it would be very difficult to engage with people and it would just be another overwhelmingly white campaign. Of course, things had developed. In the

'80s and '90s there had been a politicisation of the Black community, which had thrown up a new generation of young, progressive Muslims as well. That was our big involvement at Friends Meeting House. We helped shape the demands of the Stop the War Coalition from the beginning. I was one of the National Officers. I suppose I was in the inner cabal right from the beginning to February 15.

Shahed Saleem, Just Peace: At the meeting there were all the different organising groups together – so nurses, lawyers and other different interest groups. And there wasn't any Muslim interest group. So I gave a slip of paper to the table saying "If anybody wants to organise a Muslim Against War group please get together afterwards". So that's how Just Peace started.

Shahedah Vawda, Just Peace: So we all met and decided to set up Just Peace – predominantly young Muslims along with people such [as] Dr [Ghayasuddin] Siddiq from what was then the Muslim Parliament. A lot of the people involved were people who had never been political before. There were nine or ten core people.

Shahed Saleem: The thing about starting a Muslim interest group within Stop the War was that I felt lots of people were speaking about islamophobia – that was one of the key mandates of Stop the War Coalition – but there were no Muslims involved. So there were people defending Muslims rights, but no Muslims defending their own rights. It felt like Muslims should be there. So that's one of the reasons I thought it was important to have Muslim representation. Not for the Coalition itself, but from a Muslim point of view. Muslims needed to be there.

Lindsey German: We were all very pleased with this [the 21 September meeting] so said "Ok, let's have an organising meeting next week", thinking maybe 50 people would turn up. So we booked the big hall in Friends Meeting House again and 400 or 500 people came to the organising meeting. It was one of the worst meetings I've been to. I chaired it. It was an absolute disaster in lots of senses. It was completely out of control. Most people didn't know each other. And there were people getting up and you didn't know if they had a very serious point to make, or whether they didn't want to say anything. CND came along, or some representatives of CND, and said they didn't want us to form a Stop the War Coalition – because I think they saw it as they were the permanent peace organisation. They said: "Fair enough if you just want to have a meeting but you shouldn't do all this". So there was huge controversy going on in the meeting – people shouting.

John Rees: Andrew Burgin, who became the [STWC] Press Officer, who was working at [the radical London bookshop] Housmans, was in the meeting and just walked off the floor and said he wanted to get involved. Andrew Murray, who's now the chair [of STWC] and at that time was the Press Officer for the train drivers union ASLEF, walked off the floor and introduced himself. It was an incredible confluence of different things that all had their point of origin at that huge meeting really. It was the right thing at the right time.

Andrew Murray: I suppose my political history goes back to 1976 when I was 18 and when I joined the Communist Party. I was a journalist on the *Morning Star* newspaper for some years down to the 1980s, roughly through to the end of the [1984–5] Miners' Strike. I was active in a number of other areas – miners' support, the campaign against the Poll Tax, issues that activists of my generation have been involved in. I came to work at the T&G in 1987 in the press office, and stayed here until 1998. At the time the Stop the War Coalition was set up I was working for ASLEF, the train drivers union, in a similar capacity. I've since returned to T&G – now Unite. So I suppose you could say I've been involved in politics all my life really. I can't claim to have been one of the virgin activists involved in Stop the War.

Andrew Burgin, Press Officer, Stop the War Coalition: Originally I was a member of the Worker's Revolutionary Party – in the '70s, the '80s and the '90s, I suppose. It was an organisation that had a very serious internal division – after the Miners' Strike in 1985. I worked on various campaigns – the Miners' Strike, the question of the defence of Bosnia during the Balkans crisis in the '90s, and many other different issues – with offshoots of that organisation. But in 2001, after 9/11, I felt the organisation I was part of, which was by then a very small organisation, wasn't up to the job. [It] really couldn't contribute anything to what I thought was a very serious situation that was created by 9/11, that would lead to war. Big war. If there was going to be a big war, I thought we needed to have a big anti-war movement. So I left the organisation I was part of and started working in the Coalition... Normally when you have a big public meeting, people say "We need to do a public campaign, who wants to get involved?" and you have a meeting a week later and it's 20 or 30 people. But it was another mass meeting – 500 people had come along...

There were people there from different political tendencies. At the September 21 meeting many people spoke, but of course the person who spoke with most authority and vision was Tariq Ali, who at that meeting spoke well. The political organisation at that time was predominately the Socialist Workers Party... Many political organisations were there, but what happened at the organising meeting is that there was a political struggle over the nature of the Coalition. The SWP really led that. Many of the smaller left-wing groups wanted the Coalition to engage on a number of different issues – difference aspects of imperialism. They wanted to make it very complicated, whereas I felt we needed to organise, and this was expressed by the Socialist Workers Party people, against the war, [for] the defence of the Muslim community and against the attacks on civil liberties. So it was to keep it on those key questions and not have it go off into other areas that would have limited the growth of the Coalition. You could say the demonstration on February 15th, the largest ever in British political history, the foundations were laid then, by making sure that the Left had learnt the lessons of previous struggles, that they weren't going to exclude people and were going to do it on the broadest possible basis. We would create a situation where you could bring in Greens, Lib Dems, you could keep it as broad as possible. It was the key to the whole thing.

Albert Beale, Militant Pacifist: Within a couple of meetings the party cadres from our dear comrades in the SWP had sown it up. There was some of us in what you might call the ongoing, existing peace movement who stuck with it a little while. Different people stuck with it for different amounts of time. I didn't run away after the first meeting, but I didn't stay as long as some people. I did go to some of those attempts at networking for a little while. It turned out, in the end, not to be terribly productive – in the sense I thought it was important to do what I thought was valuable. I'm not against getting a million people in the street for goodness sake. That's great, that's excellent. But in as much as that submerged a lot of other politics then it seemed to me that I would rather be one of a smaller group doing something smaller but what I thought was more important. Like people like Gabriel Carlyle.

Gabriel Carlyle, Peace Activist: The thing I do remember is that a platform was put forward, and a vote taken not to vote on the platform, which seemed a bizarre way of doing things. My recollection was that I went away from that meeting thinking there wasn't much of a place for me in that particular structure. I went away with the clear feeling it was undemocratic. That didn't mean I went away thinking I wouldn't do anything, or that I was going to go away and try and piss on their parade and screw things up for them. It just meant I went away thinking there wasn't a way I could constructively put my energies into that particular organisation.

Milan Rai, Activist, Author and Co-Editor of *Peace News*: One of the things about the 2002/2003 mobilization that is not so well-known is that it came out of the anti-sanctions movement. To some extent the skeleton structure of the mobilization was laid down over the previous five years by local groups organizing around Iraq and getting to know a lot about Iraq: responding to the Desert Fox attacks in 1998, responding to the February 2001 attacks, responding to the no-fly zones.[ii]

So there was an anti-sanctions and anti-strikes movement that had built up a considerable amount of knowledge about Iraq and had mobilized a certain amount of people. That network was obviously one tiny fraction of what eventually developed but I believe that network of anti-sanctions campaigners helped to accelerate the growth and knowledge of the anti-war movement in a way that wouldn't have happened if they hadn't been there. The fact they had already been doing that campaigning and had already developed a certain level of awareness and mobilizing – and had a certain amount of knowledge about Iraq – helped the anti-war movement a lot. I think that is part of the roots of the mobilization. There were various groups around the country in Birmingham, Cambridge, Bristol and London that had been campaigning against the sanctions and strikes. Those groups helped and strengthened the anti-war organizing that happened in those places. And because of the work that they did in their areas – educating and mobilizing people – that helped to lay the groundwork for the local groups that sprang up. They also supplied speakers who could go and speak to groups about the knowledge they had acquired in the previous years. There was a lot of contributions that the anti-sanctions movement made both locally and nationally to the anti-war mobilization. How much of that ended up in national Stop the War I don't know, but at the local level there was a considerable influence.

---

ii During the period 1991–2003 the US and UK (with the sometime participation of France) imposed two "No-Fly Zones" over parts of northern and southern Iraq, ostensibly to protect the Kurdish and Shiite populations. Neither zone was ever authorised by the UN. In December 1998 the US and UK launched Operation Desert Fox – a four-day bombing campaign against Iraq. On 16 February 2001 the US and UK bombed Iraq, supposedly in response to increased threats to US and UK aircraft.

"I remember being reasonably heartened by it": Anti-war activism against the war in Afghanistan

Salma Yaqoob, Chair of Birmingham Stop the War Coalition in 2003: In the immediate period following 11 September 2001, the ideological campaign was intense. The genuine sympathy and solidarity felt across the world for the innocent lives lost was cynically exploited in the drive to war. It was not easy to be a dissenter during these first few weeks and months... The ability of the anti-war movement in Britain to galvanise opposition among huge numbers of people was, in part, a defence against this type of ideological repression in the name of patriotism. Street politics became the order of the day – stalls, flyposting, door to door leafleting, internet campaigns, public meetings, as well as direct action, all carved out a space in which dissent was possible.[9]

Kate Hudson, Campaign for Nuclear Disarmament Chair 2003–10. General Secretary 2010-present: The first demonstration against that war [in Afghanistan], against it happening, in early October [2001], was called by CND. It was a vigil at Downing Street. I think it was called something like "Shoulder to shoulder" or something like that. It was at this time when Blair was saying we must be shoulder to shoulder with the US. We were saying shoulder to shoulder for peace... at around that time Stop the War Coalition was set up, which of course CND has never affiliated to. We are not part of Stop the War Coalition. So we began to cooperate with them on various things. But they didn't really emerge as the main force until slightly later. The vigil outside Downing Street had around 5,000 people at it. That may have been in September [2001]. And then the first march was in early October.[iii] That was a march led by CND and the Palestine Solidarity Campaign – an unusual combination. It came about because CND had already booked a demonstration slot on the question of National Missile Defense,[iv] so we had a date and a march booked, and the Palestine Solidarity Campaign had some kind of vigil or protest booked for the same day at the US Embassy or somewhere like that, so we decided to combine the slots and make it a 'Don't Attack Afghanistan' demonstration. I think it was probably supported by the Stop the War Coalition at that time.[10]

Mark Steel, Comedian, Journalist and former member of the Socialist Workers Party: By the time they bombed Afghanistan [in October 2001] there was quite a sizeable opposition to it. Which again I think is lost from history. Again I suspect because of subsequent events. Because it has become very commonplace to regard the war in Iraq as a disaster, and the war in Afghanistan as being a much healthier, reasonable war, it's forgotten there was a

---

iii On 22 September 2001 "An estimated 3,000 protesters gather outside Downing Street... to call for a measured response to the terrorist atrocities... with placards carrying the slogan 'Stand shoulder to shoulder for peace and justice, not more violence'." 'Anti-war protesters take to streets', Guardian, 22 September 2001, www.guardian.co.uk/world/2001/sep/22/september11.usa4 [Accessed 9 August 2012]. On 13 October 2001 the BBC reported a "CND-led march from Marble Arch to Trafalgar Square" was attended by around 20,000 people according to the police. 'Anti-war protesters rally in London', BBC News, 13 October 2001, http://news.bbc.co.uk/1/hi/uk/1596810.stm [Accessed 9 August 2012].

iv National Missile Defense is the antimissile programme the United States has been developing since the 1990s.

really sizeable opposition to the war in Afghanistan in 2001. Obama typifies it. He always opposed the war on Iraq, but the war on Afghanistan was something different. But it wasn't like that at the time. I opposed the Falklands War when that was going on and the numbers were small and confined to the Left. Worse than that, the people who supported the war weren't just in support of it but running up and down the road singing the national anthem and getting up in the middle of pubs and bursting into Rule Britannia. It certainly wasn't like that. So I remember being reasonably heartened by it.

Kate Hudson: Then we were working together with the Stop the War Coalition to have a further demonstration, in November 2001, against the attacks on Afghanistan.[v] Kabul fell a week before the demonstration was due to take place. I remember a discussion about whether we should cancel the demonstration because people wouldn't come because Kabul had fallen. But in fact we went ahead with the demonstration and it was much bigger than the previous one. I think the first one [on 13 October 2001] had had maybe 30–50,000 people on it. The second one [on 18 November 2001] was more like 70–80,000 people. Much broader, as indicated by the banners and placards and things like that. People from all different kinds of groups and backgrounds and so on coming out to express their opposition. Whereas the first one had been [a] more "of the

v "Organisers estimated that 100,000 had marched from Hyde Park to Trafalgar Square" for the anti-war march on 18 November 2001 "although the police say the numbers were nearer 15,000." 'Thousands join anti-war march', BBC News, 18 November 2001, http://news.bbc.co.uk/1/hi/uk/1662656.stm [Accessed 9 August 2012].

movement" kind of thing, more sort of narrow in its participation. This second one was remarkable really. That was the first phase of the development of what became the big anti-Iraq war movement.[11]

Sean Wallis, Web Manager, Stop the War Coalition: Campaigning against the war in Afghanistan was very interesting. I'd been involved in campaigns over, for example, the [1999] Serbian conflict, where to a great extent public opinion supported the war. We'd have tiny demos – 10,000 would be typical. People would abuse you for protesting against the war. But leafleting local Tube stations over Afghanistan in the autumn of 2001 showed me that something else was going on. If you had enough people and made a big enough splash you could get 90% of people to take the leaflets. This told me that we were not alone. The audience for the anti-war movement was the majority.

The roots of the British Muslim mobilisation

Anas Altikriti, Muslim Association of Britain Spokesperson in 2003: I'm very heavily involved in politics by virtue of birth. I was born to a very political family. My father hailed from Tikrit in Iraq, the same village [as] Saddam Hussein. He went to school with Saddam. My grandfather was the school headmaster. When the Ba'ath Party came to prominence and Saddam started to rise to power through the party my father was living in fear because the Ba'athists were particularly brutal with their detractors, and particularly so with those who came from the same clan. So when he saw an opportune moment in 1970 he left Iraq and came to the UK. I was about a year and a half old... It was during my 'A'-Levels and early college years – 1985–1987 – when I became heavily involved in local politics, and particularly student politics. It wasn't 'Muslim' politics, it was just politics. But I was a Muslim and I worked with all sorts of people. At the time the Muslim community wasn't really a tangible element. But what I think shifted that from mere politics in general to a more Muslim politics was the Salman Rushdie affair in 1989.

Shahed Saleem: Muslim social action in Britain reached its zenith at that time. It was the biggest issue around which Muslims collaborated and came on to the streets. Interestingly, it was very much an 'us' and 'them' scenario, a very polarised situation. "The Western world doesn't support our values and what is important to us blah blah blah". From an outsider perspective it was very much "These people are unsophisticated and illiterate and don't understand literature". There is truth in both perspectives, but it was a polarised situation.

Anas Altikriti: There was an incredible debate within the Muslim community itself about what we should do and how we should express our anger and frustration. I was one of the few that was against the protests and demonstrations in the manner they took place. I was one of the very few controversial people who at the time outspokenly criticised the fatwa against Salman. Not because I had any kind of favour with Salman Rushdie or his book, but because I thought at the least he wins the publicity. I recall the absurd argument of a very angry, quite well-off young man who went and [bought] 200 copies of *The Satanic Verses* and gave them to be burnt. Such absurdity! It just cemented my view that this was all wrong and that we needed a new direction. But I could also see at that time – I was about 20 or 21 – the emergence of something quite unique – the Muslim voice. The young Muslim men and women being on the streets – I hadn't seen this in my lifetime.'

Shahed Salaam: After that came the first Gulf War, then the Bosnian War. So through the 90s there were lots of issues that really reinforced the polarisation. That's why in the 90s you had groups like Hizb ut-Tahrir becoming very popular on campuses, because their rhetoric was one of Muslim separatism. Their argument was basically "It doesn't matter how much you live amongst non-Muslims, they will always turn against you." This was their selling point. To demonstrate this point they would point partly to the Gulf War, but specifically to the Bosnian War, saying these were European people who are being persecuted and, even though they are white, the fact they are Muslim means they are being persecuted. From the Rushdie affair through the '90s there was a sense of growing Muslim radicalisation. The rhetoric was very much about separatism. So that is what we were up against in 2001.

Anas Altikriti: After the Salman Rushdie affair I started working with Muslim youngsters, trying to do two things. First of all, to present an Islam I recognised – coming from an Arab heritage but being raised entirely in Britain. I was often frustrated by the way Islam was represented. My local imam, [to whom] my father used to take me every Friday, spoke a language I couldn't understand. Although his words were in English, he was talking to a different kind of audience... My experience was entirely different. I wanted someone to speak from the British perspective in Islam and also to present a version – if that is the word to use – of Islam that did away with the cultural ties... In 1997 I think the real serious step to what I had envisaged took place when myself and a few others – a few dozen up and down the country – came together and founded the Muslim Association of Britain [MAB]. The idea behind this was basically to address serious societal, economic and political visions from the Muslim perspective. We were trying to prove Muslims weren't just here as consumers, but here as people who have a future in this country and a say in its future. And also possibly have some solutions – either from our religious background or values or because of our own experience which [we] have carried to Britain. These are experiences that ought not to be wasted. And at the same time we wanted to talk about an Islam that is essentially British. That speaks in English and addresses people in a British kind of mentality or attitude. There were 200–250 founding members. By 2002 we had a membership of 450–500. The figure may have been up to 1,000 by 2003. It wasn't a huge organisation per se, but it was the kind of size that we thought was capable of carrying a message. Once you get lumbered with thousands upon thousands of people it gets fairly bureaucratic.

9/11 and British Muslims

Anas Altikriti: A number of things happened after 9/11. The terrain evolved.

Salma Yaqoob: Before 11 September 2001 my immediate concern, as a mother, was naturally the wellbeing of my own family. I was interested in the world, and had opinions, but never saw myself as a "leader" or a spokesperson. But within a few short months I was involved in political organising on a local and national level. How this transformation occurred is but a small example of how many Muslims, and others, had their lives transformed by their response to those big events. My story begins with the shock of 11 September and its immediate aftermath. It is difficult to describe in words the feeling that I experienced after hearing about the horrific attack on 9/11. The sheer scale of the attack produced an unprecedented level of media coverage, with many turning quickly to expression[s] of anti-Muslim sentiment. Within a few hours, Muslims were being blamed for the terrible attacks, and the words "Islamic terrorism" were being screamed from every media outlet. Suddenly I was not Salma any more, but a terrorist somehow connected with these despicable acts. My fear was very real and I felt isolated and a stranger for the first time. Returning to my home I was spat upon in the street. I was shaking with anger. I had my three-year old son with me and I feared for his safety. Nobody said or did anything – they just looked and passed by. I felt helpless, and the indifference of the witnesses was the greatest shock. It was clear that I was not being seen as a person any more. I clutched my son closer and from that moment decided that I would never be passive again. I would never be like those people who saw but just walked on by.[12]

Ruhul Tarafder, London-based community activist: It suddenly became apparent, whether you are a practicing Muslim or not, that you are a Muslim. It was drummed into you at every opportunity by the newspapers, the TV, everywhere you were looking. People who worked in the City who thought their Muslim identity wasn't very important, suddenly they became aware because everyone at work was saying "Oh, right, so you're a Muslim". Some people had genuine curiosity and wanted to know what people's views were on these things: "Do you support September 11th?" – silly things like that. Some kind of inherent racisms that existed, suddenly came out – "You're responsible", "You have to apologise for what happened, otherwise you must support it". After September 11th, the climate was such that Muslims had to become very apologetic and we were under pressure. Racism towards Muslims increased without a doubt. Working at 1990 Trust I used to see racism cases all the time, in terms of hostility towards Muslims. Even within my own family I can think of incidents. For example, one of my sisters was walking in Kent and someone – and this is how stupid some people are – rolled down his window and said "You F'ing Israelis!" She found it quite funny because they are so ignorant they said "You F'ing Israelis", but obviously they meant to be anti-Islamic because she was wearing the hijab and it was just after September 11th.

Islamophobia and Anti-Muslim Hate Crime: UK case studies report, European Muslim Research Centre, 2011,

University of Exeter: The phenomenon of increased suspicion, hostility, bigotry, intimidation and violence towards Muslims in the UK can be traced back to 9/11. In the last twelve months we have interviewed Muslims with different theological, ethnic and cultural backgrounds in many parts of the UK and there is already significant evidence to suggest that 9/11 marks a dramatic and negative shift in attitudes and behaviour towards Muslims from within virtually all other sections of UK society.[13]

Anas Altikriti: What people often don't mention is the fact the Muslim community was hand in hand with anyone else throughout not only Britain but the world of feeling the shock and the horror of the 9/11 events. Very few people mentioned this. We had to deal with a number of issues at the same time. We were shocked and horrified. We were totally in a state of collective shock. But at the same time we were commanded to come out and sort of explain ourselves... MAB had our general assembly a few weeks after 9/11. There were calls to the office saying "This is not the time, let's cancel"... Our take was that there is no reason for us to hide. It was as though we were admitting something we hadn't actually done. So there was a meeting that took place between the main organisations. I recall people speaking from all corners and all points of view. And one of the most alarming speeches was from someone I have incredible respect for – who has a long history with the Muslim community in Britain. And he stood up and said his advice was to stay at home. And if you can afford to take time off work do that, and if you can afford to keep the womenfolk at home do that – because of the hijab thing women can't get lost in the crowd. And I remember that same person talking about stocking up with canned foods – it was like back to the bunkers! I was sitting there and thinking this was going to take us back way beyond the 70s. This is bad, because what was being proposed was for the Muslim community to impose a siege upon itself. That was exactly what we had been trying to fight for the last thirteen, fourteen years. And now most mosques who had opened up to the community were receiving floods of interest from people in the neighbourhood, sports clubs, the police and the local council, we were suddenly talking about hiding at home? It just didn't make sense. I remember saying something that was quite impassioned and possibly out of place because there w[ere] some elders present. Others also spoke in the same vein, and I'm glad to report that by an overwhelming majority that was the decision made – that now is the time to open up and hit the streets. The meeting was some time around the 20th September [2001]. A couple of weeks after 9/11. I think it was one of the most important, milestone decisions in the evolution of the Muslim community in Britain. Thereafter we were propelled forward.

Salma Yaqoob: The response to 9/11 went broadly along three lines. One, which was quite a large proportion of the community, was that things are really bad so let's keep our heads down. Don't say anything in public because it will make people even more angry at us. This is not the time. Bury your head in the sand and it will all blow over at some point. In fact it would be irresponsible if we did speak out because it would bring even more harm and negative attention and focus to the community because we will be seen as traitors if we criticise the Government. Don't get involved. There was also a fear about being put on the books of MI5. There was a huge combination of paranoia and genuine fear. They didn't want to do anything that could be viewed as counterproductive in terms of how British Muslims are viewed by [the] wider society and the Government. So there was a lot of pressure to not say anything. For example, the mosques didn't want to discuss this stuff. Nobody wanted to draw attention to the community. You have to remember people had worked for so many years to be accepted in this country. And by criticising the Government about the war it might reinforce some of the negative stereotypes about Muslims not belonging and that we are outsiders. Another response, a small proportion but vocal, was that "It is 'us against them', the West against Muslims. They are going to kill our brothers and sisters. There is no point in joining non-Muslims in opposing this because they will always hate you and will always be your enemy." There was this idea of Jihad, of being anti non-Muslim. So the mainstream anti-Muslim sentiment that was expressed in the media was used as a recruiting tool for some of these groups, as if they were the vanguard for Muslims and they were defending the Muslim cause. But it was very negative and anti-Western. To me this was counterproductive. So the two responses – one of complete passivity, and one that appeared to be active and assertive – were both complete cul-de-sacs. I thought both were a morally flawed perspective to start with and at the same time politically counterproductive. I saw there was a gap, where yes we were feeling this pressure but we should speak up, but how do we do that without being further isolated? For people like myself, even if we were further isolated it was the right thing to do. For me that is what Jihad is – struggling for what's right.

Jenny Pickerill: Muslims have not previously been associated much with political engagement in Britain. There have been one or two prominent Muslim politicians, some observers might have recalled that angry Muslims in Bradford had burned copies of Salman Rushdie's Satanic Verses in the late 1980s because it had allegedly insulted Islam. They participated in demonstrations against the first Gulf War in the early 1990's, and others will have remembered Muslim youths participating in the Oldham riots during the spring of 2001. But on the whole Muslim groups have had a low public and political profile focusing on their communities and keeping out of issues and areas that might cause controversy.

Richard Phillips, Researcher into anti-war movements and Islamophobia, University of Liverpool: I think it's quite useful to take a step back. For one thing whenever you talk about 'Muslims' it is always a problematic category in the sense that identifying as Muslim in the movement is something some people do at certain moments in strategic ways. So many of the people who chose to identify as Muslims in the demonstrations against the wars in Afghanistan and Iraq and the war on terror were individually involved in other movements and took stands many times before in their lives, it's just they may have done so under a different framework. So although they may not have been presented publicly as 'Muslim' and may not have presented themselves as 'Muslim' they were still there. So I think the idea that there wasn't any Muslim involvement before then is not entirely right.

Abjol Miah, Community activist in Tower Hamlets and Respect parliamentary candidate for Bethnal

Green and Bow in 2010 general election: We had to work very hard to get some of the mosques involved. The problem is that many of the mosques and many of the community projects are within the framework of, or get funding from, the council. And anywhere there is funding attached, projects get very scared. It was "The Government aren't going to like us" or "We will lose our funding". So it was a tough battle for the anti-war movement to get the message across. We were telling them this was safe ground to express themselves.

Salma Yaqoob: It was not until a friend of mine, quite by coincidence, came across a group of Socialist Workers Party activists campaigning in the city centre against the proposed bombing of Afghanistan, that things began to turn around. At a time when we were feeling powerless and were being told to keep our heads down, it was reassuring to be approached by people who were sympathetic to our stance and predicament. She told me of an anti-war meeting to be held and persuaded myself and another friend to attend. Things began to unfold very quickly from there onwards. That meeting was a ray of hope, and my friends and I had a renewed sense of optimism. For the first time our views and thoughts were being heard and taken seriously, and the fear and frustration of being constantly misunderstood began to lessen.[14]

Abjol Miah: The [anti-war] marches [in 2001 and 2002] helped because they really tested the leadership in the community: "Are you there or are you not there?" The Muslim leaders were tested. You can have coffee behind the scenes and work with different politicians but as a community we wanted to see where they stood. So the marches were a testing ground.

Asad Rehman: The first demonstration [against the Afghanistan war, on 18 November 2001] was an important demonstration. Important because we were able to have a lot of influence on how it was shaped. I would say that pretty much laid the foundation for the fact it was more diverse than any other anti-war movement the country had ever seen. The demonstration happened at the same time as [the Islamic month of fasting] Ramadan, so we went around the Muslim community collecting a lot of food and we did a symbolic opening of the fast in Trafalgar Square in solidarity with the people in Afghanistan. We made a space at the demonstration for prayer. We got an Imam to do a call for prayer off the platform in Trafalgar Square. All big, symbolic things to engage the Muslim community that had never been done before. Plus we went out and brought the mosques on board and really drew out people and got people engaged. At that point it was about the war in Afghanistan, not the war in Iraq. So that really laid the foundation and laid the groundwork for the diversity of the anti-war movement – one of the marked achievements of the anti-war movement.

Ruhul Tarafder: I remember one of the first demonstrations was during Ramadan. Asad [Rehman] might have mentioned it to you. We got thousands of Muslims to attend and we provided Halal food for everybody to break their Iftar.[vi] I remember a friend of mine managed to sort out a deal with Tahira Foods. There were four trucks of food for Trafalgar Square. But there was one problem – when it all arrived it was all frozen. So I had to ring another friend

---

vi Iftar is the evening meal when Muslims break their fast during Ramadan.

of mine who owns another big catering business called Chutney's in Barking, who have big kitchen facilities. And I have never worked so hard – through the whole night we cooked these four trucks of food in all their different fryers and things, and then we took it to Trafalgar Square. And we had prayer facilities – just to make people feel welcome and involve them. It was after that that MAB and other Muslim organisations got involved from what I saw.

Female Muslim anti-war activist: The march that sticks in my mind was the first march. It was Ramadan. I was with some friends – non-Muslims and Muslims and some of the non-Muslims were fasting with me. That was quite amazing. Then when we arrived in Trafalgar Square there were Muslims providing food for breaking the fast. I remember there was a section in Trafalgar Square where people could pray. And for me that was the most amazing thing – in the middle of London you have Muslims marching, fasting and praying. Someone on the platform was calling for prayer – in the centre of London! I don't think anything could have beaten that. So the rest of the marches was the same kind of stuff, except it was getting bigger and bigger.

Jenin and the Muslim Association of Britain's April 2002 demonstration

Asad Rehman: Jenin happened.[vii] There was a group called the Muslim Association of Britain. They were interesting

vii Between 1–18 April 2002 Israel invaded the Palestinian refugee camp in Jenin killing over 50 people and damaging hundreds of buildings.

because they were mainly drawn from Arab Muslim backgrounds. So not from South Asian Muslim backgrounds, which was the dominant [Muslim] community in the UK. But they say politics is about being in the right place at the right time. They called a demonstration about Jenin. There was a massive outpouring in the Muslim community. Some people say 75,000 people, some people say 100,000 people came out on the demonstration. It really cemented MAB as the mobilising arm of the Muslim community, in the sense that it gave them a position.

Anas Altikriti: In April 2002 there was the Jenin massacre. We decided to do something that hadn't happened for years and years – since the Salman Rushdie affair. That is, call for a demo from the Muslim community. Emotions were flying high. What was happening in Palestine was really gruesome, and people were very, very angry. And we said "Let's call a demonstration". I recall going with the President of MAB to the police before the demonstration. It was the very first time we had done anything like this. In their book Andrew Murray and Lindsey German described us as being "amateurs" in terms of demonstrating or marching. It wasn't something we did everyday! We were told we had to go and get a permit, so we went to the police. And the application form asked "How many people do you expect to attend?" And I looked at my friend and he looked at me and I said "How many do you think? 5,000?" And he said "Come on, let's say 10,000". And we were discussing this between ourselves – we didn't want more police than demonstrators. So we decided to put down 10,000, and then as soon as we walked out the door my friend said "You know what, we should have put in 5,000. Never mind". It turned out to be more than 125,000 people! I think it transformed most people's views about the size, the potential and the weight of the Muslim community. And the level of anger at a time when we were still under the kosh because of 9/11 – because of the accusation we were a fifth column and people to be suspected. To come out in the way they did, and travel from so far, was absolutely phenomenal.

Shahedah Vawda: MAB really went for it, which is great because someone had to do it. But I think other organisations were more aware of the subtleties of working with the government and community at the same time. Initially, when we started organising, a lot of the community was scared – scared of the backlash, scared about what this meant for them. When Anas [Altikriti] came on board they were able to justify anti-war activities from a Muslim perspective, so Muslims were comfortable. At that time the MCB [Muslim Council of Britain] was seen as a Government lackey. Much more institutionalised; it didn't really have any credibility. So MAB were able to exploit the vacuum. Their background is from Egypt, the [Muslim] Brotherhood. So they have a very conventional, religious interpretation. That's why they were able to convince people.

Salma Yaqoob: MAB, as part of their theological understanding, have this concept of 'jihad' as standing up for justice. So not being afraid to be political. For me it is extremely political to not speak. Often you are seen as political if you do something but I think it is sometimes more telling, and has greater consequences, if you choose not to... MAB, because they had this as part of their original thinking, stepped up and helped organise things. So that's why you hear about MAB. It's not that everybody came on coaches with MAB, but they were an organising cog. They had that disciplined, organising approach, in the same way the SWP [Socialist Workers Party] has. They [MAB] had a certain philosophy and organised members, so they could organise effectively.

Female Muslim anti-war activist: The Stop the War Coalition, the SWP and CND are not representative of the British people, but no one mentions this. MAB were given an opportunity and they took it. Ultimately you have to give credit to people when they did good things. And I think MAB grabbed the opportunity.

Anas Altikriti: What was important [on the April 2002 protest] was that we were joined by a sizable non-Muslim contingent, which worked wonders in the long run. Also, most of the speakers were not Muslim – we had Jeremy Corbyn, Tony Benn, Lindsey German, Andrew Murray, George Galloway. Those Muslims who weren't entirely convinced about marching alongside the Left were suddenly listening to these people, who were actually talking their language. It made our job much easier. First of all the boost of confidence in the community was beyond imagination. I can't describe the outpour of emotions from people who said they were really scared before that march. Things that now we would think were silly – think of the context of the time. People would say: "I took my wife and kids and we had a very nice conversation with the police." To him that was something to write back home about. It broke many, many barriers and created a lot of confidence within – and trust with – the authorities.

Building the anti-war movement: The Muslim Association of Britain and Stop the War Coalition form a coalition

Anas Altikriti: Just to remind you of the context – the Muslim community had been catapulted in this. Before this there had been a huge reluctance, particularly from the Salman Rushdie affair, which was particularly bruising from a PR point of view – a lot of resistance to actually coming out overtly in the name of the Muslim community. That was one point of view. The other issue was taking Muslims, many still very devout and hanging on to baggage from their homeland, and trying to convince them to stand on the very same platform as gays, as atheists, as communists – which in the minds of many Islam was diametrically against. So therefore, first of all we had to convince the Muslim community that to come out and be seen as the Muslim community wasn't a bad thing. And that if it was run well, and managed well and done in a disciplined manner we wouldn't have a repeat of the Salman Rushdie affair, with crazed-eyed youngsters shouting in front of the camera "I'm going to kill him, I'm going to kill him!"... The other question was whether we could bring the community to stand alongside people whom they have never had any dealings with. From a religious perspective we should be allied to the Right – we believe in family values, faith and religion. But we know how the Right had failed not just ourselves but the entire country. And therefore we felt this was an opportune moment. We went round trying to convince people saying "So you disagree with people. So what? So people have their own beliefs. So what? So people have a particular lifestyle? So what?" Saying these things, to many it was borderline blasphemy. We were declaring ourselves to be outcasts of Islam. So we did it in a way that made sure we weren't isolated. Wherever I went to a meeting, I wouldn't go alone. I would bring with me an Islamic scholar and someone from the grassroots. So I wouldn't be seen to be speaking on my own whim, but would be seen as someone who had the backing of the community and has clerical backing. It was very, very tough. Very difficult... The important thing after that [the April 2002 march] was that Stop the War realised MAB had a hefty mobilising power and energy. And therefore during the demonstration – as I was chairing it – I could hear Lindsey German, Andrew Murray and Andrew Burgin whispering with the MAB leadership, talking about holding something together before the Labour Party conference in September [2002].

Mike Marqusee: People have re-written the history of this. I was at the meetings and there was a lot of confusion, including the SWP leadership who had no particular idea what to do about this. And their members were confused. I got a lot of grief from a lot of their members about excessive religious symbolism and religious rhetoric on the [28 September 2002] march. These people are life-long atheists and secularists, and they have a right to feel that way, although I don't think you can impose it on people at a demo. It was understandable. Their leaders were going in a different direction because they saw a model they thought they could repeat cookie-cutter style endlessly.

Asad Rehman: There was a lot of ignorance. You've got to remember the backdrop to all this was that in the 70s and

80s the SWP had the Anti-Nazi League. In the late 80s and 90s there was an explosion of Black community politics, so you had had Black community organising, basically saying "Hold on a minute, we are not canon fodder for you Left groups. We control our own struggle" etc. There had been a putting in place of the SWP. They were not the dominant people in community politics. In fact most of them didn't know how to speak and engage with the community. What they were good at was being in public sector unions. Good at being in the trade unions, good at being in the local authorities. Very much in the public sector unions. So it didn't come easy to them. So partly we were showing and teaching them how to engage with the Muslim community – making the right introductions for people, explaining how they could leaflet during prayers on Friday lunchtime and asking the mosques and Imams to make announcements. And over the years the SWP formula of public meeting, demonstration, public meeting, demonstration, whilst it had many flaws, played well to what they could do. They are very good at leafleting and organising meetings. Also, for a long time they had been speaking to themselves. So they would have a meeting and maybe 10 or 20 people turn up and they would think it is successful. In community organisations you don't think it is successful until you have 200 or 300 people there. And these are meetings in the local communities, not in central London. So when they started speaking to the Muslim community, it was very interested in this issue – there was a historical relationship with Afghanistan, there were lots of family connections with Afghanistan. So there was lots of crossover that made it an easy sell. There was an immediate connection for many people within the Muslim community. So suddenly you would go to a meeting and there would be 200, 300 people. So to some extent they were like rabbits in the headlights – suddenly speaking to bigger audiences than they had for a very long time.

Anas Altikriti: Remember this was the first time we had come together as equals. It was difficult for us as well as them. For instance, the very first meeting we were invited to by Stop the War, they invited us to a pub. So I called and said "We'd love to come, but not in a pub", and they said "You don't have to drink", and I said "I realise that I don't have to drink, but if it is at all possible could we meet somewhere else?" If in a personal capacity I had been invited with a friend to meet where there is alcohol I might not have a problem, but at that time I was representing the Muslim community. And you must always understand every single step I took I was always dragging the entire community behind me. And I'm being stabbed in the back by numerous people and if I was found to be meeting in a pub that would confirm every single apprehension and myth that was being put on me. So Stop the War kindly suggested a community centre, which was absolutely fine. And that was the last time, as far as I know, that Stop the War met in a pub. I think that shows the maturity in how we were dealing with each other.

Shahedah Vawda: There was a great deal of goodwill, especially from the non-Muslims. They would go to great lengths to accommodate us. To think the SWP, which is so fervently anti-God, were even able to discuss working with Muslims was amazing. It was a real shift. There was a lot of rumbling throughout the time the Coalition was together. Generally there was a lot of goodwill. For Muslims like us who have been raised in the West – we can play both games, being equally comfortable in the Muslim community and in Western society.

Richard Phillips: What I discovered [from my academic research] was that you can have strategic political actions which can have a moment but don't necessarily change things forever. You can have a moment where things become so extreme – or they take a particular shape where people will form coalitions and behave in ways they don't normally do. So the relationship between the Muslim Association of Britain and the Left in particular made some people in both groups uncomfortable. Certainly Nick Cohen has talked about the latter.

Nick Cohen, Journalist: The Muslim Association of Britain... whose members are mainly Arabs, isn't a strong force in British Islam. It is a branch of the Muslim Brotherhood which wants a religious tyranny to enforce Islamic law. A supporter explained to the communist Weekly Worker that existing Muslim governments were far too permissive. "We see no genuine Muslim states in the world today – Saudi Arabia and places like that profess to be Muslim states but this is untrue." The association believes the punishment for Muslims who abandon their faith should be death and that Israel should be abolished. Although it didn't support the 11 September atrocities, it refused to condemn the al-Qaeda killings in Mombasa [in November 2002] because Israelis were the target... Single-issue campaigning always brings strange alliances and it's silly to be over-fastidious... It's one thing, however, to see the upholders of sharia law join your demonstration. It is quite another to invite them to co-host your demonstration and embrace them as brothers.[15]

Female Muslim anti-war activist: Coming from a French background, the interaction between the Left and Muslims was very interesting, and the most inspiring element, for me. In France it is close to zero. I was coming already coming from a left-wing background and before 9/11 I hadn't done much work with Muslim organisations in this country. I have spoken to a lot of people, and there seem to be several factors. The attitude of the Left in this country was much more inclusive than in any other part of Europe. The Stop the War Coalition was very inclusive. Also, Muslims had been in this country for several generations. They got involved in the Salman Rushdie affair in 1989. And in the 1990s organisations like MAB and the MCB started addressing issues for Muslims in this country. In terms of their identity, Muslims are less stigmatised in this country than they are in France. They are also much more assertive than they are in France.

Mark Steel: One thing I think they [Stop the War Coalition] got absolutely right was the attitude towards religion. There was something very poignant about it. When I was in the SWP, when it was really dynamic, you would get talks or pamphlets about religion or something like that. And on this issue the socialist point of view, as I understood it, was far from being the stereotype that socialists despise religion and see it as the opiate of the masses – the Stalinist view. That was never the tradition of socialists towards religion. For example, I've read very moving accounts of how the Left in the 1930s in America would join and make alliances with evangelical churches and preachers, who even though they were very religious, were committed activists against segregation. All of this was seen as just theory and people condemned it as "Bloody lefties talking about absolutely nothing". But when it came to this march and the movement more generally, that attitude towards religion had an absolutely fundamental impact. You could easily have taken the view that Islam was something that you were thoroughly opposed to and therefore we are certainly not going to involve ourselves with those sorts of people. And I think the people leading the Stop the War movement were absolutely, completely right in taking the opposite view and saying we can argue about whether mountains move or whether the Koran should be strictly followed or whatever another day, but now if you are opposed to the war in Iraq then we want you to be part of this. It wasn't automatic at all in the Muslim community. It wasn't automatic that the Asian or Muslim communities would side with the Left. All sorts of things could have happened. In France for example, although they were opposed to the war so it was a slightly different business, the Left has traditionally been hostile to Muslims. So on a big scale it means anyone who is opposed to this war for the reasons we are all opposed to it came on the march. And I think it was absolutely right that they did that. Without that it wouldn't have been anywhere near so effective. When people are scornful about this I find it incredibly smug and patronising. The idea that all Muslims are all crazy jihadis or that all Muslims hate women is such a repulsive idea. I play cricket with a load of Pakistanis, and the idea you shouldn't go on a march with them if they want to oppose a brutal war is so absurd. I think they were absolutely right to do this. It was a very important thing that they did.

Lindsey German: Andrew Murray always puts it quite well. He says, if you were having a campaign around anything you wouldn't demand that people are pro-gay.

John Rees: I'm old enough to be in the Left in the 70s. The Left at that time was having a love affair with Afro-Caribbean militancy and with Rastas, who were religious and also had exactly, [the same] if not worse, ideas about gays and women as the Muslims. But I don't remember a single debate at that time about what are we doing deifying Rastas. I've only ever really thought this now, because I've had to answer questions about the Muslim community that I never had to answer back then about that.

Lindsey German: I think the real jihadi, extreme fundamentalists don't come anywhere near Stop the War. One of the things that happened in 2002/2003 is that one of the extreme Muslim groups would produce leaflets saying "Don't stop the war, except by Islamic means." They would hand out these leaflets in Whitechapel markets saying don't go on the marches. Those people never come near us.

'DON'T STOP THE WAR Except through Islamic Politics' by Hizb ut-Tahrir, Britain, 22 January 2003: It is clear that many of the heads of the Stop the War campaign are atheists, communists, anarchists and believers in sexual freedoms. These are people who believe that Allah does not exist, that the Prophet Muhammad (Sall Allahu Alaihi Walallam) was an imposter, and that religions such as Islam are barbaric, oppress women, forbid sexual expression and remain as the 'opium of the masses'... their agenda and vision for what values, systems and policies Iraq should have are as corrupt to Muslims as any right wing hawk residing in Washington. Hence it is Haram (forbidden) for Muslims to march… under such a banner.[16]

Mike Marqusee: The history of this is important to get right. What had happened was MAB had been instrumental putting together a very big demonstration in spring 2002 against the Israeli invasion of the West Bank – utterly brutal. It was a good demonstration. At that time one of the biggest we had had on the Palestine issue. It was particularly noticeable that MAB had mobilised lots of young Muslims. That was a great breakthrough and very welcome. That gave them a lot of confidence, and already there had been extensive Muslim participation since 9/11 – before MAB came on board. Then MAB picked the [28] September 2002 to hold a demonstration to mark the second anniversary of the beginning of the second intifada. So they wanted to hold the demo that day, and we were also looking forward to that date for our next big anti-Iraq war demo. They came to see us. At that stage almost nobody knew anything about them, apart from the name and a few basic things. There was confusion about what to do. I think that we all felt we couldn't possibly have two demonstrations and divide those two issues on that day. That would be very damaging to the movement. Secondly that we couldn't possibly have a separate Muslim anti-war demo and a non-Muslim, or white, anti-war demo. That it had to be one anti-war movement. So after discussion we all agreed to pool our resources and do it all together. And it required a lot of work because there was different emphasis, different methods, and so forth. Overall it was very rewarding and it did work.

The warm up: The 28 September 2002 anti-war march in London

Tony Blair, Prime Minister 1997–2006, introduction to the 24 September 2002 dossier on Iraq: What I believe the assessed intelligence has established beyond doubt is that Saddam has continued to produce chemical and biological weapons, that he continues in his efforts to develop nuclear weapons, and that he has been able to extend the range of his ballistic missile programme... I am in no doubt that the threat is serious and current, that he has made progress on WMD, and that he has to be stopped ...his military planning allows for some of the WMD to be ready within 45 minutes of an order to use them.[17]

Greg Dyke, *BBC* Chairman 2000–4: The September dossier was only a public relations exercise designed to persuade sceptical Labour MPs and a sceptical public to support a policy of going to war in Iraq.[18]

***Observer*, 26 June 2011:** The senior intelligence official responsible for Tony Blair's notorious dossier on Iraq's weapons of mass destruction proposed using the document to mislead the public about the significance of Iraq's banned weapons. Sir John Scarlett, who as head of the Joint Intelligence Committee was placed "in charge" of writing the September 2002 dossier, sent a memo to Blair's foreign affairs advisor referring to "the benefit of obscuring the fact that in terms of WMD Iraq is not that exceptional".[19]

Andrew Murray and Lindsey German: September 2002 marked a turning point in the movement, which gained in confidence as the case for war looked shakier. The demonstration was planned in London for 28 September, the day before the [Labour Party] conference was due to begin in Blackpool.[20]

Anas Altikriti: Stop the War wanted it to be about Iraq, because clearly there were preparations for war. We still thought Palestine was very important and didn't want people to forget about it. There was a very lengthy and often heated discussion amongst ourselves.

Andrew Murray and Lindsey German: This was a challenge for everyone. Most people in the Stop the War Coalition had no problem with linking over these two issues. We had ourselves campaigned on Palestine, organising a march and rally in January outside the Israeli embassy on one of the wettest days of the year. So it was felt we could easily combine the two slogans. But we had never worked with MAB, and there was some hesitation and nervousness, no doubt on both sides. However, in the interests of building the biggest possible protest which could have a real impact on the Labour Party and hence on Government policy, we decided to go ahead with the unity.[21]

Anas Altikriti: We said to them "What's the problem with carrying two banners – Iraq and Palestine?" And they said "It wouldn't work. People don't come to a demonstration that calls for two things. Those that are against Iraq might not agree with our views on Palestine, and vice-versa. Why are we dividing people? We can have another demonstration at another time about Palestine, but this time it should be about Iraq." And it was a very, very heated debate. And ultimately we came to an agreement that we would have the two banners: Iraq on one side and Palestine on the other side.

Mike Marqusee: One of their [MAB's] suggestions initially was that it be called the million man march. We shouldn't make a big deal out of it, because in the end it was rejected, but clearly that was no good for us because firstly it was a sexist formulation. Secondly it was taken from the [1995 million man Louis] Farrakhan march in America and had those associations.[viii] And thirdly, my key objection was that we weren't going to get a million people there. If we got 500,000 they would say we failed. So commonsense prevailed on that.

Anas Altikriti: In our very naïve optimism, once we had seen 125,000 people on the April 2002 demo, we said "This is a serious business, we can bring out a million people on to the streets". This was rubbished by Stop the War. It wasn't just politely dismissed, it was rubbished. I recall Andrew Murray – a very, very good friend who I consider quite wise and learned in activism and left politics – saying "It will never happen in Britain. The problem is that even if you bring out 500,000 people which would be a miracle in itself, people would say you didn't get a million. That would

---

viii The march, in support of atonement and personal responsibility in the African-American male community, "was without doubt the largest gathering of African American men in Washington, outnumbering even the famous civil rights marches of the 1960s." The protest was led and addressed by Rev Louis Farrakhan, the leader of the Nation Of Islam, who has been accused of homophobia and anti-Semitism. James Coomarasamy, 'Marchers recall moment of unity', BBC News, 13 October 2005, http://news.bbc.co.uk/1/hi/world/americas/4339388.stm [Accessed 9 August 2012].

be the story. And we would have failed". He said therefore it would be entirely wrong. So our first publication that went out actually called for a million man march, but then because of the consultations we then had, we withdrew the publication. But it was out there! And a lot of people came to the march calling for one million people because they had got the earlier publication.

Mike Marqusee: I liked them [MAB] and enjoyed working with them. We had some very funny discussions about all kinds of things. That is one of the joys of mass politics – that you get to meet people who are very different from you. But that involves a genuine exchange, not just a pat on the head and saying "We love you, you are a Muslim and you get to be a speaker at the next demonstration".

Anas Altikriti: I remember working with my opposite number at Stop the War – Mike Marqusee, who wrote the Muhammad Ali biography, a Jew.[ix] A wonderful friend. And it was one of the most enriching experiences I've been through.

Mike Marqusee: A week before the September 2002 [anti-war] demonstration the Countryside Alliance had put on its pro-foxhunting demonstration [on Sunday 22 September 2002], and there was a large turnout at that.[x] The media was obsessed with it. In our media briefings running up to the

---

ix Mike Marqusee, *Redemption song: Muhammad Ali and the spirit of the sixties* (London: Verso, 2005).

x The Countryside Alliance's figure of 407,791 people marching was accepted by the Metropolitan Police. Tania Branigan, '400,000 bring rural protest to London', *Guardian*, 23 September 2002, www.guardian.co.uk/uk/2002/sep/23/hunting.ruralaffairs2 [Accessed 15 April 2012].

demonstrations it was constantly "Oh you will never get as many as the Countryside Alliance". And I pointed out that they probably had 100 times more money than we had. Certainly a lot more vehicles! Plus the advantage of all the publicity running up to it through the press. But I was still pretty confident we would match them... From the media angle we had very few resources: myself and a few other people working for no money. But we put a concerted effort in and we got a number of NUJ members to help out to press the media like mad in the weeks running up to it, so they couldn't pass over it and say it was the usual suspects.

Sean Wallis: The real turning point in my view was the September demonstration in 2002. This was the first 'mega' demo... and it was bigger than any other demonstration that anyone could remember, at 400,000. It shocked the police who had only given us half the road, and it shocked people on the demonstration itself just how large it was. I was stewarding at the back saying "Please wait in an orderly queue as you have quarter of a million people in front of you", and people started cheering.

James O'Nions, Stop the War Coalition Steering Committee member in 2003: The real surprise for me had come on the September 2002 demonstration. I forget what the figures were, but I remember waiting and waiting at Embankment. We thought the police were stopping the march from leaving, but actually there were so many people there it was taking forever to get everybody moving. We were stood there, and then we had hardly set off and we heard the front of the march had already reached Hyde Park.

Mike Marqusee: It had a big impact. First of all it made the Countryside Alliance march look small, and more importantly we were now established as the major issue of popular protest of the day. A far bigger constituency than the fox hunters can put together. Also it showed that even with our small resources we could reach an awful lot of people.

Sean Wallis: I think it was extremely important that the Muslim community was involved in an organised way. The MAB had organised their first demonstration – over Jenin – in April 2002 in London and 100,000 people turned up, mostly Muslims and the Left. Before that point, Muslim organisation tended to be local, via the mosque, and divided by nationality and denomination. Pakistani Muslims would see themselves as Pakistanis and not be part of the same organisation as Arabs. The MAB mobilised Arab Muslims and drew in many many more. That demo was a very young demo! I spent most of that demonstration just smiling because I remembered how Muslims felt after the Iranian fatwa against Salman Rushdie – pushed into a corner and attacked in the press and told that they believed in the fatwa even when many didn't. This was the first time that Muslims in Britain stood up for themselves (and the Palestinians), from a low point in 1988 when they were vilified and isolated. On the September 2002 demo, Muslims came up and joked that the Stop the War Coalition was now the biggest Muslim organisation in Britain. After the September 2002 demonstration, the anti-war movement really hit the mainstream. The *Mirror* woke up to the fact that opinion polls were showing 70-80% opposed, and came out against the war.

Lindsey German: I think the September one was a very important demo. Again the figures vary from a quarter of a million to 400,000. It was very big. It was lots of Muslims and lots of trade unionists. In a way that laid the basis for February 15th to be as big as it was. So after the September demo CND asked if they could be joint organisers.

"Once Piers Morgan decided he was going to go for something then he went for it": The *Daily Mirror* and the anti-war movement

John Pilger, Journalist: The *Daily Mirror* of the 1960s/70s is unlikely to come back – although it did so for 18 memorable months from October 2001 under [editor] Piers Morgan, proving that nothing is lost forever…The *Mirror* played an important part in helping to galvanise the anti-war movement in the build-up to the Iraq invasion.[22]

Former senior Mirror executive: It was very much driven by Piers Morgan. I'm pretty certain he had a brother who was a serving officer in the army. And I'm fairly sure he came from a military background. His father was in the armed services. The military was not unknown to him. He was editing the only left-wing tabloid paper in the country. At the time he was looking to have a clear point of differentiation with the *Sun*, which as you know is very jingoistic. And whilst it was a Labour paper he was very uneasy with some of the things Blair was doing, particularly the foreign policy.

Piers Morgan, *Daily Mirror* Editor 1995–2004, 27 October 2001 diary entry: I was sitting bored on the back bench at lunchtime when a mad thought came to me. "Get me John Pilger's number", I shouted. Who better to cement our new brand of journalism than the great radical ex-*Mirror* legend himself? I rang him, and he sounded immediately sceptical – not surprisingly, given that we've spent the last few years slagging each other off in print. "Look John, there's no agenda here. You know what we've been doing. I know you'd write a great piece with us, and your return would be great for the paper." He said he'd think about it and call back. Five minutes later he did. "OK, I will do it, but I want absolute control over my copy, and the right to make all cuts myself." "Great John – you can write up to fifteen hundred words and I'll pay you a pound a word."[23]

Former senior *Mirror* executive: Pilger was an interesting choice and not an uncontroversial one. He was an ex-*Mirror* man but very critical about the way the media worked, then and now. A man of very, very firm opinions which brooked no argument. So he wasn't a universally popular figure even though he had been a *Mirror* man.

Carmel Brown, Press Officer, Stop the War Coalition: Pilger is one of the great *Mirror* columnists. Him and Paul Foot were recognised as their great writers. When I was growing up, you certainly knew of Pilger and if you were a bit older you knew about Paul Foot. And there are lots of journalists I've worked with, especially men, and all they've wanted to be is John Pilger. I was genuinely excited that Pilger was back – the opportunity for proper journalism. And Pilger's stuff was very good. Phenomenally hard on the lack of Weapons of Mass Destruction.

Chris Wade, Press Officer, *Trinity Mirror*: I was a press officer for *Trinity Mirror*, the *Mirror*'s parent company. From time to time we would get involved with supporting the papers, especially the *Mirror* when it had a major exclusive or was running a big campaign. The paper had taken a strong anti-war line... I recall the mood was very good, and most staff were supportive. There was a real sense that the paper was doing something important, and that it had caught the public mood.

Former senior *Mirror* executive: I look back with genuine pride on that period. Part of the reason is that Piers managed to unite the whole staff behind this. It was something he felt very personally about, felt very strongly about. And that's not always the way. It's a Labour newspaper, it doesn't mean everybody on the staff is Labour. But on this issue, the whole paper felt like it was working together for the same thing. There was an amazing sense of doing something for the right reasons. And doing something that flew in the face of everyone else but being aware of the fact we spoke for a vast section of the populous. There was something going on here which a large part of the country was deeply uncomfortable with. We were the only people saying that. We were the only people giving them a voice... Very, very often it felt like we were a voice crying out in the wilderness. The *Guardian* was broadly anti-war but not in the same nail your colours to the mast kind of way. The other papers, certainly the other tabloids and most of the broadsheet papers, had switched to jingoistic mode and were really quite gung-ho about a lot of this. Looking back I think it was quite a serious failure of the British press. Not enough questions were asked in a way they should have been.

Piers Morgan, 29 October 2001 diary entry: We ran a pretty fierce leader to go with the Pilger piece today, attacking Blair for not dealing with Al Qaeda the way he dealt with the IRA – by diplomacy not bombs. Alastair [Campbell] rang, furious. "What the fuck are you doing?" "Being your conscience", I said.[24]

Former senior *Mirror* executive: [Alastair] Campbell had made a series of strategic errors with the *Mirror* quite early on where he had openly favoured and courted the *Sun* by giving them stories. He repeatedly failed to do this with the *Mirror*. He treated the *Mirror* as a newspaper which they could rely on and wouldn't go away whatever happened. And actually the more that happened, the more Piers dug in. And part of the friction with the Blair camp prior to Iraq was all around the way they were treating the *Sun* and the way they were ignoring their own. And that was very much Alastair's call. So in a way they sowed the seeds of what came later. That was so easily avoidable but they chose not to do it. They chose to put all their eggs into the one basket which was the *Sun* newspaper and keeping it on side. The *Mirror*, I can't remember what it was exactly, was 65 percent read by Labour voters, which is a pretty high proportion of any newspaper. I imagine we ended up doing them quite a lot of damage actually. I'm not particularly proud of that but it was the side effect of having been ignored by the Labour Party in government. They just didn't take us as seriously as they should of, and as seriously as they historically had. So it was odd. They were very angry with us. Piers got a lot of abuse from Alastair.

Carmel Brown: 28 September 2002 forced a sea change in media attitude towards the Stop the War Coalition and those who were protesting the war... Following the September demonstration the *Daily Mirror* commissioned an inhouse survey which revealed that 40 percent of the country were against any war with Iraq, but that rose to 60 percent amongst *Mirror* readers.[25]

John Rees: Carmel [Brown] rang up the *Mirror* and got us in to see the people at the *Mirror*, and the three of us went down to the *Mirror* offices down at Canary Wharf and talked to them about supporting the demonstration, about producing posters and placards.

Carmel Brown: I just went and interfered; did what I thought I could do from Liverpool with email and a phone and a nose for a news story. One of things I did is that I wrote Piers an email. Didn't hear anything. Everybody in London didn't expect me to hear anything. I must have written him three emails in the lead up to February 15 march. I wanted to get back in touch with the *Mirror*. John [Rees] said he thought that was quite dangerous because if the UN resolution did go through we wouldn't agree with it and Stop the War would carry on, and the *Mirror* might turn on us. And my thought was "Nice problem if that happens. And first of all they would have to join with us." So I wrote to Piers again asking if we could link up. And I got an email back, "Thanks for your email, thanks for the work you are doing, these are the people on my news desk, come in and have a meeting." I was like "Oh shit!" And they [everyone at Stop the War] were all a bit "Oh shit!", because it gets big and you are not controlling it.

Former senior *Mirror* executive: I wasn't particularly involved. My guess is what had happened is that it probably coincided with Stop the War Coalition becoming more prominent and probably upping its game as well. I imagine the two things came together at the time as Stop the War Coalition upped its game, and as it became more obvious what was going to happen, it was clear the politics were heading towards war. Probably the two things coincided.

Carmel Brown: The *Mirror* meeting. I remember dropping my kids off at school and dashing down to London wondering how I would find Canary Wharf... I remember Andrew Burgin came and Lindsey [German] was supposed to come but she didn't come. I thought this was really big time stuff. If we got this right this would be a breakthrough moment for publicity. If you had the *Mirror* on board it would push other news desks and journalists. And I found out when I was coming down that Lindsey wasn't coming to the meeting and I could have crashed the car I was so cross. I felt really let down. Andrew [Burgin] is lovely, but how much of a lefty does he look? He has his flowing coats and is hugely eccentric, and I just thought this is going to be so the wrong image – which does make me sound too much like Blair for my own good, talking about image and dressing etc. But it mattered to these people... So I remember calling John [Rees] and said "I can't believe I'm dashing down to a meeting with the *Mirror*, having fought for this for so long, and Lindsey is not coming." I pushed the door, and I could tweak a conversation back in a way that would produce it, but I didn't have all the details. I didn't know where the demonstration was starting, where it was finishing, who all the speakers were going to be. So John

[Rees] came, for which I was very grateful... Andrew [Burgin] was great when he was there. He said "We need £20,000 from you if you can do it." I wouldn't have asked for that, but he got it. So the *Mirror* gave £20,000 for the staging of the February 15 demo.

Andrew Burgin: They [the *Daily Mirror*] agreed to do certain things in support of the demonstration and in support of the lead up. So on February 14 we had a series of very high profile events throughout London. There was a welcoming party for [US Civil Rights leader and former candidate for the Democratic presidential nomination] Jesse Jackson, there was a trade union meeting, there were artistic events. There were a whole series of cultural and political events the night before. And the *Mirror* devoted a whole four pages of the paper advertising those events. On the day the *Daily Mirror* produced placards, thousands of placards.

Former senior *Mirror* executive: It had a massive impact on the content of the paper because once Piers Morgan decided he was going to go for something then he went for it. That meant we would be doing a spread, two spreads, sometimes three spreads a day, by which I mean double pages, analysing what was going on, reporting what other people against the war were saying, calling into question the evidence, asking questions about why Hans Blix wasn't being given enough time. Why this rush to war?

Mark Steel: The time leading up to it [15 February 2003] was thrilling. I'd been on demonstrations and tried to mobilise people for demonstrations for 25 years and suddenly now there was something that is nationally seen to be something you should go on. Rather than the demonstration being seen as something a bit peculiar, it was just so, so far into the mainstream. It was absolutely in the mainstream. The *Daily Mirror* played a role in that certainly. The *Daily Mirror* was publicising it the way a tabloid paper might publicise a big concert or something. It was a staggering atmosphere.

Building the anti-war movement: The Campaign for Nuclear Disarmament joins with Stop the War Coalition and the Muslim Association of Britain

Carol Naughton, Campaign for Nuclear Disarmament Chair 2001–3: I was elected chair the weekend after 9/11, so it was a pretty intense time to become chair. I was kind of thrust into it.

Kate Hudson: I was nominated to be a vice-chair of CND, which I accepted, with enthusiasm. I was elected in September 2001, at the annual CND conference. Interestingly, that annual conference, which is where CND's policies are decided and its leadership is elected and so on, it was the Saturday after 9/11... one was dropped into a situation totally unlike one had expected. Because one thought there were these things going on like NATO and missile defence and so on, but one didn't realise it was going to be starting off as a vice-chair post-9/11. It was the main thing. It was really the biggest possible deal. I remember, maybe it was my hustings speech – candidates do a hustings speech – and I started off talking about that, and I said one deplored this criminal action and that the perpetrators should be brought to justice. But I deplored it in the same way we deplore state terrorism, which results in the death of innocent civilians, and acts such as the bombing of Hiroshima and Nagasaki. So linking it to that and then saying that the appropriate response was not to bomb Afghanistan and kill more innocent civilians. That the international community, or whoever, should seek down and bring the suspected perpetrators to trial, and that war was not the answer to that. And that was the position that was taken up by the CND conference, I think. I'm not aware that anyone disagreed with that perspective.[26]

Carol Naughton: The first decision I had to take was, does CND take the lead against any retaliation for 9/11... People looked to CND. We were getting thousands of phone calls. People were calling our offices all over the country saying "What's going to happen? We don't want retaliation". It seemed natural that, in the first instance, CND should take a lead. It was the weekend after 9/11; I was elected and the first decision I had to take was will we do that. And I said sure, why would we not? And therefore we called a vigil outside Downing Street immediately to say "No retaliation and no war". It was amazing. It was done very quickly – in the space of a week, with email. I could not believe the thousands and thousands that turned up. It wasn't on the scale of the big one on February 15, but this was done so quickly and thousands turned up. It was an indication there was an immediate appetite out there to say "no we do not want military action". Immediately after that we had already planned a demonstration about missile defence. That was about to happen, and we took a decision in CND to turn it into a 'Don't start wars' demo. We used Trafalgar Square and there was about 30,000 there; that was before the invasion of Afghanistan. That was the background – CND was out there taking a lead.

Tony Myers, Campaign for Nuclear Disarmament Campaigns Officer 1995–2003: CND had to take an interest because nobody knew what was going to happen, especially after 9/11 when everybody was asking "What's the response going to be?" It's ridiculous now but at the time people were asking whether someone was going to get nuked because of this. It sounds ridiculous but you still have to take it into account.

Kate Hudson: CND was founded as an anti-nuclear organisation; that is what it is. Its focus is that. But nevertheless it has, to a certain extent throughout its life, always had a peace movement characteristic as well. So while the core is anti-nuclear stuff we have always touched on other things, largely related to nuclear weapons. We don't do any old war or some humanitarian thing. We have tended, on occasion, to take an anti-war position. The obvious example is Vietnam, and subsequently the first Gulf War and Yugoslavia. Partly because a nuclear power is involved in the war, and partly because when those types of war happen they are the most pressing issue of the day.

Bruce Kent, Campaign for Nuclear Disarmament Vice-President in 2003. CND Chair 1987–1990: It is often difficult to make the connection, but in the case of Iraq it was quite easy. War began because Iraq allegedly had nuclear weapons – it was a nuclear issue. So I think there was a very good case for CND getting involved. You can get much thinner cases for CND getting involved in things! We once got involved in the American blockade in Nicaragua. But in this case it was very clear – WMD was the reason for the war.

Kate Hudson: There has always been a tension in CND around the extent to which we become involved in anti-war campaigning. Always a little bit of a row about it. And it is always the case that the vast majority think it is right to get involved in it. And basically this was exactly the same pattern. There was a small tendency among the wider leadership to say our core issue is nuclear weapons and we shouldn't be taking a position on the Iraq war. A small tendency – all the votes at conference and all the votes at CND Council were overwhelmingly that we should be involved because it was ostensibly a war about the development of WMD, disarmament, and UN Resolution 687 after the first Gulf War, calling for a nuclear weapons free Middle East. So very much lined with the nuclear weapons issue, plus CND basically does take a position on wars in which nuclear weapons may be used.

Minutes of CND National Council – 1–2 December 2001: Carol Naughton reported on the actions taken by CND after 11 September, and the reasons why CND had not joined The Coalition to Stop the War, but were working closely with it. Concerns included lack of democracy (decisions taken before planning meeting), failure to condemn terrorism and lack of commitment to non-violence….Among the wider membership, there were those who felt that the war was nothing to do with CND's strategy, and on Council opinions were divided as to whether or not CND should be part of the Coalition to Stop the War, now that it also had condemned terrorism. Some felt that our aims do not conflict, that opposing the war was the most urgent issue at the moment, that there were strong links with our own objectives and we need their power to mobilize. On the other hand, opposing the war was a temporary activity, and CND needed to remain apart and financially independent to continue with its core activities afterwards. It was noted that, in Scotland, CND had led the formation of the anti-war movement, but it was felt that CND does not have the resources to do that in England. Partnership was put forward as the best model.[27]

Bruce Kent: It amazed me that this Stop the War lot had started. I've always been nervous about CND getting involved in other campaigns, because it is traditional that you split them. My experience is groups like the SWP do their best to latch on to any big group, and so whenever CND get in to partnership with others I get a bit nervous as to what is going on.

Carol Naughton: Some people within CND wanted us to become part of Stop the War Coalition. The choice was do we become part of the Stop the War Coalition and sign up to it. The alternative viewpoint was there were very useful things CND could be doing as CND, and although we wanted to work closely with the Stop the War Coalition and the Muslim Association of Britain – strength comes from working together – there were useful things we could do: one was the court case where we took the Government to court, the more traditional silent vigils, the creative ideas. We felt we could be doing this as CND separately to Stop the War Coalition, and it was better for us to be doing that as separate. Many people in Stop the War might not have wanted to go down the High Court route because they had a specific role, which was to mobilise millions of people across the country to come out and do stuff. Stop the War are very good at mobilising people. That is a huge strength that they have. CND didn't have that ability then. But we could bring a different element to it because of our long history and tradition; we brought a certain historic element in to it. That is why we took the decision not to join Stop the War Coalition, but to remain as CND working very, very closely and collaboratively with the bigger group. And everybody accepted that. It was a council decision that went through and everybody respected that. I think personally it was the right decision because it gave us freedom to do extra things.

Anas Altikriti: During that time Stop the War approached CND, and CND – according to the sources that we were talking to within Stop the War – had a problem. Amongst their ranks and leadership were people who thought it was totally unacceptable for CND – a liberal movement and essentially pacifist and includ[ing] the gay movement – to be in partnership with ourselves. We were also told that the leadership of CND led by Bruce Kent and Kate Hudson and others were in favour of joining. But they didn't win the argument at the time, so therefore they decided to sit on it.

Tony Myers: I'm sure there were individual people in the general peace movement who might have thought this, and within CND, but that certainly did not come up in any meetings I attended. I don't remember people talking about this.

Kate Hudson: Then in the run up to September 2002 the Iraq issue was becoming a big deal. We were, at that time, working with the comedian Mark Thomas to back a legal challenge against the Government going to war on the basis of [UN] Resolution 1441. Stop the War and MAB proposed having a demonstration in September which I proposed to CND campaigns groups and then to CND Council: that CND should jointly organise the demonstration with Stop the War and MAB. The then Chair of CND [Carol Naughton] was opposed to doing that, so we didn't. So we supported it. It was formally described as organised by Stop the War and Muslim Association of Britain, supported by CND. Because CND was a longstanding, better known, bigger organisation with money, they were keen for us to be involved. And it broadened out the alliance against the war, as CND brought different things, politically, to it. So the CND leadership at that time decided not to organise it, but to support it, which I think was an error. Then it became clear the September 2002 demonstration was going to be massive. There were about 500,000 people on that demonstration. That's when the anti-Iraq war thing really took off. So from September 2002 to February 2003 it was the main issue on the political agenda.

Anas Altikriti: Our figures show more than 500,000 people marched on 28 September. It was an incredible feat. The media coverage was sensational. I recall being contacted by friends in Egypt who were watching the march live. They were saying the image of London with waves of demonstrators in the streets was absolutely unbelievable. I think this was the moment CND decided to come on board. It was after the 28 September. We had Bruce Kent and Kate Hudson come and speak on the platform and we got to know them better and they got to know us better. The mood changed.

Carol Naughton: We began to talk to Andrew [Murray], who I knew already, about joint efforts with Stop the War... So by the time it got to the big February 15 demonstration we had taken a decision. I had a meeting with Andrew in a pub in Whitehall. We said we really needed to come together and look at doing a massive demo. There was an appetite out there – people wanted to demonstrate and wanted to have their say. So we planned the huge demo. That was a really positive thing to do as it brought in the CND types, together with the Stop the War Coalition and the Muslim Association of Britain... CND is seen as being at the forefront of the wider peace movement. I'm not saying that we are bigger or better than anybody else, but people see the CND symbol of peace and that we should be taking a lead. We also had a track history of involvement in anti-war activism going back a long time.

Andrew Murray: The anti-war movement from 2001 onwards, and especially in early 2003, represented the biggest such mobilisation of public opinion in British history. At the heart of it was a three-way alliance between Stop the War Coalition, the Muslim Association of Britain and CND. Each organization brought unique contributions to the overall development of a movement, which came within a hair's-breadth of stopping Tony Blair backing Bush's war. Each mobilized people the others would have had difficulty reaching. CND particularly brought not just its universal recognized identity as Britain's historic peace movement but its wealth of support among liberal, Christian, environmental and pacifist activists. Without that support the overall movement could not have reached as far as it did into the mainstream of public opinion.[28]

Setting the date of 15 February 2003

Andrew Murray: There had been a certain degree of international coordination so we could have all these protests around the world on the same day. I wasn't directly involved in those discussions. It was obviously driven by the perception of what the timetable was for Bush actually attacking Iraq. There were various United Nations dates in the mix... I can't remember exactly why February 15th was chosen, but it had to be a Saturday, and it had to be in that time frame, and it had to be coordinated internationally. That was roughly the criteria.

John Rees: The date was essentially fixed at the anti-war assembly at the European Social Forum in Florence in November 2002. There was an anti-war activists' assembly and Chris [Nineham] and I and Lindsey [German] were at it. It was proposed, and we were part of the people proposing it, that there should be an international coordinated day of action. I can't remember exactly why we wanted to go for February 15, but we did. There was an argument about that, with the Italian delegates definitely want[ing] to go later than that, I think. The reason we wanted to go earlier was because we were pretty certain of when the attack would take place and we didn't want the demonstration to take place after that. We did eventually settle on February 15. It was clear from the beginning it was going to be an international day of action.

Lindsey German: We had the meeting there where we had a big row about whether it should be the 15 February or 18 January. The Italians wanted to go earlier, they thought it would be over by February. 18 January: there was a demo in Washington that day, it wasn't a random date. Their argument was the war is going to happen very quickly; we said no we don't think it will come till the spring, because usually it's around then they start invading countries. It was only a little meeting, 25 people, an organising meeting.

Chris Nineham: We had already fixed our date: February 15. We went to Florence in November trying to convince everyone that this was the date. And there was a very, very fraught meeting. Some people thought the date was too late, and it was very, very tense. But we finally got an agreement. At the end of the Social Forum they had a million people on the demo, which at the time was something completely new in terms of this generation of activists. There was a meeting the next day with 5,000 activists in this disused factory in the centre of Florence. It was essentially an assembly of the movement, and it ended with an announcement – well I made the announcement – calling on the world to protest on February 15 2003. And as the meeting was coming to the end the other organisers behind me started singing 'Bandiera Rossa', an Italian resistance song. And they started very, very quietly, and then the whole meeting started chanting this incredible Italian partisan song.

John Rees: I then proposed [the 15 February date] at the [anti-war] Cairo conference in December 2002, and it was taken up and endorsed by the Cairo conference, which was symbolically very important – that a conference of activists, which included Iraqis, in the Middle East, endorsed the call. I think it then went on to Porto Alegre at the World Social Forum. It wasn't that it had been called in any mechanical sense, but there was a kind of rolling sensation in the social movements that this was going to happen.

Chris Nineham: At the end of January 2003 we went to the World Social Forum in Brazil, where again there were 150,000 activists from around the world. At that event we publicised and polemicised the February 15 2003 date. And people were coming up to us and saying "Yes, Guatemala will have a demonstration!", "Yes, Canada will have a demonstration!" We were ticking off country after country. And then someone would come up and say "I live in a tiny town in Paraguay. We will have a demonstration." By this stage the European Social Forum backing it in 2002 was enough to confirm the date. But it was a question of making sure people around the world understood the importance of this date for everyone. [US dissident] Noam Chomsky and [Indian novelist and dissident] Arundhati Roy did a meeting at the World Social Forum in a basketball stadium, with 20,000 seats. It was absolutely rammed. An absolutely phenomenal meeting. 50 of us from Britain. We all sat in this meeting in one high up corner of the stadium. Roy and Chomsky were fantastic. There were 5,000–10,000 outside the stadium who couldn't get in. At the end of the meeting the organisers put on *Imagine* by John Lennon over the tannoy system, which we all thought was fairly banal. Then we unfurled this massive banner – in Portuguese – saying "Don't Attack Iraq – demonstrate February 15". In Portuguese, unless someone was taking the piss out of us, "Don't Attack Iraq" is "No Attacki Iraqi". And then we started chanting "No Attacki Iraqi". The whole stadium, 20,000 people, started going "No Attacki Iraqi". It was an amazing moment – the coming together of the anti-capitalist movement and the anti-war movement. From that moment on we were completely mobbed with people telling us about their demos and giving us phone numbers and emails. That definitely had a big impact because it meant Latin America was on board and some.

John Rees: There was a very, very strong sensation of the movement building, drawing on the previous resources of the anti-capitalist demonstrations, the international dimension, of the scale of the feeling about the war.

Building the anti-war movement: Getting the trade unions on board

Paul Mackney, National Association of Teachers in Further and Higher Education (now UCU) General Secretary 1997–2005: I was elected in 1997 as the first of a wave of new trade union general secretaries who were more on the Left, less frightened by unemployment, which had cowed a lot of others – unions tend to be very weak when there is a lot of unemployment. There was a succession of general secretary elections – myself, then Mick Rix at ASLEF, Billy Hayes for CWU, Jeremy Dear for the journalists, Mark Serwotka from PCS, Andy Gilchrist with the FBU and Bob Crow for RMT. We started to meet – something the press dubbed "The Awkward Squad". So you had this group who were meeting initially in the Lucas Arms at Kings Cross and then down the road and eventually in a hotel. An organised group – we would meet to discuss common problems, but it wasn't a Bolshevik organisation or anything! We didn't have a strict line that everyone pursued because unions are democratic organisations and come up with different policies. Some unions were in the Labour Party, some weren't. But we were all against the war. All in favour of justice for the Palestinians... The people by and large wouldn't be seen as pacifists. They would be seen as people opposed to – and I know this sounds like a jargon term – imperialist wars. I think all of them would have supported people fighting for national liberation, for example. That group were instrumental.

Andrew Murray and Lindsey German: Initially, however, trade union support for the Stop the War Coalition was pretty thin. Aslef, the train drivers' union, was strongly supportive from the start under Mick Rix's leadership, as was NATFHE, the lecturers' union, and its General Secretary Paul Mackney. The RMT's Bob Crow was another early stalwart. The largest unions – Unison, Amicus (then the AEEU and MSF in the process of merging), the TGWU and the GMB – held aloof initially, as did the TUC itself.[29]

Bob Crow, Maritime and Transport Workers (RMT) General Secretary 2002–present: RMT got involved very quickly. There were Stop the War meetings taking place – people like Andrew Murray. The actual Stop the War committee was set up and RMT actually met as an executive committee, and decided to support the Stop the War committee and the demonstrations. I went to some of the meetings. On top of that a lot of work was done from the RMT building. A lot of the placards were made up here. We've donated money.

Paul Mackney: NATFHE was affiliated with Stop the War and we provided the premises for Stop the War. For various reasons, which are now more apparent with expenses scandals, and because it made it more formal with our committee structures, we had a formal agreement for rent. They had a big room and an enormous basement where they could store all their stuff for about £100 a month in central London. So it was not quite a peppercorn rent, but almost a peppercorn rent.

Billy Hayes, Communications Workers' Union General Secretary 2001–present: The one thing that is most striking about the anti-war movement today compared with previous wars has been the level of support given by the trade union movement. It is quite surprising really, because I can remember the Falklands. I was living in Liverpool and the whole of the country was behind the war. Whereas this time there was clearly a desire not to go to war. We took very tentative steps as a union to support the ceasefire in Afghanistan. We then decided to get involved in the anti-war movement and speak where we could. I don't think I've ever had one letter complaining about the union's stance on the war in Iraq, which was really different compared to say 1982 with the Falklands/Malvinas. In 1982 most people supported the war in Falklands. It was seen as a big thing to support 'our boys' as it were... I think you have to think about it in terms of the British labour movement. Traditionally, in the first world war and the second world war for example, the Labour movement has supported imperialist wars. It is often said [Labour Party leader] Keir Hardie broke his heart over the British labour movement supporting the first world war. So to get the trade unions' leadership and the trade union movement to be anti-imperialist is a victory in itself. I don't want to over play it, but it is an important change in the thinking and psyche of the trade union movement.

Paul Mackney: It was seen as terribly against normal TUC procedures, but Mick Rix and myself exchanged texts that were then taken to the special general council in January 2003, which led to the TUC being against the war. I think that was the first time in history that the TUC was against a significant war. It was possible they had qualms about the Cyprus insurgency or had things to say about the Crimean War, but in terms of significant international wars, that was the first time.

Statement on Iraq, General Council, Trade Union Congress: The General Council recall and reaffirm the positions adopted by Congress in 2002, the key points of which were that the emphasis should be on a multilateral approach working through, and only with, the explicit authority of the UN Security Council; that they unambiguously opposed any military action being contemplated by the US or any other country on a unilateral basis; that the Government should seek to align with our EU partners its response to any initiative by the US Administration; and that military action should only be an option as a last resort, if all diplomacy failed, and if there was evidence made generally available which clearly demonstrated that Saddam Hussein was developing weapons of mass destruction and delivery systems and posed a real threat to world peace. On the evidence currently available, the General Council do not judge these conditions to have been met and for war to be justified.[30]

Billy Hayes: The TUC came out against the war, which was historic. I don't think it had ever happened before that the TUC had come out against a war.

Paul Mackney: That said, partly because Brendan Barber, as head of the TUC, felt he had to stay close to new Labour otherwise he felt the unions wouldn't win anything – you could say they haven't won a lot anyway – he never spoke on a platform against the war. But, of course, we were able to say we were speaking in line with TUC policy... Of course, at the same time was the campaign against tuition fees. The Government said they hadn't got any money for education, yet they were spending all this money on Iraq. If you want to do a really interesting interview, go and interview Margaret Hodge – although you always have to take what she says with a pinch of salt. I remember Margaret Hodge at the TUC in November 2002 walking round with a beaming smile on her face because she was the Minister for Universities and she had got the budget to do the expansion of 50 percent of the population going to universities. A month later Margaret Hodge was head in hands, doom and gloom, got no money, had lost it all – obviously to fund the war. Some of it is loans and borrowed, but the rest of it they go round the different departments chopping their budgets...They never denied it. If you did a forensic examination of the budgets the figures would probably match up.

"We went on the road": Public meetings and activism around the country

Lindsey German: We've always had the same attitude as the Suffragettes apparently had, which was they said they would go and do a meeting for anybody, anywhere around the country. They never refused to do a meeting. And we always try to never refuse to do a meeting.[31]

John Rees: A lot of the way we did that, we went on the road. Me and Lindsey [German] and Chris [Nineham]. George Galloway was very important at this stage. Tony Benn and Jeremy [Corbyn]. We built the marches out of rallies. Essentially what we did was take that first London rally [on 21 September 2001] and reproduced it around the country. So we did it in Manchester, an absolutely huge meeting in St Georges Hall in Liverpool. And we did this around the country. And we did it more than once. In many ways we still do it. It was a way in which the emerging collective political leadership of Stop the War shaped the movement's responses and its political responses, gave it arguments which were then repeated in radio interviews, people's houses, in trade union branches, in the colleges. And that's how we created an educated and informed cadre of the anti-war movement, which would then go out and build and organise the demonstrations, book the coaches.

Jeremy Corbyn, Labour MP 1983–present: I was very involved. From April 2002 onwards it became obvious we were into something big. Blair and Bush had clearly had a discussion about Iraq... We organised a demonstration in September 2002 that was a lot bigger than expected –

maybe 200,000. From then on I was flat out doing public meetings and rallies all over the country in opposition to any future attack on Iraq. I spoke at over 200 public meetings in six months. It got bigger and bigger. Young and multiethnic audiences.

Mike Marqusee: I did a lot of speaking on platforms right up to February 15. I was very inspired by the attendance at these meetings. This is why I knew the national demos would be big. The media had no idea what was already bubbling underneath. You would go to a meeting in Derby and there would be 80 people there on a Tuesday night. Many places like that. And with an intensity of commitment and a diversity of attendance – young and old, different styles, different ethnic groups.

Philip Steele, Peace Activist based in Bangor: Most London-based reporters were hopelessly out of touch with the strength and breadth of the growing peace movement, which they represented as naive and misguided: they claimed that peace campaigners were apologists for the crimes of Saddam Hussein – whereas many of them had been longstanding and outspoken critics of the Iraqi regime. Media prejudices would have been confounded if they had witnessed the quality of informed debate and expertise to be found in any of the small peace groups springing up across the country.

Mark Steel: I remember speaking at meetings at the time. I spoke in Croydon at the Labour Club. And because I've always lived around this area and I was active in the SWP in that area, I remember [Arthur] Scargill coming down in about 1988 and there was 200 people there and I remember thinking "200 people – that's bloody good". Or Tony Benn would come down and speak and 200 people would come out. So I went down and spoke at this thing and there was so many people there – 400 people maybe. It was like an underground train in the morning. Absolutely squashed. 50 people or so couldn't get in. Everywhere was like that. And I was probably the best known person speaking at that. And that certainly wasn't why people came. It could have been anyone. The wrath of people at this meeting was incredible. I've never, before or since, known anything like it, where protest and rage was so mainstream. There have been times when the wrath and the rage has been more militant, but not so widespread and not so mainstream.

Yasmin Khan, Stop the War activist, London School of Economics and Political Science, 2001–5: I feel incredibly privileged to have been part of the anti war movement and the Stop the War group at the LSE. It came at the perfect time for me. As a socialist activist who had just arrived in London from three years in Sheffield not knowing anyone, I ended up in one of the most active and dynamic Stop the War groups in the country... We were incredibly active on campus. You couldn't go a week without some stunt, meeting, direct action or teach-in taking place. Being in central London we got our fair share of high profile speakers and media attention so I think it's fair to say we weren't your average group. We even managed to get the first occupation of LSE since the 1960s. It was an incredible time – so intense, so active, so urgent. October 2002-March 2003 was the most intense bit of the years from 2001-2005 (when I would say my anti-war involvement took place): I did anti war activities almost every day; there was a fantastic energy and enthusiasm on campus.

Anas Altikiriti: Up until mid-January [2003] I remember being extremely stressed. MAB had a meeting. We were, I wouldn't say underprepared, but we had the feeling this was very, very serious and we hadn't done enough and we didn't have enough time. That kind of feeling. I was living in Leeds and lecturing in both Leeds and Edinburgh, and spending two to three days in London away from my family. It was very hectic. I was ordered to leave everything by MAB. And I did; I simply left everything – I resigned my position in Edinburgh and reduced my load to one day a week in Leeds, and I spent about five days a week in London. The feeling was that there was an incredible appetite for what was to come. I was speaking, on average, at a meeting a night; sometimes it would be two or three a day, particularly on weekends, and at every single meeting there was never enough seats. There was one meeting, I think in Redbridge, where I commented to George [Galloway] "Can you see there are three empty seats?", and he replied "Yeah, it's disgraceful!" That was how the meetings were. Everyone was really angry. People who I knew voted Conservative and were from the middle classes, their overall take was that they were extremely upset and angry with what was happening – the preparation for war and the dossier and all that.

Yasmin Khan: So what anti-war activities was I involved in? What wasn't I involved in more like: writing leaflets; designing and printing leaflets; organising meetings and teach-ins; flyering outside Tube stations; organising motions at the union; talking, talking, talking all the time to anyone, anywhere about it; going on demonstrations, blocking roads, writing letters to newspapers; disrupting meetings or threatening to disrupt them if there were any "warmongers" i.e. politicians who supported the war scheduled to speak at LSE; making banners and T-shirts and talking, talking, talking some more. That's the thing I remember most, talking about it and trying to convince people all the time. I just knew I had to convince the most number of people that the war is wrong so they took action and tried to stop the war. I don't know if that was the moment, or the urgency or my youth, but I know I don't have that energy anymore and I often wonder if the anti-war movement took it out of me.

Mike Marqusee: For anyone who had campaigned on the Left, as I had, all of this had been a long time coming. It was very exciting and it revealed the scale of this thing. I count that time as some of the most rewarding activism I have ever engaged in.

"Absolutely essential to get the message out": The importance of artists and celebrities to the anti-war movement

Andrew Burgin: The political campaign against the war has been marked at every stage by a huge creative energy. Artists, actors, poets, musicians, film-makers, authors and playwrights – all have contributed enormously to the flowering of the movement.[32]

Carmel Brown: Celebrities were absolutely essential to get the message out; they were really good about it. You needed them, but you also needed to keep quite a hard political message in the core of it. What I remember about it was that people were really kind with their time, and generous and cool. Alex Cox the film director was helpful. He was good because you had Alex Cox and Ken Loach – so film *directors*.

Kim Manning-Cooper Campaign for Nuclear Disarmament Staff member 2002–3: Part of my job was to get celebrity support. It was very important. Celebrities, members of Parliament, journalists – we built a huge movement. With the support of celebrities the campaign became very relevant to young people. With the support of the celebrities we worked with we were able to reach out to a wider demographic than we would have been able to. In particular Damon Albarn [from Blur] and Robert Del Naja from Massive Attack: at the time they were the only celebrities who were willing to go out on a limb and speak out against the war. I will always be eternally grateful to them for that. It was very difficult in the beginning because there was a real reluctance among the artistic community to speak out against the war in Iraq.

Carmel Brown: I was told by Regine [Moylett, Bono's PR agent] when I asked about Bono and Bob Geldolf getting involved – I thought, why not? – she said "They don't get involved in British domestic affairs".[ix] They do this world stage poverty thing, but not the war in Iraq, which

xi Regine Moylett says she has no recollection of this conversation. Email to author, 7 February 2012.

was seen as very political. In fact Geldolf spoke in favour of the war, so he was far from a saint for me at the time. So clearly he did get involved – just on the wrong side.

Ken Loach, Film Director: Most of them [artists and celebrities] aren't political. When I say political I mean making a political analysis of it. They will see themselves as vaguely on the Left and vaguely humanitarian, but it is not enough. You've got to try and place events in the course of history and think about why they are happening. It is not enough just to be anti-war. Who isn't anti-war? We are all anti-war. In order to fight the drive to war you've got to understand where it's coming from and why it's coming and what interests it's representing. I don't think many people take the trouble to do this; it's a pity.

Damon Albarn, Musician: The looming invasion struck me as a very dangerous development. I didn't feel it was the way to address the problem, which was more to do with American imperialism than [Saddam Hussein's] actual threat to anybody. And obviously oil. I thought it was very dangerous and it would only perpetuate the problem for five more generations or something. The point is, Iraq was never an easy fix; you don't just go in there and get rid of Saddam Hussein and then the problem in solved... I don't get involved with those sorts of things because I am a celebrity. You may have a slightly inaccurate idea of why people do this kind of thing. One, the word "celebrity" is a little bit condescending. I don't think you will find there were many "celebrities" involved; it wasn't an easy subject. I hope there wasn't any showbiz involved. I come from two generations of conscientious objectors, so it is not something I just decided a few weeks beforehand that I fancied getting involved in. One of my core beliefs is passive resistance. Also, my father and mum brought me up to have an understanding and respect for Islamic culture. So I was trying to defend the right for an Islamic voice. So it is not just as clear cut as "the war". The war is a symptom of something that is ongoing, which is an ignorance about other people's core belief systems.

Kim Manning-Cooper: Those two [Damon Albarn and Robert Del Naja] were amazing. As I said I'll always be eternally grateful because right at the beginning when no one else was speaking out, they did. They funded two double page adverts in the *NME.*[xii] We got together and talked about what they could do. They were always very clear it was not about them or their bands, but purely about them putting their weight behind raising the profile and PR of the march. They said they wanted to help get as many people there as possible. Back in December 2001 the Gorillaz did a gig at Fabric as a fundraiser for the Red Cross after the bombing of Afghanistan. Then Damon wore a CND T-shirt to the MTV awards when he went to collect his prize. He spoke out at the microphone about his opposition to Afghanistan; I think that went down like a lead balloon. From the beginning they were doing stuff far beyond what we had hoped – such as getting an award on TV wearing a CND T-shirt in 2001 and saying "Fuck the war". I remember his manager phoned me up and said "Can you get a T-shirt to the airport – Damon wants to wear it at the MTV awards?" We were like "Of course we can". I thought

xii The adverts appeared the weeks before the 28 September 2002 march and the 15 February 2003 march.

he would wear it, but to state on live TV his opposition to the bombing of Afghanistan was quite something. We continued to work together for the next couple of years on what they could do and how we could best utilise them. We wanted to do something strategic that would have the most campaigning impact. They are smart, politically savvy people who wanted to do something strategic. That is when we settled on the *NME* ads. Putting an advert in the *NME* – twice – in the run up to the demos unquestionably increased the number of young people who attended. They always wanted as many people as possible on the march, and they were in a position to speak to young people through interviews. There was an interview in the *Independent* a couple of weeks before the march and they were wearing CND T-shirts and stickers. CND hadn't had that kind of exposure for a long time. CND wasn't very cool at the time, and they helped us make CND cool again.

Tony Myers: Celebrities? It's a bit of a double-edged sword because people can get fed up with being talked at. It depends how they are used and in what way they are going to cooperate with you. Bono and Bob Geldof are always banging on about something – it's an ongoing joke. So it can backfire and you need to be careful... It depends who you are aiming at. Those of us who are hardened activists get a bit fed up with it, I think. If you are going to help, just donate a month's salary or something like that. But again I think you have to remember lots of people are involved for the first time, and they have a different take on it. It can make a difference to them... It does help get publicity. Whether you like it or not this is the way the media works.

"It was like Monty Python": The Government attempts to ban the march from Hyde Park – January-February 2003

***Guardian*, 29 January 2011:** Organisers of a huge anti-war rally yesterday vowed that it would go ahead despite a decision by the culture secretary [Tessa Jowell] to ban the events from London's Hyde Park. A spokeswoman for the Stop the War Coalition said it would vigorously contest the decision, taken with the direct authority of Tessa Jowell, to outlaw the event on health and safety grounds. The manager of the royal parks, Steve Edwards, wrote to the STWC on Monday to say that an emergency liaison team had decided that Hyde Park was not a suitable site for a rally at this time of year because of the condition of the ground and the number of people involved.[33]

Mark Steel: What a magnificent excuse to disrupt it – grass… when cabinet member Tessa Jowell made the announcement she might as well have assembled the press and said, "Here is my statement – will you STOP going on about this BLOODY march. It's ALL I bloody hear about.[34]

Lindsey German: I got on the *Today* programme for some reason, which is a rare occurrence – the don't like demonstrators for some reason. But obviously the mood was such they had me on the *Today* programme. And they were going to have Tessa Jowell on as well, who was the minister responsible for it, but she wouldn't turn up in the end. Then a guy called me from *ITN* and it all kind of snowballed.

***Times*, 30 January 2003:** A leading anti-war protester has threatened riots if ministers do not allow a rally in London to go ahead… The Labour MP George Galloway, a vehement critic of war in Iraq, said "This is an extraordinary turn of events. I would want to warn Mrs Jowell that she can either choose between half a million people at the rally or half a million people in a riot because that is what will surely happen if we tell them that, thanks to the British Government, they are not allowed to attend a meeting at the end of the march."[35]

Jeremy Corbyn: We had an absurd argument with the Department of Culture; I remember like it was yesterday. Tessa Jowell phoned me up at home on Saturday evening; the phone rings and they say "Downing Street switchboard here, we've got Tessa Jowell on the line". So she comes on and says "Tessa here. We've arranged the park for you and it's ok for the rally". She said "You'll find your way there alright?" And I said "We won't have any problems finding Hyde Park". And she said "No, no Battersea Park". I said "No – we aren't going to Battersea Park, we want to go to Hyde Park". And she said "That's not on because of the damage to the grass, and the Royal Parks' authority and Royal Parks' police are against it." So I said "Tessa this is ridiculous. You are going to have an awful lot of people there. I think you better have a rethink about this."

Lindsey German: Because it [Hyde Park] was a Royal Park you have to negotiate with the Parks authorities and the Parks' police. And they've got a little house in Hyde Park where we had meetings when there had to be a decision.

John Rees: The Parks' police are a kind of separate department to the Metropolitan police. The Parks' police aren't the Flying Squad. All the meetings were in this kind of gingerbread house in the middle of Hyde Park.

Jeremy Corbyn: It was like Monty Python; they just didn't understand.

Andrew Murray: I tend to get brought into these meetings when there is a log jam, because it is felt that having the chair there adds some weight. This had gone on, we had conducted a lot of propaganda around it – in the sense that it is absurd we have this huge demonstration and its going to be barred from holding a rally on the grounds the grass might be damaged. Completely fatuous. And the police knew it was fatuous. So we discussed various alternatives like holding the rally in the Mall at Buckingham Palace, but the police weren't terribly keen on that.

Public Order Branch memo, Metropolitan Police, 3 February 2003: It has been suggested that the Mall be considered as a possible location for the rally. However, when consideration is given to all the security implications – the proximity of Buckingham Palace, St James's Palace, Downing Street, Horse Guards and Wellington Barracks together with high level of threat that currently pertains, the area is a particularly target rich environment which brings particular and challenging problems to police and protest.[36]

Jeremy Corbyn: The whole idea of pictures going round the world of a huge Stop the War stage and rally in front of Buckingham Palace – well I was really tempted. But I said

"Actually there is going to be a problem with numbers. If we get the kind of numbers we are expecting – at least a few hundred thousand people – then it has got to be Hyde Park."

Andrew Burgin: More and more people got involved. Previously Chris [Nineham] and I were going to these meetings. Then it was Chris and I and Andrew Murray and Lindsey German. So our delegation became larger and their delegations became larger, to the point we had a big meeting where there must have been 30 or 40 people there. We were trying to put pressure on the Secretary of State, who at that time was Tessa Jowell, but there were cracks appearing in the cabinet. Clare Short had made a statement saying she thought it was a bit ludicrous. Cracks about where the march would go, not obviously on any more serious question! Michael Foot, at that time, who did speak on February 15, had said this was an attack on our most fundamental liberties and that he would lead the march personally into Hyde Park should it come to it. And once people like Michael Foot said they were going to lead hundreds of thousands of people in an act of civil disobedience, they seemed to change their minds fairly rapidly.

William Weston, Chief Executive, Royal Parks 2000–5: It was an unsustainable position for us to maintain given the significant degree of public pressure. DCMS felt we had to accept the reality of the public demand.

John Rees: It's always resolved in this way: we always refuse not to do it. What it is always resolved by is weight of numbers. It gets to a certain point where they realise these people aren't going to agree to this and if there were ten of them we would tell them to fuck off or arrest them or whatever, but they've been putting out posters and leaflets and there are going to be tens if not hundreds of thousands of people arriving. And we are either going to have to confront them in a poll tax riot way or we are going to have to let them go.

Tessa Jowell, Secretary of State, Department for Culture, Media and Sport in 2003, 4 February 2003: I have today agreed that Hyde Park should be the venue for the Stop the War rally on 15 February. This follows several days of intensive work by my Department to find a better venue for the Rally. Everyone agrees that Hyde Park is far from ideal for an event of this kind at this time of year. The right of protesters to organise and take part in peaceful marches and rallies has never been questioned. The issue has only ever been to find a venue that is as safe as possible for those taking part.[37]

Jeremy Corbyn: There was a lot of people around the Royal Parks' authority and Royal Parks' police who feel the Royal Parks should be just that – Royal Parks, and are not terribly keen on the way Charles II allowed people into the Parks. So there is a lot of history there. Secondly, there were a lot of people in the Government who were keen to put a spoke in the works of any kind of anti-war protest.

John Rees: I don't understand why they do this. They don't seem to have understood that that conflict built the demonstration in a very big way, because one of the big sentiments feeding the demonstration was: not only is this wrong, but the Government is behaving in an undemocratic way because it isn't listening to people. The questions of are we being properly represented, is the Government behaving democratically, are fused with the question of this war is wrong. The madness about refusing to let us have Hyde Park simply demonstrated the authoritarian nature of the Government to a whole new layer of people who were maybe ambiguous. And it just drove forward the anger and desire to demonstrate... I would have thought there must be someone clever enough in Government saying "Look, you are not helping here."

Chris Nineham: Obviously it did a lot of damage. It was a terrible move on their part. They had added a secondary issue – the right to protest, civil liberties. We had kind of predicted this development, because Stop the War was founded on three principles, one of which was the defence of civil liberties, because we knew war and attacks on civil liberties go together. I guess it added hundreds of thousands to the demonstration.

"A lot of negotiation and anxiety": Choosing the speakers for 15 February 2003

Andrew Murray: On February 15th we had a lot more people who wanted to speak than we could fit in given the time constraints – being in February dusk fell fairly early. But you have to remember, although it was fair to say Stop the War was the lead organiser on February 15, CND and the Muslim Association of Britain were also there. So the speaker list was gone over with them.

Kate Hudson: Between the choices of Stop the War and choices of CND there is a huge amount of overlap. With the Muslim choices they were very different. We would choose who we would want on the basis of their representativeness of the movement and wider elements in society. This is a generalisation, but we would always want someone from all the parliamentary parties you can get: definitely a Lib Dem, the Scot and Welsh nationalists, a Labour person, preferably a minister or former minister – have it as broad as humanly possible. Then we always want religious types: a Bishop, preferably a Rabbi or something. Our thing is that we want it to be as broad as possible: a male/female balance, an ethnic mix if possible.

Mike Marqusee: Everyone wants to have the widest and most representative platform, in principle. Everyone also wants to make sure the platform includes those they particularly agree with, they endorse or whatever. That is natural; it's not wrong. But juggling these two things is often quite difficult. Then there is the bottom line, that you can't have an infinite number of speakers. That would solve everything.

Tony Myers: It's difficult to go through it without talking about how the SWP works, but it's just the way they are. They can be a nightmare to work with and can have a similar attitude to George Bush: "If you are not with us you're against us". So that can come through sometimes. Anybody who has been involved in this process with them [the SWP] will tell you that you end up with a list of speakers a mile long, because every single interest group has to have a speaker. I don't like that particularly because it's boring but I can see that if you are working with different groups of people, one of the things they are going to want is a speaker. But I think it gets a bit boring because you end up with the same thing being said over and over again... My view was that it didn't really matter as a lot of people weren't going to see them anyway.

Carol Naughton: The first list of speakers had 50 speakers on, of which three were women, and I was going "Wait a minute!" The three organisations each put suggestions forward. Stop the War came with a list already, and it was very heavily male-dominated. We very quickly fed other ideas into it and narrowed it down. If we had everybody we wanted to have the speeches would have gone on for three days. So trying to narrow that down to have a representation of all the different organisations – the trade unions for example, the outspoken MPs, celebrities. What you want are speakers who will resonate with your audience.

Mike Smith, Secretary's Department, Trade Union Congress: You ask why the TUC did not put forward a speaker for the 15 February 2003 rally. The invitation was given careful consideration but declined on the grounds that the TUC policy, as adopted by Congress the previous September [2002], had emphasised the importance of working through the United Nations and had not ruled out military action against Saddam Hussein in all circumstances. This was not the policy of all the march organisers nor that of some of the organizations that had been prominently supporting the march.[38]

Bob Crow: The TUC didn't even speak! [TUC General Secretary Brendan] Barber never spoke. I can't believe that.

A million people on the streets and the TUC General Secretary didn't even speak. Madness.

Mike Marqusee: So there is inevitably a lot of negotiation and anxiety accompanying this and there certainly was in the run-up to September and in run-up to February 15... I'm not sure how much people come for the speeches anyway, but I think it is important when you've got people's attention to use it effectively. Some speakers do and some don't. I felt it was important that there be women speakers because there were so few of them. I thought it was important that there were younger speakers and also that there were people from ethnic minority communities. I think we made a good effort on all those things, but of course who gets to represent all these constituencies is an impossible question to answer. It is always problematic because of course no one person does represent these things. Another factor you weigh up is who is a good speaker. So there is always a compromise. So people start with formulas and the best of intentions and the formula is shredded an hour into the discussion.

Asad Rehman: There was a lot of jostling for space... from the Black and Muslim perspective; for short-term gain people had defined that the only people to speak from a Muslim perspective were the religious Muslims. Many of us were saying "We are progressives. We are in the religious space, but we don't define ourselves purely in a religious framework. You are also playing this dangerous game of saying the Muslim community is homogeneous, and that people speak for it. No, there are multiple voices and the anti-war movement needs to represent that." And that was one of the many criticisms people made of the SWP: SWP speaker, religious Muslim speaker, MP – the platform it has for every public meeting around the country.

Andrew Murray: At one point we did think we might need to have two stages in Hyde Park. In the olden days before amplification you used to have thirteen or fourteen platforms for mass rallies in Hyde Park and speakers would go from one to the other. And we thought that the numbers were going to be so overwhelming that we might need two platforms, with some speakers on one and some on the other and some going from one to the other – the most popular speakers. There was quite an argument about that, but in the end we didn't do it.

Carmel Brown: Ghada is the reason Jesse Jackson was at the February 15 2003 demonstration.

Ghada Razuki, Office Manager, Stop the War Coalition: I was going out with a bloke, and we were meant to be going to New York for a lovey-dovey weekend, but that didn't work out. I would have lost my money so I went with my best mate to a peace demo in Washington in January [2003] instead. I was at the demo as an ordinary punter, although when I was out there I was asked to look at [Vietnam veteran] Ron Kovic, to see if we could get him over. And at the time we had had a few people interested in speaking at the demo, but for the big cheeses it has to be really big for them to come over. So anyway, we are on this demo in Washington, bloody freezing, and saw Jesse Jackson speak. And I thought we have a problem with this demo. We are getting hardly any black people on it and we need to find a way of doing that; and whether Jesse Jackson says very little, the way he delivers inspired me. Me and my friend were leaving the demo, and at one point I passed Jesse Jackson and I went "Alright, Jesse mate" and shook his hand. So I got back to London and emailed his office and said we would get half a million people, which I estimated it would be at the time – we would get members of Parliament blah blah blah. And I got a phone call from a member of his office and they said he would come over. Brilliant.

Carmel Brown: People were quite resistant to it. People weren't quite sure about whether we should have Jesse Jackson here. I thought it would be fantastic: he had marched with Martin Luther King. From a press point of view it gave us a very different picture. He was an international celebrity, a civil rights guy, he had marched with Martin Luther King. He was a Black American being beamed back in to American homes, so I thought it would improve our international coverage as well. He was rather high maintenance. He did get invited, and bless him – American politicians work so differently than our own – he wrote back saying he needed an entourage, he wanted a car, he needed to be picked up at Heathrow airport. He was demanding. Celebrity demanding. Stop the War just didn't have a budget for this. And I remember Andrew Burgin saying "We just have to let him know even the Mayor of London travels on the train. And the Prime Minister's wife travels on the Tube". It was put to Ken Livingstone that London could host him, and Ken was very good. The Mayor's car was sent to pick him up at Heathrow airport and he was the guest of the Mayor.

Ghada Razuki: There was resistance from Lindsey [German] and John [Rees]. I didn't understand why. We had an Officers' meeting and I was so excited he was going to come over... John Rees and Lindsey argued against it, and I couldn't really understand it. They said "What has he got to add to the demo?" And I said "Quite a lot". Everyone else kept quiet, and I said "We can get a lot more press, which will build the demo, but more importantly will get more Black people on board". And he said "We are getting so much press, we don't need anymore". And I said "Well John, let's close down the press office, shall we?" Anyway, they dropped it. I wonder if it was because Ken [Livingstone] got involved. A loss of control?

Andrew Murray: I don't remember anyone being vetoed by one organisation or another. There were obviously controversial suggestions like having the leader of the Liberal Democrats, Charles Kennedy.

"The party had to fight Kennedy to go on the peace march.": How Charles Kennedy ended up speaking on 15 February 2003

Donnachadh McCarthy, Deputy Chair of the Liberal Democrat Federal Executive in 2003: I was involved almost from the beginning. The days after 9/11 happened to be the Liberal Democrat party conference. So there was an emergency motion and I was involved in the drafting of that motion. I don't have the wording to hand but my memory is that we were trying to call for a measured and mature response and not to leap to war immediately. That was the party's activist- and conference-endorsed response. So therefore we were opposing war and that included, obviously, the

Afghanistan war. Within weeks of that conference decision Menzies Campbell announced our backing for the [2001] Afghan invasion. So that was the first major divergence of approach between the party membership-activist base and the leadership. When it comes to Iraq, my understanding is that the party's membership was enthusiastically opposed to the war. I didn't come across any enthusiastic pro-war people in the party leadership; there were only a couple of MPs who were vaguely pro-war at that time. But there was a leadership reluctance to take a position. It was their natural tendency: "Let's sit on the fence".

James Graham, Member of the Liberal Democrat Federal Executive 2003–5: There was definitely lots of talk in the run up that basically we needed to make sure the party didn't get stuck down the rail tracks of supporting the Government with its foreign policy blah blah blah. There had been lots of moves in the run up to the autumn 2002 conference. That was a fairly crucial conference, at least from Charles Kennedy's point of view, because we passed a motion which talked through the criteria by which we would support an Iraq intervention.

Menzies Campbell, Liberal Democrat MP 1987–present. Liberal Democrat Foreign Affairs spokesperson in 2003: We were preaching to the angels. The Liberal Democrats grassroots was wholly behind our position. There was a resolution in the September [2002] conference which I think I summed it up. I didn't move it but I summed it up. Essentially it set out the position we had adopted.

***BBC News*, 25 September 2002:** The Liberal Democrats have passed an emergency motion insisting military action against Iraq should only be taken as a last resort and with UN and Commons backing. Echoing the words of leader Charles Kennedy during Tuesday's Commons on the crisis, the party's conference demanded evidence that Saddam Hussein was a threat. And it said action should only come with full UN backing and after approval by the Commons. The conference also dismissed the government's dossier of evidence against Saddam, claiming it did not constitute evidence of an immediate threat.[39]

James Graham: The tension from that conference onwards was very much around that motion and to what degree those concerns had been met.

Jenny Tonge, Liberal Democrat MP 1997–2005. Liberal Democrat spokesperson for International Development in 2003: I was getting a lot of letters and support in my constituency because I was totally against military action from the start. Then there was all the debate about whether the UN resolution [1441] permitted military action or not. There was really quite a lot of quarrelling within the party as to whether it did or not. In the end it was decided it didn't and the Lib Dems, led by Charles Kennedy and advised by Menzies Campbell and the Foreign Affairs team, said that it really didn't permit military action: so we decided to oppose the war. It was pretty straightforward actually, it really was. The only thing I would say is Charles was very hesitant as to how public it should be.

James Graham: We are talking January 2003. We had this motion from the autumn [2002] conference that spelled out the criteria. It was very clear the criteria wasn't being met. We were in a position of at least supreme scepticism, if not outright opposition. We were in a position where someone basically had to make a stance. As a new, enthusiastic member of the Federal Executive my instant response was "Well, surely the FE [Federal Executive] should be doing this." I ended up drafting some stuff. I can't remember – it probably went round by email a few times with a few individuals. We agreed on a line. It was very deliberately myself and [future Liberal Democrat MP] Susan Kramer that were proposing and seconding it.

Excerpt of Federal Executive motion, January 2003: The executive... encourages Liberal Democrat members to voice their concerns about the Iraq situation, in particular by participating in the Stop the War demonstration on Saturday 15 February. Calls on the Party to publicise this fact through the press, the party's email and internet facilities and Liberal Democrat News. Requests that the Parliamentary Party send one of their number to speak at the post-demonstration rally on behalf of the Federal Party.[40]

James Graham: So we got that agreed and almost instantly found ourselves at war with the party centrally. Specifically, [on] every single substantive part of that motion we weren't making any headway on whatsoever. The Press Office wouldn't mention it; wouldn't put out a press release about what the position had been.

Donnachadh McCarthy: He [the Liberal Democrat Chief Executive Chris Rennard] said "I don't know what has happened, but since last night they've all got" – I can't remember the phrase exactly – but basically "they've all got scared and don't want this motion to go ahead." I can't remember the exact wording of the rest of that conversation but I made the decision that as an officer of the Federal Executive I was going to implement their decision… I took a decision that if it meant sacrificing my political career to help oppose the war, I was going to do that. I felt on very clear moral grounds to do what I did. Because there is no constitutional reference that says the leadership can veto any decision of the Federal Executive… This house [the interview took place in McCarthy's house] became the campaigns headquarters for the Liberal Democrats, unofficially, for the next two months… we got significant funding from various senior party members. My email became the contact email for the party's participation in the march. I was flooded with emails and support… James Graham set up a website to advertise the party's participation in the campaign, as access to the party's website had also been blocked… crucially, I told nobody that the leadership was attempting to block the party's participation.

James Graham: I built a website, which was absolutely awful, to mention that we had this motion agreed at the Federal Executive. Bear in mind this was in the days before Facebook or anything like that, so it was all sort of hand coded. It looked atrocious… It [the website] was very much done in a way to force the issue… We were dragging them by the short and curlies; it was very much resisted.

Donnachadh McCarthy: What happened then is, in a spare moment in the middle of all that madness I fired off a letter in my capacity as deputy chair to the *Guardian*... The [Liberal Democrat] leadership, in my opinion, wanted to sit on the fence until such time as the UN had taken its view. My understanding is that once that vote was taken and if it had authorised war then the Liberal Democrats would have endorsed war. I was determined to brand us as the anti-war party so when that came he [Kennedy] could not do that.

Donnachadh McCarthy letter, *Guardian*, 7 February 2003: The Liberal Democrats do not believe that there is sufficient evidence to date to justify a pre-emptive war against Iraq. As Charles Kennedy has said, "we are being bulldozed into a war not of our choosing". While a UN resolution is necessary, it is not sufficient... following this lead by Charles, the party's federal executive has called for all members and supporters to attend the peace march on February 15 to demonstrate the depth of our concern.[41]

Menzies Campbell, quoting from his autobiography: Charles has gone to lunch with the senior editorial team at the *Guardian*, who gave him a hard time about not going on the march. When he returned to his office he decided to take part in that and rang me to let me know his decision. I said "I wouldn't have done that", because of the demonstration's strong anti-Americanism and because some of the other groups taking part didn't exactly aspire to liberal values. I added "But now you've decided to do it, it's become the right decision and we must defend it."

Donnachadh McCarthy: I'm not aware of the *Guardian* lunch. What I am aware of is… I wrote a letter on the Thursday; it was published on the Friday. On the Saturday the *Guardian* quoted that letter in an editorial.

***Guardian*, 8 February 2003:** A week from today, London will be the scene of a national demonstration against the government's policy. If the advance publicity is right, it will be one of the largest in memory, rivalling the countryside march last autumn… Remarkably, no senior or significant political figure has managed to place themselves anywhere near the head of this oppositional movement… This ought to be a Charles Kennedy moment. He leads a party which officially supports next week's protest. He has spoken out in parliament and in interviews for a different approach to Iraq. By any normal standards of political engagement, Mr Kennedy ought therefore to be on the platform in Hyde Park next Saturday. Bu he is not going to be there. He has not been asked to be there and he does not appear to want to be there.[42]

Donnachadh McCarthy: So you are left with a situation that if it is not Kennedy who is going to be a spokesperson on the march, who is it going to be? There was nobody else. You had to symbolically have somebody in parliament representing the movement. If you hadn't Kennedy, who were you going to have? Backbenchers in the Labour Party, which would be dismissed as the usual suspects.

Andrew Murray: The main controversy [when choosing speakers in Stop the War Coalition] was around Charles Kennedy...The Liberal Democrats were against the war, but they hedged their opposition in the sense that if the United Nations had passed a resolution they would have switched. That was the reason for the controversy within Stop the War. Some felt it was a hostage to fortune. We put this guy on a platform and next week he might switch his position.

George Galloway, Labour MP 1987–2005. Respect MP 2005–10 and 2012–present. Vice President of Stop the War Coalition 2001–present: I was personally in favour, though I knew the Liberal Democrat's position was an opportunistic one. I knew that as soon as the war started, if it did, they would jump ship, which they did. But I took the view that it was better to have Charles Kennedy – drunk or sober, sincere or opportunistic – on the platform, in terms of the lift and publicity we would get.

Andrew Murray: So we wrote to his office and we didn't hear a response. And within the Liberal Democrats a lot of people were putting pressure on him to speak, and he popped up on one of the Sunday political programmes on television a week or two before the demonstration and said "I haven't been asked". He didn't really want to get involved, I think.

Charles Kennedy, Breakfast with Frost, 9 February 2003: As concerns the peace march itself, personally speaking I'd be very happy to participate in that. As a matter of fact I've not been formally invited, and I would want to make the Liberal Democrat case, which is the pro-United Nations case. It is not anti-war, come what may...[43]

Donnachadh McCarthy: Which was bollocks because I had been conveying the invitation from the peace movement to Kennedy. I rang Lord Newby who was his head of office at the time, and said "You know, for fuck's sake, that there is an invitation. I am confirming absolutely, categorically that the invitation stands from the peace movement to Kennedy."

James Graham: From what I understand what happened was Kennedy, thinking on his feet and backed into a corner, said "Yes, of course we are". Literally within an hour of that interview the floodgates opened. We suddenly got the link on the front page of the website. An email went out to all Lib Dem supporters promoting the march; they went into overdrive; it all started happening. But it was only after that interview that we saw any cooperation whatsoever from the party centrally.

Jenny Tonge: To do justice to Charles it is a big decision to make: whether a party leader should go on a popular march. Because up until that time party leaders didn't do things like that... Some of the more senior members of the parliamentary party thought it was undignified to speak at a rally.

James Graham: They were very anxious about being associated with the hard left. That was almost the point blank line in the sand problem. There were lots of other factors but that was a fairly compelling factor. Part of the reason I felt it was worth pursuing is because it looked to me, even as far back as September/October [2002], that this was going to be more than just the hard left. Inevitably the hard left would want to take all the credit, would want to be seen to be the vanguard of it, but actually the people who would actually be on the march would, broadly speaking, drown out the left.

Donnachadh McCarthy: In that generation of politicians on the centre/centre-left there is a huge collective nightmare folk memory of what happened to Michael Foot: "The longest suicide note in history." Anything that was perceived as pacifist, anti-nuclear, on the left, was seen as a disaster for any political party to be associated with. I think that generation of the party is terrified of the tabloids. Terrified of what I call the Murdochracy… If I was arguing their case for them against me, I would also say "Look what happened with the Falklands." A week before the Falklands nobody had heard of the Falklands Islands and didn't give a damn about Argentina. Then suddenly, within days, you had 83–85 percent support for the war. So if you are a party leader and you have that swing in public opinion, you could have your party wiped out. So those are the real political arguments taking place on the other side… The party had to fight Kennedy to go on the peace march.

Andrew Burgin: Kennedy was a breakthrough speaker. Getting Kennedy to speak was very very important… There were some Lib Dems involved in the Coalition, and they were organising a contingent. I spoke to them and between us we tried to put as much pressure as possible to get Kennedy to speak. We were very happy that he chose to speak.

Andrew Murray: I think it was a good thing he spoke, because then our focus had to be on trying to persuade a Parliamentary majority to vote against the war by some means or other; which always seemed like a long shot given the Conservatives were strongly backing Blair. So clearly the Liberals were an important part of that, so binding them into the movement was important.

Menzies Campbell: At that time we were having a pretty hard time, Kennedy and I. I had some sleepless nights and I think he did too because when the country's going to war the last thing the people who are going to risk their lives need is the notion there is any kind of dissent or fracture in opinion behind them. We had to accept the positions we were taking were opposed to that. We were helped, I think to some extent, by the way public opinion was moving.

"The politics of fear and exaggeration": The Government deploys tanks at Heathrow Airport – 11 February 2003

***Guardian*, front page, 12 February 2003:** Heathrow was last night being patrolled by 1,500 anti-terrorist police and troops after intelligence warnings identified it as a likely target for an imminent attack by al-Qaida-linked militants armed with anti-aircraft missiles... The prime minister was told of the threat and rubber stamped the deployment of 450 soldiers from the 1st Battalion the Grenadier Guards and the Household Cavalry... Investigators regard the Heathrow threat as more significant than the alert following the discovery of ricin in North London last month because the warnings refer to a specific target within a specific time limit. They indicated it was the most worrying terrorist threat to Britain since September 11.[44]

David Blunkett: They'd moved armoured personnel carriers – the equivalent of tanks as far as the public were concerned – and of course all this frightened people to death, particularly women. You could feel that: the minute it was described to me. I knew it was a mistake.[45]

Andrew Burgin: My father, who has been a *Daily Mail*-reading Tory all his life, phoned me up when the tanks were at Heathrow and started laughing and just said "They are trying everything to stop your march, aren't they?"

Clare Short, International Development Secretary in 2003: At the time, and today, I feel cynical about them. I think people rarely, absolutely, explicitly say "We are going to lie about this" and then hype it up. I think they get themselves into a hyped-up atmosphere and obsessed with the media, and sort of semi-convince themselves of the falsity they are about to engage in. That is the human condition. I don't think many humans sit there and say "Let's tell an absolute lie". They say "It might be like this, it's dangerous, and these are very tense times". At the time I felt full of doubt, and I made a comment to that effect in the media. I didn't have any inside knowledge. That's the politics of fear and exaggeration, which New Labour has engaged in. I think people convince themselves of the hype, rather than set out to deliberately lie and exaggerate. But it is a lie.

Jeremy Corbyn: If you think about it, putting armoured cars at Heathrow is actually ridiculous. If someone has a SAM-7 missile that they want to fire off at a plane, then they are not going to do it from the car park of Heathrow, they'll do it from somewhere else. So then you think why? What is the point of all this? Unless it is to create a kind of national anxiety about people's safety and security.

Tariq Ali: The Heathrow business was all part of the setup to justify the war on Iraq… I remember I was travelling to Heathrow and I asked a cop what this was all about and he said "It's sort of 9–6 tanks – that's when the threat exists" with a smile on his face. So after 6 o'clock they disappeared. They weren't working overtime! That was all part of the propaganda campaign to build fear in the country so no one could question the Government.

***BBC News* online headline, 14 February 2003**: What if a dirty bomb hit London?[46]

Sir Rodric Braithwaite, former head of the Joint Intelligence Committee: The campaign to win round a sceptical public was not conducted primarily on the basis of intelligence dossiers. In the first months of this year we were bombarded with warnings that British cities might at any moment face a massive terrorist attack. Housewives were officially advised to lay in stocks of food and water. Tanks were sent to Heathrow. People were unwilling to go to war to uphold the authority of the United Nations, to overthrow an evil dictator in a distant country, or to promote democracy throughout the Middle East. But in this atmosphere of near hysteria, they began to believe that Britain itself was under imminent threat and that we should get our blow in first… Fishmongers sell fish: warmongers sell war. Both may sincerely believe in their product. The prime minister surely acted in the best of faith. But it does look as though he seriously oversold his wares.[47]

George Galloway: Our political class, our political system, was so debased by going to such a war on such a pack of lies, that they might as well be hung for a sheep as a lamb. I think our political leaders sank lower than any in modern times and they would have been prepared to sink lower still... I wouldn't have believed these people if they had told me today was Tuesday [the interview took place on a Tuesday]. So debased was that Government at that time, so desperate, almost Shakespearean really – the spot that will not out.

Mike Marqusee: Tanks at Heathrow! It was clearly contrived by the Government to provide justification for the war on terrorism, to promote the climate of fear they had been promoting since 9/11 and thereby to deter people from protesting against it. The amazing thing was it didn't work. I was worried at the time, and thought "Oh god, how are people going to respond to this?" Some people clearly were affected by it, but on the whole people weren't and it didn't stop the movement from gathering pace at all. In fact the manipulation of opinion, the dodgy dossier being the most extreme example, backfired. It built up such a level of distrust in the Government. An interesting lesson. There was a certain amount of overkill by the Government that made people suspicious. Anyway it certainly didn't stop the movement from developing.

"The *BBC* was absolutely petrified of the Government": The *BBC* and wider media coverage of the anti-war movement and the march

Mike Marqusee: After 9/11 it was extremely hard for any anti-war voices to get into the mainstream media, including the *Guardian* and *Independent*. Even to get our demonstrations noticed was very difficult.

Ian Mayes, *Guardian*'s Reader's Editor, 20 October 2001: It is the paper's general policy not to cover marches.[48]

***Guardian*, 11 February 2003:** Rupert Murdoch has given his full backing to war, praising George Bush as acting "morally" and "correctly" and describing Tony Blair as "full of guts" for going out on a limb in his support for an attack on Iraq. The media tycoon, who has developed a close relationship with the prime minister, said he was full-square behind Mr Bush and Mr Blair, who are now facing critical opposition from Germany and France over war. Mr Murdoch described the prime minister's stance as "extraordinarily courageous" but branded the Labour party as a hotbed of "knee-jerk anti-Americanism"... On the war Mr Murdoch was equally unequivocal. "We can't back down now. I think Bush is acting very morally, very correctly, and I think he is going to go on with it," he said. "The fact is, a lot of the world can't accept the idea that America is the one superpower in the world," he added.[49]

Mike Marqusee: As we put more people on the street the pressure increased on journalists and broadcasters to reflect that somehow.

Andrew Burgin: Two national newspapers took a broadly anti-war position – The *Independent* and the *Mirror*... *Al Jazeera* were ever present and *Sky* carried reports of our work continuously. The *BBC* were more difficult. Their coverage was almost all uncritically pro-war.[50]

Tony Benn, President, Stop the War Coalition. Labour MP 1963–2001 (with a brief spell in 1983–4 not in Parliament) and former Labour Cabinet Minister: The *Observer* came out for the war. I gave up the *Observer* after that and haven't read it since. Nick Cohen and people like that – I simply couldn't read them. The *Guardian* was a bit wobbly. The *Guardian* is always "On one hand and on the other hand, we hope wiser council will prevail". Sort of wishy-washy liberal stuff. The *Morning Star* was the only paper that gave systematic day-to-day reporting.

Alastair Campbell, Tony Blair's Communications Director: The left of our media, that basically just was opposed to the whole thing and very aggressively ran the kind of "Blair is Bush's poodle" line... the *BBC* became very, very hostile in its coverage of Iraq.... It is true that there was opposition and hostility. There was also a considerable amount of support for the government's position, and I think there still is, but it just doesn't get much airtime.[51]

Carmel Brown: *Sky News* was an easier nut to crack because of 24-hour rolling news – they just take a lot of stuff. People were quite surprised at that at the beginning. The *BBC* were difficult, were quite sniffy about the whole thing. They only wanted news filtered through a celebrity. They were massively behind *ITN* and *Sky News*. The [*BBC*]

Today programme were really hard work. From our point of view they were the least helpful to us. [Alastair] Campbell's notion that the *BBC* were anti-war from top to bottom was a complete joke. I would have loved them to be anti-war from top to bottom!

Greg Dyke, *BBC* Chairman 2000–4: You shouldn't underestimate the role played by [Alastair] Campbell in the whole thing. I'm not sure Campbell believed in the war but Campbell is very much "He said it so my job is to deliver it". Campbell bullied. Campbell was a thug – an old-fashioned thug who bullied all sorts of people. He tried to bully the *BBC* and failed… It's a very interesting phenomenon – it will never happen again – where someone who runs the publicity machine becomes the second or third most powerful person in the country.Very dangerous… He tried to pressure us a lot. He hated the *BBC*… He told me one day. I went in to see him about something else and he told me he how much he hated *Panorama* and how much he hated the *Today* programme. He'd stopped listening to the *Today* programme you see – he only listened to *Five Live*.

Kevin Marsh, *BBC Today* programme Editor 2002–6: Alastair Campbell was a complete control freak as everybody knows… Campbell would deluge us in letters.Anything and everything: a single word, a phrase, the way in which a headline was presented – all the way through to "You're lying". The whole gambit. And this was a regular thing. I genuinely don't know how he and his office found the time to send as many letters and faxes as they did. Because they must have been faxing other people as well, it can't have been just us. So when you talk about the tremendous amount of pressure the *BBC* was under from the Government, when parliament returned in 2002 it was pretty much daily pressure from Alastair Campbell: "You've got this wrong", "You've got that wrong", "This isn't true".

Lindsey German: The *BBC* were awful, absolutely awful. We got much better coverage from *Sky*, we got much better coverage from the *ITN* news channel. I think the *BBC* was absolutely petrified of the Government. The second thing is that they have this kind of ethos that demonstrations are beneath them, whereas the more commercial channels go with what they think is interesting. Lots of the *BBC* people were sympathetic, but there was a clampdown from above. I think they [the *BBC*] absolutely went out of their way not to upset the Government. It's an absolute classic. It's a bit like when you read what happened with the [1926] General Strike with Lord Reith. The impartiality of the *BBC* actually becomes "We have to defend the Government, or otherwise what vista does this open up – there may be anarchy or revolution or whatever". And that's really how they responded to it.

Lord Reith, Founder of the *BBC*, diary entry during 1926 General Strike: They [the Government] want to be able to say that they did not commandeer us, but they know they can trust us not to be really impartial.[52]

Tony Benn: The *BBC* – take them as a symbol, as a mouthpiece of Government – they accepted the broad thrust of the argument that Saddam was a threat and they went along with it.

Greg Dyke: I'll say back to them [critics of the *BBC* coverage] what I said to the Prime Minister in my [21 March 2003] letter to him, and what I've said to all sorts of groups over time, which is: I'm sorry, but you can't be the judge of impartiality. There is a brilliant quote from John Simpson, the foreign affairs editor of the *BBC*, which basically says at the time of conflict the *BBC* is inevitably under pressure from the Government of the day. Enormous pressure. And that this is not a problem as long as the *BBC* doesn't fold. *ITN* or *Sky* or *Channel Four News* wouldn't know what pressure is compared to the *BBC*. For example, the Gilligan affair.[xiii] Jon Snow could have done what Gilligan did and no one would have said a word, no one would have noticed. The *BBC* is in a different league to anyone else. Why? First of all, governments know how powerful it is. Secondly, governments often mistakenly believe it belongs to them. But it doesn't belong to them at all; it belongs to the people. It doesn't belong to the Government. It's not their money, it's the people's money... The pressure is intense and enormous and your job is to be balanced.

Kevin Marsh: I can see where those criticisms come from. But I do think they come from, in most cases, a bit of a misreading about what the *BBC* is and how the *BBC* sees its role. In some of the criticisms we received at the time I got the feeling we were being criticised for not doing things we don't really do... I think it is absolutely the case that we didn't have the same proportion of coverage of the Stop the

xiii On the 29 May 2003 edition of the *BBC Today* programme journalist Andrew Gilligan reported on allegations that the 24 September 2002 dossier had been "sexed up". Gilligan's reporting led to several official inquires into the intelligence that led to the invasion.

War demonstrations, the big one and the smaller ones, as *ITN* or *Sky* did. But I think in total we had more coverage – because we had more airtime. So if you look at straightforward gross time of how many minutes' anti-war voices and narratives got on the *BBC*, it is more than on *Sky* and *ITN*. Where the Stop the War Coalition had a point is that the *BBC* tends to think very hard before it covers demonstrations as demonstrations. It is partly because we are more sceptical about the motives of demonstrations. You've got to remember the *BBC* has been in the firing line for a long time... We don't just cover a demonstration because it is noisy, or because there is a lot of people there. We are not guided by the numbers of a demonstration. A couple of years prior to the big anti-war march – in 2000 I think – there was a huge teachers' demonstration. I've forgotten what it was about but I got a lot of flak from my wife, who is a teacher, because we didn't cover it at all. But in our view we had covered the arguments; we felt we had covered the arguments. Having a big demonstration does not in itself get it on to a programme... So did *ITN* or *Sky* do more? I would agree that it is probably the case. *Sky* and *ITN* have a much more traditional journalistic view. They take the view that part of their job is to grab people's attention. Numbers grab people's attention. Demonstrations grab people's attention, even if they don't turn violent. So that is part of the answer. The other answer is, and this is certainly true of *Today* [programme] and *Radio 4* and to some extent true of the main bulletins on *BBC 1*, there was a hell of a lot going on. Real things happening. UN talks on the second resolution, trying to get France on side, meetings between Bush and Blair and so on. We felt that that was our priority: to look at the real movements that were happening that meant that war may or may not happen. If you remember, the huge troop movements beforehand made some sort of conflict almost inevitable. Did we cover the popular view well enough? Possibly not because we felt there was so much going on over here; capturing the mood and will of the people, while it was there on the agenda, it was probably a notch or two down. In hindsight it should probably have been higher… since we, rightly or wrongly, see ourselves as public policy journalists then necessarily we look at what is happening in public policy i.e. politicians and officials. And it is probably true that we would think more about what politicians and the military and so on were saying to us than we would think about those who were not in a position to make decisions, like the anti-war movement. This is the important thing. These are people in a position to change things. The thing about the Stop the War Coalition was that, although it was a very large coalition, these were disparate voices. And again I think there is a weakness in our way of doing journalism. So you sit down and take a phone call or read a letter and you think "Yep, I understand this argument. But if I put this on air is this one voice even within Stop the War movement? Does it matter? Is it important? Will it change anything? If I think it won't change anything, does it nevertheless deserve to be heard?" So there are all of these considerations going on in my mind. But I have to say, at the end of the day – certainly the programmes that I was responsible for – we did see ourselves as commentating on public policy and on the people who were in a position to make decisions.

Lindsey German: It's obvious from what we know subsequently that they [the *BBC*] did make an agreement that they would always try to find pro-war people to balance – that was the letter Greg Dyke wrote to Tony Blair.

Greg Dyke letter to Tony Blair, 21 March 2003: I believe we have made major efforts to ensure that the issues and events surrounding Iraq have been properly reported. Let me explain how we have done that. Some weeks ago I set up a committee… it was that committee which insisted that we had to find a balanced audience for programmes like *Question Time* at a time when it was very hard to find supporters of the war willing to come on. And it was that same committee when faced with a massive bias against the war among phone-in callers, decided to increase the number of phone lines so that pro-war listeners had a better chance of getting through and getting onto the programmes. All this was done in an attempt to ensure our coverage was balanced.[53]

Greg Dyke: If you looked at the polls they were pretty 50/50. So there were supporters of the war, they just didn't get on the radio or television. So we decided we ought to try and reflect what the polls showed – that there was a fair proportion of people that bought and believed in the Government line and supported the case for war, and that their opinion should be reflected. So therefore you shouldn't have on just people who were opposed to the war.

Kevin Marsh: It's difficult to know where to start with this one. The *BBC*'s promise is about impartiality. It is not about balance or neutrality or fairness or objectivity. It's about impartiality which is a different thing... And what Greg [Dyke] was getting at here was the *BBC*'s promise of impartiality. Therefore, we take any issue, whatever the issue is – it could be the second resolution, it could be the troop movements – and try to locate the significant views along the axis of that disagreement. You're not trying to balance that in a numerical way. You are not trying to say "If we have ten voices on this side we must have ten voices on the other side". What you are trying to say is "We must hear the significant views and we must go out and seek them". That is the key thing. If a significant view, a powerful view, an important view isn't being heard for whatever reason it is the job of an impartial *BBC* journalist to go out and look for that view... What I know we were aware of was [John] Major's victory in '92, which was down to a lot of people voting Tory but not admitting it in polls. There was some evidence that there was more support for the war than we were finding. More diverse – people supporting the war for different reasons. It wasn't just the Government. We also had a sense – and I don't want to make too big a thing of this – of two things. Firstly, by definition an anti-war movement is more visceral, more heated and more committed. People see something that is intolerable about to happen, something vile, and they feel much more emotionally attached to it. And therefore they are much more likely to call phone-ins, much more likely to turn up at *Question Time* to get themselves in the audience or whatever. And that is not to say this is a bad thing and they shouldn't have done it. But it is nonetheless the case: the energy and vehemence of the anti-war case was clearly at a different level. And there was a little thing that was lurking in the back of our minds, which might sound unconnected. A few years before, we had the MMR scandal[xiv] where we got it really wrong. We had allowed the emotional appeal of the anti-MMR case to dominate. The diversity of the voices – there were parents and campaigners and lawyers on one side and boring old doctors on the other side. And we were absolutely aware we had got that wrong. It was not a 50/50 split.

Andrew Murray: The *BBC* actually instructed their journalists not to attend the march unless they were there in a professional capacity, which was an extraordinary injunction considering they haven't issued any other injunctions on any other occasion as far as I know. The *BBC* is more prone to pro-government pressure... I think the *BBC* is an arm of the state.

***Guardian*, 11 February 2003:** Senior *BBC* news presenters such as Huw Edwards and Fiona Bruce and journalists including Andrew Marr have been ordered by bosses to stay away from Saturday's anti-war march in London. The *BBC* deputy director of news, Mark Damazer, yesterday sent an email to newsroom staff listing which categories of journalist should not attend the march… these include all presenters, correspondents, editors, output editors and "anyone who can be considered a 'gatekeeper' of our output"… The *BBC* director general, Greg Dyke, has also reminded staff they should remember their duty to be "independent, impartial and honest" in the coming weeks as a possible war with Iraq looms.[54]

---

xiv The MMR scandal was a media-driven 1998 health scare about the safety of the Measles, Mumps and Rubella vaccine.

Kevin Marsh: Senior figures did go on the march. I didn't. Partly because I don't do that sort of thing. For example, journalists like Hugh Sykes went on the march. And I am aware of two or three editors on the *Today* programme who went on the march. We were heavily discouraged from going on the march but, at the end of the day, certainly, I as an individual, had to say to people "I can't really inhibit your freedom to express yourself." It just felt wrong to me. I can't stop people believing what they believe in... It's appearance. That awful, dreadful thing that I hate where it is actually the appearance of the thing rather than the substance. I knew that the people who had been on the march would come in to work on the Monday and they would not scream "Stop the War!" but would consider the issues and make rational judgements. But at the end these things are very much about appearance.

Greg Dyke: If you look into history of the post-war period you'll find it there every time. It was the same thing at the time of Suez, the Falklands, Northern Ireland and Kosovo. Politicians in power want the *BBC* to support them basically. And the *BBC* doesn't. So in the end they always fall out. It's only a matter of time. There is a great quote from a woman called Grace Wyndham Goldie, who was in charge of *BBC Current Affairs* at the time of Suez [in 1956], and who wrote a book in the '60s, and she basically said broadcasters and political parties are different animals. They have a different role in society and therefore conflict between the two is inevitable. It's just a matter of when. If they are both doing their job properly, the politician will believe he is doing something devoutly and the broadcaster will question him or give airtime to those who question him.[xv]

"The phones went bonkers. It was 20 hour days": The Stop the War Coalition, CND and MAB offices in the final days before the march

Tony Blair: The political pressure was just enormous at that time in December, January, February 2002/2003.[55]

Andrew Murray and Lindsey German: In the build up to the march, the Coalition worked from two offices. The first, in the Brick Lane brewery, was our mobilising centre where a small army of volunteers was presided over by our office coordinator Ghada Razuki, a former firefighter from an Iraqi family. Her organisational skills and endless energy were invaluable assets. From here publicity was distributed, placards prepared and logistical issues resolved... All the logistics of the demonstration were in the hands of our Chief Steward, Chris Nineham, an experienced organiser who was centrally involved in Globalise Resistance.[56]

---

xv Dyke seems to be referring to Wyndham Goldie's 1977 book *Facing the nation. Television and politics 1936–1976*, in which she writes "Political pressures... are inevitable. For the aims of the political parties and those of broadcasting organisations are not the same. Broadcasting organisations, generally speaking, want to interest their audiences and to inform the electorate by presenting facts and opinions relevant to a particular situation regardless of any effect these may have on the future of the political parties. The political parties, generally speaking, want to use broadcasting, and particularly in recent years television, to persuade the electorate to support certain policies and people in order to win elections and gain power."

Carmel Brown: Ghada was a phenomenon. A real phenomenon. She was described by Ken Loach in the *Observer* as "a Catherine Wheel of energy".

Ghada Razuki: It became obvious the demo was going to be enormous in mid-January [2003]. I had come back from Washington where I had seen Jesse Jackson speak, and the phones went bonkers. It was 20 hour days. It was getting closer and closer. The UN in December [2002] had taken a stance that was not great. The press picked up on it. They were suddenly all over us. There were people ringing up from towns that I'd never heard of. You could feel the escalation of calls really rising. But it was the quality of calls that was key – i.e. people who had never been on a demo in their lives. It wasn't the usual people, but ordinary punters, kids.

Sean Wallis: We were registering around 250,000 hits a day on the home page, a level which is unheard of for a campaigning website.

Ghada Razuki: From the national office 1.5 million leaflets, 500,000 posters, 150,000 stickers and 20,000 window posters were also produced. For the demonstration the Stop the War Coalition put together 30,000 of their own placards and 15,000 of the *Daily Mirror* placards.[57]

Kim Manning-Cooper: In the run up to the demo it was extremely hard work. We were working very long hours and not getting very much sleep. As it got closer to the demo it became very clear – in terms of discussions with the police and with the other coalition partners and the number of phone calls we had to the office – it was going to be very, very big.

Anas Altikriti: We formed what we called the Operation Room within MAB, from the Sunday prior to the demonstration to the demonstration itself. There were between eight and ten people manning that Operation Room 24/7. People were taking it in shifts. I recall I'd done a meeting in Bolton and arrived back in London at 01:00 am and I got to the office at 02:00 am and there were about five people on their feet, about three under the tables having a kip and two having a bite to eat because they had been working for the past six hours non-stop. This was all about the poster and banners and taking phone calls. There were people from Glasgow who had booked four carriages of the train that came all the way to London. It was immense. We were getting calls from corners of Britain where we didn't have any branches, but people had heard about us.

Ghada Razuki: I remember the day when I realised it was going to be big. I had a phone call from a ten-year old called Colin who said he had put stickers up all over his school and he was getting into trouble for that, so he asked if I could talk to his headmistress and tell her it was ok to do this. I had to explain to him I couldn't do that, and he asked if I could send him some more stickers. An hour later a woman called up and said "I can't come on the demo because I'm very old and not very mobile". So I said "That's ok. What if I send you a few fliers that you can have in your home and if someone comes round you can give it to them?" And she said "No, no my dear you don't understand – I'm going to go and lie down on the M3". It was absolutely brilliant. Inspirational.

Alice Kilroy, Stop the War Coalition Finance Officer in 2003: The phone calls were incredible because it was obvious there were a lot of demo virgins who intended going. There were worries about bringing dogs, what if you wanted to walk in the opposite way to the demo, were tickets needed etc.

Phillip Steele: In the weeks before the February 2003 march our phone never stopped ringing, all day long and into the night. We were soon aware of a rising swell of public revulsion for the policies and deceit of Bush and Blair. I had never experienced anything on this scale before. Many strangers rang in or stopped by the high street stalls just to talk about it, to let out their anger. Sometimes a call would start "I am an old soldier..." or "I served in the Second World War..." – I would brace myself for criticism, only to receive warm messages of support. This was especially reassuring, as the government and media propaganda was succeeding to some extent in dividing the loyalties of families and friends. It was later said that it was the STWC and colleagues in the peace movement who could claim credit for this surge in opposition to the war. I would say that it was not down to any of us activists – the public had motivated themselves.

Chris Nineham: The problem was that none of us had experienced anything like it. I remember saying maybe two weeks before the demo "I think there is going to be a million people", and people were like "Yeah, right". And then a few days later, as the whole grass issue developed, and it became headline news, and then the *Daily Mirror* was starting to publicise the demonstration: people started to think maybe a million wasn't too crazy. I started to think a kind of tidal wave was on the horizon. What the fuck is going to happen here? The big questions were: how are we going to deal with this number of people? How to make it as effective as possible? How to, on the one hand make sure that it has a big impact, but on the other hand make it an experience that people actually find worthwhile? Where to start and where to finish?

***Guardian*, 14 February 2003:** The Metropolitan police have cancelled all leave this weekend to help it cope with the demands posed by anti-terrorist operations and the expected 500,000 strong demonstration against the war in Iraq. But deputy assistant commissioner Andy Trotter, who is in charge of policing the protest march, insisted yesterday that the force would not need to draft troops into the capital. "We are being tested, but that will not be necessary. We will have 3,500 officers policing the march and others in reserve. We expect this to be one of the biggest marches of recent years, but we have experience of handling big occasions like the Notting Hill Carnival."[58]

Carmel Brown: Three days before the demonstration I was in the Stop the War office in London. I was worried about how we could monitor press coverage if we didn't have a TV or radio in the room. I think we did manage to get a radio rigged up. I come from a journalistic background and there is always a TV on in the background. I remember being bundled out by Andrew Murray to go to City Hall and meet [then Senior Policy Advisor on Equalities to the Mayor of London] Lee Jasper and Jesse Jackson's guy to discuss Jesse Jackson's itinerary. And it was "Carmel, can you go, because you have the best coat on?" They had to send me in a cab because I had no idea how to get to the City

Hall in time for the meeting. I went to City Hall. A beautiful February day. In Liverpool I'm my kid's Mum. I do my part-time work in radio stations up here. So this was an away day from rural womanhood. I found myself sitting in this car in this very beautiful coat. And my phone rang and it was [English actress] Vanessa Redgrave. She wanted to know how she could get [American actor] Tim Robbins involved in the demonstration, as he was in town filming. So she told me he was staying at the Savoy and gave me his room number. And she also told me [British fashion designer] Alexander McQueen, [and supermodels] Naomi Campbell and Kate Moss also wanted to be involved in this demonstration. So before I got out of the cab at City Hall I had spoken to Vanessa Redgrave, Tim Robbins and Alexander McQueen's PA! I just had to pinch myself, it was so funny. This is about as dynamic and glamorous as it gets in London – and I'm with Stop the War and the lefties!

Andrew Murray and Lindsey German: Special efforts were made to build the atmosphere around the demonstration. A broad programme of events was organised for 14 February, the eve of the protest, including a reception hosted by Ken Livingstone, two central London political rallies and a poetry reading.[59]

Carmel Brown: The night before there were two events – the Ken Livingstone event at City Hall and another event at Friends Meeting House. Jesse Jackson spoke at Friends Meeting House and moved to City Hall later. Tim Robbins came to the City Hall reception – he was a really great guy. When I called up to say "Look, let's put Tim Robbins on the platform on Saturday", they were "No, we've decided the speakers". Tim

Robbins wasn't allowed to speak, mostly because Andrew Murray had never heard of him. And I was like "Are you serious? You arse!" Nobody wanted me to upset Andrew.

Ghada Razuki: Tim Robbins spoke at the eve of demo rally in Friends Meeting House. I remember standing between Jesse Jackson and Tim Robbins and thinking "God, it can't get any better than this!"

Damon Albarn: I spent the night before at a soirée at City Hall hosted by Ken Livingstone for the people who had been working behind the scenes. I remember sitting in Ken's office with Reverend Jesse Jackson sharing a couple of whiskies, which was a new experience for me. Although Jesse Jackson wasn't going to be on the walk because he was suffering from gout.

SECTION TWO

15 FEBRUARY 2003

Travelling to the march

Alastair Campbell, Tony Blair's Communications Director, 15 February 2003 diary entry: The first thing TB [Tony Blair] said was that he has slept badly. So had I. He knew that he was in a tight spot. "Even I am a bit worried about this one," he said.[1]

Andrew Murray, Stop the War Coalition Chair 2001–11 and Lindsey German, Stop the War Coalition Convenor: As the size of the impending demonstration became clear... it was decided to split the march in two. It would have been physically unsafe to attempt to assemble everyone at our traditional point of departure on the Embankment... So a second assembly point was designated at Gower Street, near the main London railway stations, for people travelling from the Midlands and the north. The idea was that the two marches would set off simultaneously, meet and merge at Piccadilly Circus, and proceed to Hyde Park for a rally.[2]

Jeremy Corbyn, Labour MP 1983–present: I had been working flat out for several months on this, so I was exhausted. I remember going up to Tufnell Park [in north London], my local Tube station at the time, to get the train to the Malet Street [Gower Street] assembly point. I was also carrying my small bag to take with me to go to the USA that night, which was a nuisance but there was nothing I could do about it. I got to Tufnell Park station and I thought "My God they've closed the line". There was a whole queue of people outside the station: it was a queue of people to go into the station to join the march.

Ken Loach, Film Director: I was living in Parliament Hill then, just north of Kentish Town [in north London]. My wife and I went down [to the march] on the bus. The bus was full of people going to the march. We could see them outside the house. Everyone took their kids, and it was a part of London with a lot of families. You had this sense of the whole city moving to a central point.

Salma Yaqoob, Chair of Birmingham Stop the War Coalition in 2003: I know for the big march we had almost 200 coaches from Birmingham.

John Shemeld, Coordinator of Nottingham Stop the War Coalition: We took 24 full coaches to London on 15 February – over 1,000 people.

Margaret Jones, Peace campaigner based in Bristol: I went along to the coach pick-up point on the morning of the march. There were 60 coaches there – all from Bristol. I'd never been on a London demo where Bristol had sent that many people. I remember we were all so excited, just by this. I still feel moved when I think of it. Regardless of the outcome, the sight of people standing up for other human beings is always inspiring. We set off along the M4 talking and joking – feeling elated and strong.

Mark Holt, Chair, Merseyside Stop the War Coalition: On 15th February 21 fifty-seater coaches and a train packed with 650 people on board left Liverpool at 5:45am.[3]

***Times*, 15 February 2003:** It has been almost impossible to hire a coach in Yorkshire in the past few days. From the Dales to the inner cities almost 200 50-seat vehicles are making the journey south with many thousands more travelling by car, minibus or rail.[4]

Peter Offord, Founder member of Norwich Stop the War Coalition and President since 2009: 19 coaches from Norwich formed part of a convoy of 70 buses from across Norfolk.

Philip Steele, Freelance writer of children's non-fiction and peace activist based in Bangor: The Bangor group filled four coaches to London – over 200 people of all ages and backgrounds. A further coach of 50 or so was organised by the Bangor Islamic Centre, with whom we had developed close relations...The London coaches had to leave in the very early morning, when it was still very chilly and dark. The organisation and coordination over such a long journey was formidable. All five coaches met up at a motorway services in the English Midlands, and the farther south we travelled we were heartened by the sight of coach after coach festooned with signs and banners. There was a definite feeling that history was in the making.

Adrian Mole, Diary Writer: I had to stand all the way on the train. Anti-war protestors had hogged all the seats. To my surprise, the vast majority of them looked like ordinary, respectable people.[5]

Anas Altikriti, Spokesperson, Muslim Association of Britain: I remember turning up at Embankment. I was there quite early because I was supposed to speak to [*BBC* journalist] John Pienaar from *Radio 5 Live* at about 06:30, and then on the hour, every hour. So I turned up at 06:30 and our guys were starting to put up the barriers and posters and everything. By 09:30 I was getting slightly worried, because I was standing there with maybe a dozen people. There were a lot of TV cameras and very few participants! The TV cameras were picturing all the banners and posters laying flat on Embankment. I remember feeling a little bit embarrassed.

Carol Naughton, Campaign for Nuclear Disarmament Chair 2001–3: From very early in the morning I was just doing back-to-back interviews. I was down on the Embankment. There was nobody around and I was thinking were people really going to come? Then people started to arrive in droves and droves – it was amazing to see the numbers of people – and then the concern about how we were going to manage this number of people.

Lindsey German: When I was down at Embankment all the celebrities – the big celebrities – were down there. It was an amazing morning because you have people coming up to you and saying "I'd like to introduce you to Kenneth Kaunda the [former] President of Zambia". And you say "Oh hello, very nice to meet you".

John Rees, Stop the War Coalition National Officer: I went down to Gower Street first of all. It was just beginning to back up to the junction with Bloomsbury. It ran all the way from Bloomsbury Street to New Oxford Street, right past – I didn't see it but people told me – Euston station. That would have been a huge demonstration on its own. And then I went down to the Embankment. It was absolutely obvious it was going to be a huge demonstration – the whole of central London seemed to be absolutely rammed with protestors from very, very early on. I can't really remember what was happening. In a certain sense once you've got to this point, there isn't a lot you can do.

Ian McEwan, Author: I was in London. I'd already decided that the march would probably form a part of a kind of literal narrative thread in [his 2005 novel] *Saturday*. And I was coming round to the idea it might take place all on that very day, although I hadn't actually decided that yet. I went out into the crowds forming around Warren Street and Gower Street – just to get the atmosphere. I spent some time on the Euston Road watching the coaches come in. I was there with a notebook. I was very interested in the banners and the various things people were carrying... The tone of the march was almost joyous. It doesn't happen very often, but it was one of those occasions when my heart swelled with pride at the diversity and eccentricity of the English. 'The Swaffham Women's Choir', 'The Gardeners of Dorset', 'The Beekeepers of...' – every bit of civil society was there. It was unaccountably merry given the issue. The thing I noticed was how many people were there with families and how far people had come. I spent a long time on Euston Road clocking West Country buses coming in, the Midlands, Wales, North Wales, Liverpool and beyond.

Maya Evans, Peace activist: With the Stop the War national demos, I don't think the tone is quite right a lot of the time. There is a kind of party atmosphere, with live music and people dancing. I personally don't agree with that tone because we are protesting about a serious issue.

Henry Perowne, main protagonist in Ian McEwan's novel *Saturday*, set on 15 February 2003: All this happiness on display is suspect. Everyone is thrilled to be together out on the streets – people are hugging themselves it seems, as well as each other. If they think – and they could be right – that continued torture and summary executions, ethnic cleansing and occasional genocide are preferable to an invasion, they should be sombre in their view.[6]

Maya Evans: I think people are a little too light-hearted about it. If the tone was a lot more sombre it would create more of an atmosphere and make the protest a lot more powerful. It would transform into something else, and people would feel more impassioned about the actual issues, rather than going on a demo for fun. I think having people dancing around on the street is perhaps not the most powerful way of presenting a movement that does have power. I think it encourages people to have a relaxed approached to it and they will be less likely to be thinking about the issues they are protesting about. You are more likely to be taken in by the music. I love music, but I think it should be used in the right context and at the right time.

Ian McEwan: I thought the strangeness was its merriness. I don't remember that on CND marches. I was too young to go on the early Aldermaston marches. I've seen film of it and there are Trad Jazz bands, but the marches I went on in the late '70s and '80s, in the last stages of the Cold War when the two superpowers looked like they might use Europe as their battleground, the marches were sombre. Maybe everyone was already tired of marching. Whereas February 15 seemed more like an Aldermaston march. The citizenry all came out and said "No!" But they also asserted something freer than "No!" – a massive celebration of diversity... That surprised me given what was at stake. A general air of release. There is always a release of tramping down streets usually owned by traffic. I remember that holiday feeling walking up Whitehall. This was decidedly merry.

Chris Nineham, Stop the War Coalition Chief Steward: Jesse Jackson was there [at Embankment] and his people were incredibly difficult. He had a bad leg and he was late from his hotel. And then the cab couldn't get near enough because of the demo, so he had to hobble from wherever he was. And the police are saying "You have to move this demo now or otherwise people are going to get crushed".

Lindsey German: Then we set off and Jesse Jackson was late... And suddenly they all turn up and say "You have to stop the march! The Reverend Jackson is late!" We were going "Too bad, he's going to have to run to catch up".

Chris Nineham: Jesse Jackson's goons are surrounding me going "Jesse's not here, this demo is going nowhere until Jesse gets here." So we had to set off and eventually he managed to catch up. Plus the other thing was that we wanted to meet at Piccadilly Circus and then the timing was important. Fucking madness.

Marching: "Essentially the whole of London was moving from the east to the west"

John Rees: We've always had, and we did on February 15, a method of organising some of the speakers and the people who are well known at the front of the demonstration around the banner. And then building a stewards box – because otherwise the front of the demonstration just disappears into a crowd of people. And then there is always a wall of photographs and press, and for there to be any visibility for the front or for the demonstration to make any progress really, you have to create a kind of cordon of stewards that runs forward from the banner right the way forward for about 20 or 30 yards and then keeps moving ahead of the demonstration.

Chris Nineham: Controlling the front and keeping it relatively sane and bearable for people. Lots of people try to get to the front of the demonstration, so we had to develop this new system of stewarding where you have 100 stewards at the front trying to clear away people, as loads of people would try to come in and claim the front of the protest. You obviously want the front of the protest to represent as broad a spectrum of the anti-war opinion and their organisations as you can.

Tony Myers, Campaign for Nuclear Disarmament Campaigns Officer 1995–2003: I was at the back of the march near Blackfriars Bridge and I was watching this group come across the bridge to join the demo. A big group. Almost regimental. It looked like one of these well-organised hard-left groups. And then when they got closer we realized it was the Liberal Democrats! It was so rigid. I've never seen the Lib Dems that organized before. I don't think they wanted anything to do with anybody else particularly.

Donnachadh McCarthy, Deputy Chair of the Liberal Democrat Federal Executive in 2003: On the day I was the person organising on behalf of the party. We turned out a sea of Liberal Democrats. Over three thousand members turned up. My understanding is that it is the biggest meeting of the Liberal Democrats in the party's history – larger than any conference. They came from Scotland, they came from Guernsey, the came from Wales, they came pregnant, they came invalided, they came with sticks, they came ancient, they came young, they came with babies. They were there and they were absolutely excited that the party was doing something worthwhile, standing up for its principles and putting its flag in the ground and saying "This is where we stand."

Andrew Murray: The Liberals turned out a lot of people. They all turned themselves out separately near Waterloo station as far as I remember.

James Graham, Member of the Liberal Democrat Federal Executive 2003–5: There was this big Lib Dem clump, which in retrospect we kind of wished we had spread them out a bit more… In all the photographs of the day you'll see the different banners and so on but the Lib Dems were nowhere because we had all stuck together. Whereas if we had actually encouraged people to mingle then history would have shown lots of little "Lib Dems say no" banners dotted among all the other banners. That, from an historical record point of view, was a mistake, because we looked invisible. But nonetheless there were 2,000 people there.

Lindsey German: The Lib Dem MPs were like a phalanx, because they were terrified of being photographed next to George Galloway or one of us. Their whole body language was they didn't really want to be there.

Yasmin Khan, Stop the War activist, London School of Economics and Political Science, 2001–5: February 15, how do I describe it? It was such an incredible day. Friends came down to stay at my house from different parts of the country. It was the only demo my mum has been on here in the UK in the 30 years she has lived here. I remember gathering at LSE in the morning, I still have the poster actually ("LSE students and staff assemble at 11am!"). I gave the speech to the assembled group which must have been hundreds of people if not a thousand. As the LSE was such a hub of activism lots of people had decided to assemble there. My memories are blurred now, its been seven years but I remember the cold, it was bloody bitter.

Kim Manning-Cooper, Campaign for Nuclear Disarmament Staff member 2002–3: It was an amazing day. Incredible in so many ways. I remember it being absolutely freezing cold. The coldest day I can remember.

Met Office report, observing station, London St James Park, 15 February 2003: Maximum temperature: 4.9°C. Minimum temperature: 0.0°C. Rainfall: 0mm. Sunshine: 3.6 hours. Winds were mainly moderate from an east or north-easterly direction. Weather was dry with some sunny intervals.[7]

John Rees: The Stop the War demonstrations compared to most demonstrations move at an incredible rate. And partly it's because there is an incredible physical pressure, if you are stood at the front of it, on your back. It's almost like you are being propelled forward. There are people right behind you and they are pushing. They move incredibly quickly.

Clare Solomon, University of London Union President 2010–11: We were walking at a very slow pace because of the size of the crowd. I remember getting hip ache actually because you could only take very small steps. You couldn't walk properly.

Jean Perraton, retired Town Planner: I travelled by train to London with my husband. He had insisted that we should be formally and smartly dressed, to reinforce a view that this was not a fringe event; but included elderly middle-class citizens who don't normally go on demonstrations. It was splendid to find so many other marchers, but so frustrating to have to wait and wait for the mass to get moving, and then to move so slowly.

Tony Benn, President, Stop the War Coalition. Labour MP 1963–2001 (with a brief spell in 1983–4 not in Parliament) and former Labour Cabinet Minister: I joined the protest march at the Embankment just before twelve. I started at the front but gradually dropped back, and by the time I got to Hyde Park, I think I must have been about a mile behind. By then my feet were giving out. I had cramp in my legs... I had only had about an eggcup full of tea this morning, because I was terrified I wouldn't be able to find anywhere to go to the loo.[8]

Patrick Schicker, Chartered Civil Engineer: I joined the march with the several coach loads from Cambridge... My first memory is of the vast numbers of people from such a variety of backgrounds. How could Blair go ahead in face of such opposition from a complete cross section of British society? My second memory is of a desperate search for a toilet! The police had closed all the public toilets and no cafe would let us use their conveniences even when we were prepared to buy their coffee. My bladder was saved by a friendly Chinese supermarket who allowed us to use their facilities. With the vast numbers on the march and the lack of facilities for calls of nature I can't be the only one for which this agony is a lasting memory!

Jean Perraton: Since the progress was so slow and there were so many people, getting to somewhere to pee was a bit of a problem, even though the police were very good in helping people get in and out. My husband was a Friend of the Royal Academy, so we popped in there for the loo and then into the Friends' Room for a coffee and to warm up. I've never seen such a motley collection of people in that respectable sanctuary before or since.

Maggie Shevlane, Advanced Skills Teacher, Kent: This was the interesting thing because you tend to think stereotypically it will be full of students or left-wingers or whatever. But in fact it was an absolute cross-section, I would say, of the social stratum, the political divide – I remember seeing people in Hyde Park with banners that said "Tories Against the War"… there were elderly people, there were people with young families, men carrying their young children on their shoulders, there were pushchairs. It was an absolute cross-section of the country.[9]

Placards: "It was the message of the people"

David Gentleman, Artist: When the Iraq War was clearly boiling up… I was looking one day at a photograph of a demonstration somewhere on the streets of London, and with a newsprint photograph it was virtually impossible to read what any of the placards people were carrying said. All you got was the impression of a vast, inarticulate mass. I thought if you could simplify such placards down to their barest essentials – and at that point nobody here could really believe it was conceivable that we would get involved in such a war anyway – and so all the poster had to say was "No" because that is what everybody felt. But I still had to persuade the people at Stop the War, who I had no connection with, that this was a good idea.[10]

Lindsey German: He rang the [Stop the War Coalition] office and said could he help, and we were hopeless. We didn't know who he was and we had so many people phoning. Chances are we told him to come in and do some placards or something. So then he called Tony Benn and then Benn put him on to John [Rees].

John Rees: What he did at that point, he sent me a letter saying our placards are no good you can't read them.

David Gentleman: I knew Stop the War were producing placards on an industrial scale so I thought they ought to have one that people could read.

Ghada Ruzuki: We had an office the size of a large living room. Then we had to use the corridors. In any one day leading up to February 15 we would have an influx of volunteers to make placards. In the week leading up to February 15 we must have had about 50 people doing placards non-stop. They came from nowhere. They would phone up and say "We want to do something" and we would say "Fine – come in." We could have taken more but we just didn't have the space.

David Gentleman: So I got out this press photograph of the illegible march and stuck a lot of my very simple "No's" – some big ones, some small ones – so it really looked like all these people were carrying "No's" instead. And that did the trick: Stop the War said go ahead with it.

Andrew Burgin: The placards we produced were very important. David Gentleman's "No" was very important. I think that was used in many cartoons in the *Guardian* and elsewhere.

David Gentleman: Ideally I think the best placards are the ones people make themselves in their own kitchens because they are really passionate hand-done things.

Bob Crow: What I liked about it best was yes you got the SWP placards and the trade union placards, but there were people just making placards and getting their point of view over. It was the message of the people.

Clare Solomon: I used to have my own business – a number of restaurants in the Russell Square area, one in Russell Square and one in Kings Cross… I took one of my large A3 menus and on the blank side wrote the Gandhi quote "An eye for an eye makes the whole world blind", and used it as a placard. Definitely quite a pacifist statement.

Yasmin Khan: Huddled up close to my friends in the cold, drinking tea and laughing at all the home made signs and placards. It was so English, full of polite clapping, drizzle and sexual innuendos: "Bombing for peace is like screwing for chastity" was a placard carried by a particularly wrinkly old peace activist man. It made us chuckle.

Andrew Burgin: Banksy did actual placards on the day, which he handed out to school kids. They would go for thousands now!... On the day, the *Daily Mirror* produced placards. Thousands of placards.

John Rees: One of the problems we had on the day is that we convinced the *Daily Mirror* it would be a really good idea if they produced placards. Of course they didn't have a clue how to produce a placard.

Lindsey German: They were really boring.

Chris Wade, Press Officer for *Trinity Mirror* in 2003: We had more than 30,000 placards made, carrying the logos of both the *Mirror* and the Stop the War Coalition. A handful of people from the *Trinity Mirror* press office and the paper (plus a few temps and some hardy volunteer spouses and friends) were on the streets of London from about 4am. The placards were on pallets in the back of an articulated lorry and a couple of vans, and we had to manhandle them on the pavements, ready for members of the Coalition and *Mirror* staffers to hand out to marchers later that morning... The placards showed a photograph of a soldier, with the words "No War" across it, which became one of the iconic images of the day. It gave the picture editors of the *Mirror*'s rivals a headache as they had to decide whether or not to 'Photoshop' out the hundreds of *Mirror* logos. At least one paper chose to airbrush history. Some protestors, having picked up a placard, were horrified to discover they'd become a walking advert for a grubby tabloid, and tore the *Mirror* logo off the top. The vast majority, though, were happy to carry them, realising that the paper's position on the war was genuine. Happy, if not entirely comfortable: we hadn't had much experience of commissioning placards, and it turned out wooden poles had been used that were not only twice as big, and therefore heavy, as they needed to be, but also – according to the senior police officers overseeing the march – large enough to be used as offensive weapons, and therefore illegal. Not much to be done about it by then, however.

John Rees: Of course they had spent all this money and had them professionally designed, and we did it with volunteers. And they were all stacked at the side of the road. But when the David Gentleman placards turned up nobody wanted to carry these really dull ones from the *Mirror*. So we had to insist that some people carried the dull ones so the *Mirror* wouldn't be totally fucked off with it.

David Gentleman: That was the beginning of a lot longer connection than I ever expected it to be. I've done a great number of posters and placards for them in the five years or so since then.[11]

"Please note the marked absence of Iraqi exiles": Testimony from Iraqis who marched

Johann Hari, *Independent*, 15 February 2003: If you go on the march, please note the marked absence of Iraqi exiles.[12]

Henry Perowne, main protagonist in Ian McEwan's novel *Saturday*, set on 15 February 2003: Opinions are a role of the dice; by definition none of the people now milling around Warren Street tube station happens to have been tortured by the regime or even knows much about the place at all. It's likely most of them barely registered the massacres in Kurdish Iraq, or in the Shi'ite south, and now they find they care with a passion for Iraqi lives.[13]

5 September 2002 letter to the *Guardian*, signed by 100 Iraqi exiles: We are told a war on Iraq is needed to preempt a threat to the region and to free the Iraqi people from Saddam Hussein's tyranny. We, as Iraqis already free from that tyranny, living outside Iraq and in the western democracies, say that both these claims are false. As professionals, writers, teachers and other responsible and concerned citizens, many of whom have personally experienced the persecution of the dictatorship in Iraq, we say "No to war; not in our name, not in the name of the suffering Iraqi people".[14]

Kamil Mahdi, Iraqi academic living in the UK: Many Iraqis who had not previously been politically active campaigned, spoke at public rallies against the war and travelled to London on February 15. The vast majority of those people held deep antipathies towards the regime of Saddam Hussein and refused to ally themselves with Ba'thists whom they considered responsible for bringing Iraq to such an impasse. Iraqis were concerned about their families, their communities and their country and were not defending an abhorrent dictatorship.

Zainab Khan, Iraqi woman living in the UK: I am an Iraqi woman who has been living in the UK since 1982. I am a software engineer. I grew up under the Ba'ath government and have no recollection of anything else before it... Some members of my family and friends were deported, tortured and some were executed by the Saddam regime for many reasons ranging from active political involvement to carelessly saying the wrong thing in front of the wrong people. Some died serving in the many pointless wars since 1980. Some died because of a lack of simple medication during the sanctions years... My entire family here in the UK went out on the 15 February march. It was an amazing experience to see so many British people rejecting this war, and in solidarity with the Iraqi people.

Munir Al-Chalabi, Iraqi political and oil analyst living in the UK: It has been a long time since that historic anti-war march, but I still remember it as if it happened yesterday – not for the reason that it was what I sought after, but because of my astonishment at the enormous size of the demonstration and the nature of the British people who marched that day. I was completely amazed to see all these very ordinary British men, women and even children, of all ages, in their hundreds of thousands and very likely over a million, marching in such large numbers and of such mixtures of political backgrounds, if any. "For what?" I remember asking myself. To prevent a war which is going to happen thousands of miles away and which could end in the destruction of a very totalitarian regime which they, I and the vast majority of ordinary Iraqi people detested. As for myself, I always looked at the Iraqi Ba'ath regime as a fascist party with a fascist ideology. I detested that regime, especially because I and my family had suffered a lot from that party when they arrested my oldest brother and tortured him to death when they first came to power back in 1963. I left Iraq when I was still a young man in 1970, not because I wanted to go and live a better life in a foreign country, but because I was hunted by that regime as I was a political activist with a left political background who fought for a democratic Iraqi society and not a totalitarian one.

Sami Ramadani, Iraqi political exile and a Senior Lecturer in Sociology at London Metropolitan University: I was on that great march with family and many Iraqi friends. We made our own placard at home which we felt best expressed our feelings and ideas. On one side we wrote "Iraqis say no to war" and on the other "No to Saddam's dictatorship". My abiding memory of the day is that of experiencing a roller-coaster of emotions, as we marched and chanted anti-war slogans. They were feelings of extreme elation at seeing so many people saying "not in our name", but also of sadness and anger that Bush, Blair and the rest of the warmongers were bent on war and would not listen, and that the Iraqi people will be facing calamity, after decades of suffering under the weight of wars, dictatorship and murderous sanctions. Every minute of that day I went through joy, anger and deep pain.

Kamil Mahdi: The mood of the majority of Iraqis I knew in Britain varied between anger, resignation and a mixture of both. There was a very small minority who were enthusiastic supporters of the war. In one case that was well-known in the local Iraq community in Birmingham, a man went as far as recruiting members of his family inside Iraq to offer reconnaissance to the US military. There was a contrast between those in the organised exiled political groups and the Iraqi community at large. Most of the exiled parties had become dependent upon their host countries and were influenced by their hosts' policies, but the Iraqi community at large was deeply concerned about the human consequences of the planned war. Few in the community believed that the US and Britain would risk the safety of their soldiers in order to avoid civilian casualties, and many feared a repeat of the 1991 targeting of the civilian infrastructure and the consequent humanitarian catastrophe. The big division within the Iraqi community was not between the minority who were pro-war and the majority, but between those who had become resigned to the US and British war machines grinding their country once more, and those who were eager to make common cause with the peace movement in order to try to stop the onward march of war.

Haifa Zangana, Iraqi novelist living in the UK: We walked peacefully. It was a lovely atmosphere. We were all very depressed, especially Iraqis. When I rang people or Mundher [al-Adhami, her husband] spoke to people saying we were meeting [under Marble Arch] the immediate answer was "Why? What's the point?" War was imminent and Iraqis had no hope. They felt it had been planned for a long time and it was going to take place. So we had to argue, even while we were walking. Some came because they felt they had to do something regardless of how insignificant it was. They were walking, dragging themselves, as if feeling "I did it, but I don't believe in it, and I don't think it will change anything".

Nadje Al-Ali, Academic and activist. Founding member of Act Together: Women's action for Iraq: There was a whole range of opinion. Most of the people I was hanging out with and that I knew were against the war. I was aware of the fact there were people for the war. There were some people who were anti-sanctions, who were not anti-war – it was not automatic... My family in Iraq were anti-invasion – they didn't want another war. But once it happened they were glad. It is quite complex how things shifted. I wrote a modern history of Iraqi women, and I interviewed a number of Iraqi women in London about their sentiments about the invasion. There was a whole range of positions. There were those who categorically said "No, that's not going to do it, we don't want military invasion, it will just make things worse". There were some who were saying "This is the only way to get rid of the regime – we've tried everything and it hasn't worked". These people genuinely believed it would be a change for the better. There were also people who were hoping to get something out of the invasion – people linked to political parties who were gambling for a position after the invasion... Most people I knew and spoke to in my research had quite complicated views about it. It wasn't black and white. I was demonstrating and I was against the invasion, but I was also asking myself "What can be done to get rid of the regime?" It was quite painful to talk to women after the invasion who had felt it could be the way out but now felt really disillusioned. I find it really problematic when people would say "Iraqis thought" or "Iraqis wanted". Just like British people, Iraqis are complicated and complex beings. And you can't say "The Shia wanted this" and "The Sunnis wanted this" – it was much more complex than that. Even within one person there were different things going on. Lots of people were quite conflicted about it.

Haifa Zangana: On that particular day I remember we were walking in a group of Iraqis – over 20 people – and we kept meeting people as we walked. They came from all over Britain, not just from London.

Mundher al-Adhami, Iraqi living in the UK: It took us a very long time just to start moving. Because we didn't have a banner there was no way of telling where we were.

Haifa Zangana: I know a couple of Iraqis who have never joined in any demonstration because they feel they empty the anger out of people. They were apprehensive because it has been arranged with the police and the Government and you walk the streets and feel good about yourself. They felt this was nothing to do with Iraqi people. There was a feeling among the Iraqis that this was our last straw, our last hope.

Mundher al-Adhami: I think there was a slight uplift in some people's minds because they saw the antagonism to war in British society was so widespread.

Haifa Zangana: It was one of the few times I have felt at home in Britain. I thought "This is the kind of people I belong to". People trying to do something against "The regime" – the establishment. I call it "The regime" because we always called it "Saddam's regime". So it's "Tony Blair's regime".

Mundher al-Adhami: There were many old people and very young people – a lot of different people. Masses of people. So there was a sense this was "real Britain". The fact we didn't have a banner was an indication of how fragmented Iraqis were at the time.

Kamal Majid, Emeritus Iraqi Professor of Civil Engineering: I was born in 1929 in the northern city of Kirkuk, in the oil fields. When I was a schoolboy the police were after me because I was associated with the Iraqi Communist Party, so I went underground for a year while there was martial law. I was captured and arrested and spent nine months in prison awaiting trial. Then martial law was removed and I was set free and finished my studies. I got very high marks in the equivalent of 'A' Levels and was sent on a scholarship to Britain. I studied Civil Engineering at

Manchester University and got married to my wife Cathie, who was Scottish, although she is dead now. I went back to Iraq for four years, working as a Civil Engineer. And then in 1958 there was a revolution that got rid of the royal family. In 1960 I came on another scholarship back to Manchester where I did my PhD... Since I left Iraq in 1960 I have never been back because in 1963 the Ba'athists staged a coup d'etat and got rid of Qasim. I was well known politically and my family advised me not to go back. So I've never been back... I was at a disadvantage at that march and the ones before it. In 2001, just before 9/11, I became aware of the fact that my wife, Cathie, was suffering from Alzheimer's. So between 2001 and 2008 I was busy looking after her in this house and in hospital. On the big march she was in a very bad way. I took her to the march and Haifa's [Zangana] family and others looked after her – she could hardly walk. It started in the Embankment, and I took her there, and then knowing that she couldn't walk all the way to the Hyde Park, I took her by the Underground to Green Park and continued walking to Hyde Park. Also, my daughter was on the march and I left my wife with her because an Arabic news network wanted to interview a group of Iraqis. So in Hyde Park I left my wife with my daughter to organise this meeting but it never took place – it was so crowded! It was a wonderful thing.

Nadje Al-Ali: On the day I felt a sense of people coming together in their diversity. There was something positive and celebratory about it. It did feel good. I kind of let myself be swept away by the fact people came from all over, from very different backgrounds and very different politics and were struggling together. I managed to get rid of my political reservations and celebrated the event and the day with my partner and my daughter. I kept running into people I knew. I enjoyed the creativity of what people were doing with props and costumes and banners and slogans. There was something fun about it.

Iraqi living in the UK: I was planning to go on the march, but that day I received a telephone call that my mother had suddenly died. I was unable even to attend her burial... Not all Iraqis supported the war, indeed the majority were against the war primarily because of the effects of wars on humans, animals, environment etc. Regime change in Iraq should have been done by pushing hard to open up the system, not by illegal force that have cost Iraqis, the British and Americans a lot. I lived under the regime, and suffered from it, but I was against the war; force is not the solution, it leads to violence and destruction and this is what has taken place. The suffering of Iraqis is now even more greater than before, especially for women and children.

The rally in Hyde Park

Andrew Murray: Lindsey [German] and I left the front of march and walked ahead. There were already tens of thousands of people ahead of the march, already making their own way to Hyde Park. Getting to Hyde Park, there were already thousands of people sitting on the grass waiting for the rally to begin.

Michael Wiseman, Musician: I was in front of the march singing John Lennon's *Give Peace a Chance* and had stopped at the gates of Hyde Park where I continued singing and playing as the marchers entered the park. In fact well over 5,000 people at the front of the march had gone past when I stopped and asked the question "Are there any more coming?" Somehow or other the marchers following us must have been held up. When they finally arrived I played and sang *Give Peace a Chance* for about another two hours at the gate with everyone joining in as they went past. Then, because of the numbers of peace marchers going past and the increasing enthusiasm of the chanting, I did finally put my accordion down on the ground and rubbed my cold hands together.

Andrew Murray: I was focused on organising the rally, introducing the speakers, making quite a lot of announcements – lost children and so on. It was quite a lot of work. I was doing it with Anas Altikriti from the Muslim Association of Britain, and Carol Naughton, who was then Chair of CND. I think it's not bombastic to say I was the lead chair, because Stop the War was the lead organisation really. That went on for several hours.

Bruce Kent, Campaign for Nuclear Disarmament Vice-President in 2003. CND Chair 1987–1990: My memory of it is seeing Lindsey German and people and looking at the huge stage and thinking "God you've learnt how to do all this stuff quickly". It was all there. It is an enormous job to run a big demo. I thought "Good for you".

Anas Altikriti: The thing I will never forget was standing on the stage and seeing the demonstration flood into Hyde Park. I can't envisage anything beating that – it was endless.

They came through and they spilled. Beyond the front it wasn't relenting. There was a continuous flood. There was no let-up in the intensity. People got to the stage where the barriers were and they were still coming in. People were beginning to push, and they were shouting "Tell people not to push, tell people not to push!" What came to my mind was the Hillsborough disaster,[i] so I got on the mike and said "Please don't push we have a big enough park". Just about, it turned out.

Carol Naughton: One of the most emotional things for me was coming off the stage for a break, because it is very intense. I took a quiet moment to get my head together. This man kept beckoning to me from the fence, because the backstage area was fenced in. I went over, and he said "I'm Iraqi, and I am here today, and I've been on the phone to my family and friends back in Iraq, and I just want you to know they know you are doing this and they say thank you." So I went back on stage feeling really emotional about this, and before I introduced the next person to speak I tried to tell the crowd about the man and what he said, and it was such an emotional moment.

Lindsey German: Of course there are all these arguments going on right through the rally in Hyde Park on 15 February about who is speaking, because we took a very, very strict line... Particularly with this guy Tim Robbins – the American actor. We just said he wasn't speaking. We had Jesse Jackson lobbying for him.

---

i During the FA Cup semi-final between Liverpool and Nottingham Forest at Hillsborough stadium in Sheffield on 15 April 1989, 96 people died in a human crush.

Carmel Brown, Press Officer, Stop the War Coalition: Lindsey [German] was absolutely adamant he couldn't speak. John [Rees] was absolutely adamant that I shouldn't carry on fighting for this and thought I just wanted my own way. And I said "No! I want Tim Robbins on that stage because it is a good photograph". There is a tension between some lefty principles and being stupid, I think... I remember Ken Loach backstage saying "Are they going to let Tim Robbins speak?"

John Rees: It was Carmel who put a stop to it.

Carmel Brown: John's memory is really bad. I was having quiet fits, saying to John "This is really fucking stupid they won't let Tim Robbins speak". I asked George Galloway if he would help me get Tim Robbins to speak and he said "Who do I have to fall out with?" which is a great political lesson about how George works. I said "Lindsey [German]" and he said "I can't afford to fall out with Lindsey".

Ghada Razuki, Office Manager, Stop the War Coalition: Me and Carmel argued for Tim Robbins, one of my all-time heroes in terms of the films that he does. And Lindsey didn't want him to speak. And we were going "He is a big film star!"... It was embarrassing.

Carmel Brown: Jesse Jackson was in the Green Room – a rather grand name for a caravan we put people in before they spoke – really stropping about the fact there was no lectern on the stage. He was just a diva. How could he speak without a lectern?

Ghada Razuki: I remember getting to Hyde Park and behind the stage and saying "That's it, I don't want any more responsibility. I just want to digest a bit of this." And the only thing I did after this was guard the door to the little caravan where the big cheeses were. Jesse Jackson was sitting in there with his advisers, and one of them farted. In the caravan! And I said "That is disgusting!", and I walked off. I don't care if he is Jesse Jackson.

Carmel Brown: I remember holding his [Jesse Jackson's] hand and asking him if he could take Tim Robbins on stage when he speaks. And that's what they did – Jesse Jackson spoke and Tim Robbins did a power to the people salute and never spoke a word.

Chris Nineham: Tim Robbins was on stage hovering around the mike chatting to Jesse Jackson. And I'm saying to Andrew Murray "Andrew, Tim Robbins is just there". And he didn't respond. Then someone else said "Look Andrew, Tim Robbins is there". And Andrew said "I don't care. Who is Tim Robbins?"

Andrew Murray: When he went on stage Jesse Jackson was accompanied by Tim Robbins, who is a Hollywood actor, which I didn't know at the time. Jesse Jackson insisted that Tim Robbins speak and I said he couldn't because he was not on the list and it hadn't been agreed. Everyone since then has regarded this as an act of madness on my part, as apparently he is tremendously popular, but I'm very backward on Hollywood culture. In the end he appeared on stage, and Jesse Jackson drew attention to his presence, but he didn't get to speak.

The speeches – excerpts

Adrian Mitchell, Poet: Welcome to history. If Tony Blair tells Britain to go to war, don't go. Don't go to work. Don't go to school. Don't go to the movies. Don't go to college.

Caroline Lucas, Green Party of England and Wales MEP 1999–2010. Green Party of England Wales MP 2010–present: I've just come back from Iraq. Those people are already in the midst of a humanitarian crisis. I spoke to doctors who are crying out for medicines for their hospitals because they can't get those medicines because of the sanctions. People are dying as a result. Half the population of Iraq depends on food rations for survival. One in ten children die before their tenth birthday. Malnutrition kills a million children. It is a devastating situation and war will make it unimaginably worse. In the south of the country they are still living with Depleted Uranium, with the radioactive weapons we dropped on them in the last war... So when our government tells us this war is for the people of Iraq, we say this is not for the people of Iraq, this war is for imperialism and this war is for oil.

Michael Foot, Leader of the Labour Party 1980–3: Friends and Comrades, twenty years ago some of you may remember the Campaign for Nuclear Disarmament organised a magnificent demonstration here in Hyde Park. At that time we had the Programme saying "protest and survive". Well we did survive and we did protest. Now we've got to do it again. But we've got to do it again in the highest cause – of abolishing nuclear weapons all over the world!

Bruce Kent: In the first Gulf War we had soldiers – Vic Williams – who refused to serve in an oil war. And I congratulated him at the time. Our government has no right to turn the armed forces into potential war criminals. And a war of this sort will be a criminal war. They haven't even excluded the use of nuclear weapons. I say to the members of our armed forces "It is time for you to say no." You are the important ones. And my last comment is this. I speak from this platform as a Christian. I do not recognise the Christianity of George Bush. Christianity is about service, about the non-violent pursuit of justice, about equality and sharing. It is not about power, privilege, wealth and revenge.

Salma Yaqoob: If today only the Socialists had turned up they would have said "It's just the loony left." If today only CND had turned up, they would have said "It's just the bleeding heart liberals." If today only the Muslims had turned up, they would have said "It's just the fundamentalists." Well, Tony Blair, you cannot dismiss us all… United we stand, divided we fall.

Tariq Ali, Author and political campaigner: Friends we are here today to show Tony Blair and to say to him openly that if one country needs a regime change then at the moment it is Britain!... It is Tony Blair and his frightened cabinet who speak for the White House. They have forfeited all their rights to represent Britain at all international conferences. And I say to you, people have been asking me all along the march today "Do you think this will make a difference?" And I say this will make a difference in the following way: that when members of Parliament return home to their constituencies and see on the television news – there are very few of them here so they will have to see it on television – that *Sky News* is reporting a million and a half, that *ITV* is reporting a million, they will begin to worry about what will happen to them at the next election. And I say to you friends, don't let this march stop here. We have got to carry on and we have got to punish the warmongers at the election if necessary.

Tony Benn: Friends we are here today – comrades I only have a few moments – we are here today to found a new political movement worldwide. The biggest demonstration ever in Britain, the first global demonstration and its first cause is to prevent a war against Iraq. But it must also be about other matters as well. It must be about the establishment of a Palestinian state. It must be, it must be about democracy not only in the Middle East – because there is no democracy in Saudi Arabia or in Iraq – but dare I say it, some democracy in Britain as well, that allows the British parliament to decide. While we are here let us remember that 35 million people die every year in the world of hunger. That 500, that 500 billionaires in the world have the same income as half the population of the world put together. That the world in which we live is dominated by the military, by the media and by the multinationals. And what we are about is getting democracy all over the world so we can build a world which is safe for our children and our grandchildren. If there are to be inspectors in Iraq I would like to see inspectors in Israel, inspectors in Britain, inspectors in America. I want to see the United Nations, I want to see the United Nations take sanctions against the arms manufacturers who supply weapons all over the world.

I want to see the money, we want to see the money wasted on Weapons of Mass Destruction diverted to give the world what it needs, which is food and clothing and housing and schools and hospitals, and to protect the old and the sick and the disabled. My friends, that is what we are here about today. We have started something really big. And our first task is peace in Iraq but we must not stop until we have achieved the objectives that bring us all to Hyde Park this afternoon. Thank you for listening.

Charles Kennedy, Liberal Democrat MP 1983–present. Leader of the Liberal Democrats 1999–2006: For months now I've been asking questions in the House of Commons of the Prime Minister and I've not been getting the answers. What's come back has been confusing, alarming, and you are all here because like me you think it lacks persuasion. So it's no wonder that so much of British and European opinion is not convinced. But neither is a lot of American opinion convinced either. And that is all too often overlooked in the reporting that we see. Now my party has consistently argued, from the outset, for four principles. First, the mandate of the United Nations must be the one that takes the decision and gives the legitimacy. And secondly, that those decisions have got to be based on adequate information. That means full compliance with the weapons inspectors. Given the evidence that we had yesterday in New York from Dr Blix there can be, as we stand, no just, or moral case for war against Iraq. That was the message from New York. Third, if we reach the stage at some point in the future where British troops are going to be asked to enter into some form of military conflict then that has got to be achieved in a democratic way, which means that the House of Commons should be given the right which so far it has been denied... I conclude by returning to the United Nations. If the Great Powers of the world ignore it then great damage will be done to the world order and the best hope for international justice for everybody in the world. And without a second United Nations resolution based on authoritative facts from the weapons inspectors I can assure you there is no way, in all conscience, that the Liberal Democrats either could or should support a war.

George Galloway, Labour MP 1987–2005. Respect MP 2005–10 and 2012–present. Vice President of Stop the War Coalition 2001–present: And I say to Mr Blair – and I hope he is listening to this message being said by the British people today – we do not intend to continue with a Prime Minister who acts as if he is the Governor of the 51st state of the United States of America. We don't want Bush's wars! We don't want Star Wars! And we don't want to be in an alliance of an axis of evil with General Ariel Sharon either! I say to Mr Blair, if he, despite this big demonstration today, despite the overwhelming feeling around the world against war, if he takes Great Britain over this cliff with George W Bush then he will break the Labour Party he is supposed to lead. If Mr Blair breaks the Labour Party, there will be some of us ready to rebuild it out of the wreckage as a real Labour Party standing for real Labour values.

Harold Pinter, Playwright: The United States is a monster out of control. If we don't resist it with absolute determination, American power will destroy the world. The country is run by a bunch of criminal lunatics, with Tony

Blair as a hired Christian thug. The planned attack on Iraq is a pre-meditated act of mass murder.

Ken Livingstone, Mayor of London 2000–8: I want to start by saying this. I can not tell you the pride I feel that as Mayor of London I can officially welcome you here to this city in the biggest political demonstration in 2,000 years of British history! I walked along Piccadilly – it was wall to wall with people from end to end. I spoke –

Comedy Terrorist[ii] (taking the microphone from Livingstone before being hauled off the stage): Stop congestion charging! This is being hijacked by the Comedy Terrorist!

Ken Livingstone (taking back the microphone): I have to say this. Isn't it nice being able to walk through this city without being choked by fumes?

Jesse Jackson, US Civil Rights leader and former candidate for the Democratic presidential nomination: Never forget what Dr King told us: "The arc of the [moral] universe is long, but it bends towards justice". Don't you give up. And don't you surrender. Your spirit and faith will be tested. The war machine will give us fierce opposition, but faith can move mountains. That's faith. We cry sometimes and hurt. That's faith. Faith helped Moses march out of Egypt and cross the Red Sea. Keep marching. Faith helped Joshua bring the walls tumbling down. Keep marching. Faith

ii The Comedy Terrorist's – aka Aaron Barschak – most famous media stunt was gate-crashing Prince William's 21st birthday party at Windsor Castle in June 2003.

helped Jesus turn a crucifixion into a resurrection. You keep marching. Faith helped Mandela live long enough to free his jailer. You keep marching. It's not easy, but nothing is too hard for God... Stop the war! Save the children! Stop the war! Save the children! Stop the violence! Save the children! Keep hope! One world, one love! One world, one love! Many faces, many places! One people, this world is our world! Keep hope, alive! Keep hope, alive! Keep hope, alive! I love you.

Chris Nineham: Jesse Jackson was bizarre. And did the kind of "It's save the children time! It's peace time!" This kind of fake civil rights rhetoric. It wasn't a great speech.

Damon Albarn, Musician: I felt some of the speeches in Hyde Park were a little triumphant and not meditative enough. I think that is where we failed. It was almost like we had won the battle, but actually we hadn't, we had barely begun.

Asad Rehman: I remember being on the stage, but I can't remember any of the speeches! There are certain speakers who speak well and the crowd go mad – [George] Galloway, for example. But the size of the crowd was more important – the whole of London was still blocked. Of course there were some powerful speeches, but to me the speeches weren't the most important part. In other demonstrations speeches were very important, but on February 15 the most important thing was the sense you were there with so many other people. The speeches were like background music.

"Ms Dynamite, who's that?"

Carol Naughton: There were compromises made. Everybody made compromises. That was great. The Muslim Association of Britain was worried about having music. I felt it would be useful to have music, because it raises spirits, but the MAB were concerned about that.

Ghayasuddin Siddiqui, Leader of the Muslim Parliament since 1996, former Executive member of Stop the War Coalition: This is true. And this was one reason why some people weren't happy with MAB participating because it had a fundamentalist background. I was in favour of musical bands being given access to the platform.

Anas Altikriti: We had to be extremely wary as we had to carry the Muslim community. There was the issue of music. I don't have any issues with music, and most Muslims don't have an issue with music. But there are sizable sections of the Muslims community that do. I don't think it was the music, but the performance with people dancing in a particular way. That was what the fear was.

Mike Marqusee, Press Officer, Stop the War Coalition: It was interesting. I disagreed profoundly about what the MAB were saying and I also disagreed with what I thought was the too great a readiness of some of the leadership to just agree with that. The MAB claimed that many Muslims would not be comfortable with music. I don't think that is true. I've spent a lot of time in Pakistan, which is one of the world's most musical countries – popular music, classical music, all kinds. It's everywhere there, including in Muslim holy places. Sufi shrines are places of music. So I felt they were representing a particular strand within Islam which actually didn't represent most Muslims in this country. They are perfectly entitled to their point, but I didn't think we were required to fall in line behind it.

Andrew Burgin: We had Ms Dynamite who was a very popular pop act at the time.[iii] I can't remember how we got Ms Dynamite. It must have been through a friend of a friend. Or people would contact us and say "Had you thought of this?"

Carmel Brown: Getting Ms Dynamite was really important to us press-wise. Her Dad was a doorman at the Hackney Empire [in East London] that knew somebody who knew Chris [Nineham] or Lindsey [German]. Of course at this time she was absolute dynamite.

Lindsey German: We had so many of these arguments and discussions about these sort of things. So in the end we said "We've got Ms Dynamite, this is absolutely crazy". And eventually they agreed and we agreed it would just be acoustic music.

Anis Altikriti: We discussed this at length. Therefore, the decision was made – in tandem with Stop the War and CND – that after the end of the speeches and just before the music starts we would close. After that people are free to stay if they like... Those seemingly little, silly things, can make or break a day. Particularly at a time when there was

iii Ms Dynamite, a British R&B/hip-hop singer, had won the Mercury Music Prize in September 2002 for her debut album *A Little Deeper*.

pressure from without as well as within. Remember all the time there was not a negligible element within the Muslim community saying this was at best a waste of time and at worst contrary to Islam. So we were working against this at the same time as working with our non-Muslim friends. It was a really tough call.

Andrew Murray: Ms Dynamite was our closing entertainment on the day. We were all waiting for her to arrive. She got into the park through the wrong gate or something. To fill in the space before she finally arrived I had to make a rather long speech at the end. I got more and more left-wing as it went on.

Andrew Burgin: There was the fantastic situation where Chris [Nineham] and I were traversing the park on our phones trying to make contact with Ms Dynamite and her management who were there. And the time was shorter and shorter. We were making it up as we went along. She did finally get there, but we had to find her and drag her through the crowds. It was touch and go, but she did get there.

Chris Nineham, Chief Steward, Stop the War Coalition: Ms Dynamite was fucking awesome on the day. She had them in her hand. She was incredible. She was very hot at the time. She was fantastic. I think she caught the mood.

Ms Dynamite, Musician, speech before performing on 15 February 2003: How many more families torn apart? How many more will have to grieve? How many more children's hearts will bleed at the hands of your greed? How many more will you kill? How long will you steal what does not belong to you? How long will you lie and deceive this country and speak so many words but very few truths? Don't underestimate or insult our intelligence. Let the truth be told.You did the same to the Irish for their land, you did the same to my people for their gold. I believe war is not the answer – war is just death's feast. He who preaches war is the devil's chaplin – he is tarnished by the beast. An eye for an eye makes the world blind. War accomplishes bloodshed, never victory… Mr Prime Minister, I'd like to ask you, if you ever listen to your people do you hear our peaceful fight? Will you consider the views of the people before me before you sleep tonight?... Mr Prime Minister, you are just a prime minister – you are not god.

Male crowd member 1: Ms Dynamite, who's that?

Male crowd member 2: I dunno – a sort of rappy, sort of souly, R 'n' B-type, easy listening, woman, girl-type person.

Male crowd member 1: Shall we go to the pub then?

Male crowd member 2: Yeah.[15]

"It was like the demonstration was occupying central London": After the rally

***Observer*, 16 February 2003:** Despite the numbers, by five o'clock police were reporting only three arrests.[16]

Lindsey German: After it got dark people started lighting fires in Hyde Park, so you had all these people sitting round burning placards, which sent the park authorities completely bonkers.

Bruce Kent: My big memory was actually speaking while the march was still going on, but then I had another appointment. I had to get to Kings Cross, I think. And the only way to get there was to walk! So I went down to Hyde Park Corner, and the marchers were coming along Piccadilly, and I was trying to cut along a street to the north of Piccadilly, hoping I'd get by the march and get to Kings Cross, but I never could. Somehow I got to Piccadilly Circus and continued up Shaftsbury Avenue, but they were still coming down from Malet Street, and I couldn't believe what I was seeing – these people would never get to the park, and yet they were still marching along – five or six o'clock probably.

Liz Boothman, Retired Physics Teacher: By the time we got to Hyde Park (about 5ish I think) all the speeches were over and it was just a search for the right bus amongst hundreds... It was a very moving experience – there was a real sense of creating history and being part of something bigger than anything before.

Cheshire Fireman, 15 February 2003: They will take notice of a protest like this. Our MPs, and Blair himself, were voted in by ordinary people like those here today. Blair is clever enough not to ignore this.[17]

Roger Westmoreland, Landscape Contractor and Political Activist: We got as far as the rally in Hyde Park but never joined in as we needed still more beer and it was getting late. We met my youngest brother and his family by arrangement nearby. They had travelled by coach from Doncaster and were due back at the coach soon. Many others from the demo were sat outside the pub. I got the impression from the general conversation that people actually thought our actions could stop the war. In fact I believe that the only reason for the massive turnout was that the overwhelming opinion was that we could make a difference this time and actually persuade the Government to reconsider... Despite our general pessimism the demo gave us a buzz and we travelled back the following day in high spirits and renewed enthusiasm for the struggle.

Andrew Murray: I stayed around Hyde Park for about an hour after the rally. People were still coming into Hyde Park and hadn't heard any of the speeches. One or two people did impromptu speeches from the stage. After that I went to the Al-Dah restaurant, a Middle Eastern restaurant on Edgware Road which George Galloway is quite fond of. He had a table there of various people – Mick Rix, who was then my boss at ASLEF, I think Bianca Jagger. Lindsey [German] and I went there and I remember the restaurant applauding when we arrived. The stewards were meeting at a pub in Holborn – a thank you event because stewarding is very intense. So I left the Al-Dah after a bit to walk over to this pub. Edgware Road to Holborn is a fair walk. So this must have been two, two and a half hours since the rally and Edgware Road was still jammed with coaches going home, there were placards stuck in the railings all the way. It was like the demonstration was occupying central London. And that was the moment when I thought "God, did we do this? This is really something".

Alastair Campbell, 15 February 2003 diary entry: I got home [from Scotland], then later down to the canal and did an 18-mile run at just over 7mph. On the route back, I bumped into no end of people coming back from the march, placards under arms, faces full of self-righteousness, occasional loathing when they spotted me.[18]

"Opposing the overthrow of a fascist regime": Liberal critics of the march

David Aaronovitch, Journalist, 18 February 2003: Something is definitely happening. This past 12 months have seen three of the great public demonstrations in British history: last Sunday's [sic] rally, the Countryside march and the Queen Mother's walk-past. The governing cynicism of the 90s, as exemplified by writers such as PJ O'Rourke, has given way to the desire to give personal witness to historical events. It is now actually fashionable to pick up a placard with a slogan on it and walk for a few miles in the company of thousands of others. People want to say they "were there"... So in this moment of extraordinary success, I wanted to ask those who went on the demonstration some questions... Did some of the slogans bother you? Do you really believe that this parroted "war about oil" stuff is true? If so, what were the interventions in oil-less Kosovo, Bosnia and Afghanistan about?... Do you agree with Harold Pinter that the US is "a country run by a bunch of criminals... with Tony Blair as a hired Christian thug"? Is there any word in that sentence, apart from Tony, Blair and Christian, that isn't quite mad?[19]

Johann Hari, Journalist, 15 February 2003: If you are one of the many good and decent people thinking of going on the anti-war march today, I beg you to reconsider. Not for the sake of the British Government; not because of the dangers of weapons of mass destruction; nor for any of the other ridiculous reasons that have been given in the past few months. No. The only moral factor in this war should be the Iraqi people, and their needs – and the Iraqi peoples' greatest need is for our help to get rid of one of the worst dictators on earth.[20]

Christopher Hitchens, Journalist, 18 February 2003: I had hoped that it would pour with rain during last Saturday's march... During the many years I spent on the Left, the cause of self-determination for Kurdistan was high on the list of principles and priorities – there are many more Kurds than there are Palestinians and they have staunch fighters for democracy in the region. It would be a wonderful thing if hundreds of thousands of people had flooded into London's Hyde Park and stood in solidarity with this, one of the most important struggles for liberty in the world today. Instead, the assortment of forces who assembled demanded, in effect, that Saddam be allowed to keep the other five-sixths of Iraq as his own personal torture chamber. There are not enough words in any idiom to describe the shame and the disgrace of this... Just in the past few weeks, every stop-gap straw-man argument of the peaceniks has been shot down in flames. Yes, dear, I am afraid that there are bin Laden agents taking shelter in Baghdad. Yes, Mr bin Laden seems to think that Saddam's cause is, with reservations, one that a Muslim fascist ought to support. Yes there are weapons and systems, found even by the bumbling inspectors, that Saddam had sworn he did not have.[21]

Johann Hari: Life is rarely a choice between good and bad but between bad and worse. US foreign policy is, God knows, all too often terrible. You don't need to remind me about Vietnam, Chile, or the crimes being committed by the US today in Columbia [sic]. (And I hope I don't need to remind you of some of the honourable exceptions – Germany, Japan, the Marshall Plan, Kosovo). US actions can be awful but Saddam's tyranny is demonstrably worse... the writer Christopher Hitchens has raised a point that I find hard to answer. If we had listened to the Benns and the Galloways for the past 20 years, what would the world look like today? Slobodan Milosevic would be massacring the ethnic Albanians (who are mostly Muslims, by the way) in his fiefdom of Greater Serbia, instead of being on trial for crimes against humanity in The Hague. The Taliban would still be in power in Afghanistan, and their ban on all music, to cite one small but revealing example, would still be in place.[22]

David Aaronovitch: What are you going to do when you are told – as one day you will be – that while you were demonstrating against an allied invasion, and being applauded by friends and Iraqi officials, many of the people of Iraq were hoping, hope against hope, that no one was listening to you? You could still be right and I could be mistaken. A war could be far bloodier than I imagine, the consequences far worse than I believe they will be. It is just possible that a new Iraqi government, instead of moving towards democracy, might be a corrupt oligarchy. All I can say is that the signs look relatively promising in both Kosovo and Afghanistan.[23]

Johann Hari: My recurring nightmare – literally – is that, when all this is over, I meet up again with some of the friends I made in Iraq (and who I talk to everyday by e-mail) and they say to me: "You knew we hated Saddam, with his torture chambers, his secret police and his 100 per cent 'election' results. You knew we were desperate to overthrow him. You knew about the 5,000 people he gassed at Halabjah. You knew. So when British and American planes were just miles away, waiting to kill Saddam so we could begin to rebuild our country, what did you do?" How could I possibly tell them I went on the march opposing the war? How will I explain that one million people in my home town actually did?[24]

How many people marched?

George Galloway: There was Britain's biggest ever protest march – perhaps two million people in Hyde Park – just before the invasion of Iraq. This was five times the size of the second biggest – that of the Countryside Alliance – which had a budget of hundreds of thousands of pounds and the full support of the right-wing press, as well as a fair number of landowners exercising 'feudal rights' over their tenants. It was twenty times the size of Britain's most famous modern demonstration, at the US Embassy in Grosvenor Square at the height of the Vietnam War.[25]

Ken Livingstone: It dwarfed the Countryside Alliance march. It was the largest march in British history. I remember working out that it was the equivalent of the entire population of England in about 1200. Just vast.

John Rees: Billy Hayes [General Secretary of the CWU] said a very good thing about the comparison with the Vietnam War demonstrations. He said to me on February 15th on the stage "Well it might not be the Beatles, but at least we are Oasis". Tariq [Ali] put it more strongly. He said, and he is right about this, that all the Vietnam demonstrations put together weren't as big as February 15th, never mind all the Stop the War demonstrations put together.

Billy Hayes, Communications Workers Union General Secretary 2002–present: I remember Bianca Jagger being there and saying to her "There is more people listening to you today than listened to Mick [Jagger] in 1969 when the Stones played Hyde Park."

***Guardian*, 17 February 2003:** When the march organisers announced at 3pm on Saturday afternoon that 1 million people had demonstrated in London, there were loud cheers. Two hours later, the "official" number had doubled and there was widespread disbelief. "How can anyone know?" asked one man who had just arrived. "They might as well say 5 million." Yesterday the police admitted that after giving out figures ranging from 150,000 to 1.5 million or more on Saturday, they still had no idea how many people had actually descended on Hyde Park. "The figures are a guide only," said a spokesman. "They should not be taken too literally. Perhaps it was 1.5 million". Yesterday the numbers battle was being fought in newspapers with the anti-war *Sunday Mirror*, which helped sponsor the rally, estimating 2 million, but the *Sunday Telegraph* just 500,000... "It's more than an educated guess, but less than a scientific figure. What we can say is that it was one of the largest [crowds] in living memory," said a police spokesman.[26]

Tony Myers: There were people counting. It's not absolutely perfect science. You have people working in pairs and you say "How wide is this?" Let's say it's ten people wide and then we see how long it takes to click through 500 people. Then you make sure someone is timing from the start to the last person. You can then give a rough approximation. The police do a similar thing. And you always get caught in the middle.

Mark Steel, Comedian, Journalist and former member of the Socialist Workers Party: No one knows the size of the marches. The police always divided the real number by eight and Stop the War always multiplied the real number by about 50! Who knows?

Royal Parks background note to Parliamentary Question from Dr Lewis MP, February 2003: It will be virtually impossible to take an accurate count of those taking part in the rally. On 15 February many people will go straight to the rally, either because they do not arrive in time to or do not wish to march. They will enter the park from any one of over a dozen gates.[27]

***Guardian*, 18 February 2003:** This month's *Guardian*/ICM poll... shows that at least one person from 1.25 million households in Britain went on Saturday's anti-war march in London, confirming estimates that between one million and two million people went on the march.[28]

Andrew Murray and Lindsey German: A separate YouGov poll for the *Daily Telegraph* found that 4 percent of people claimed to have demonstrated on 15 February (presumably covering the London and Glasgow marches, and the smaller local demonstrations held in towns around the country by those who could not get to London). Four percent of the British population is slightly over 2 million. So 2 million it is then.[29]

The protests around the globe

***Guardian*, 17 February 2003:** Huge waves of demonstrations not seen since the Vietnam war jammed more than 600 cities around the world over the weekend as protestors from Tasmania to Iceland marched against war in Iraq. Up to 30 million people demonstrated worldwide, including around 6 million in Europe, according to figures from organisers and police, although most conceded there were too many people in too many places to count. Action began on Friday when 150,000 protestors filed into Melbourne, with thousands more gathering across the rest of Australia and in New Zealand. Protests were still swelling yesterday in Sydney, San Francisco and in Oman – where 200 women filled the streets in the sultanate's first all-female demonstration. Smaller demonstrations choked streets from Cape Town, Dhaka and Havana to Bangkok.[30]

***Guardian*, 13 February 2003:** The most unusual rally is expected to be in the international territory of Antarctica, where dozens of scientists and others at the McMurdo base on the edge of the Ross sea will take to the ice.[31]

***BBC News*, 17 February 2003:** More than 10,000 protested in India's eastern city of Calcutta while several thousand gathered in a Tokyo park. But reports from Asia's Muslim nations were of much lower numbers, with 3,000 in Islamabad, just 300 in Karachi and a thousand in Dhaka. Five hundred turned out in Jakarta, although a much larger protest was seen last weekend with about 7,000 on the streets. The Arab world's largest demonstrations took place in Baghdad itself, and the Syrian capital Damascus. Reports from the Tunisian city of Sax say police stormed into a crowd of about 3,000 people and beat them with batons and truncheons, injuring at least 20.[32]

***Guardian*, 17 February 2003:** In New York on Saturday organisers counted 400,000 demonstrators who, forbidden by a court order from marching, rallied within sight of the United Nations amid heavy security... In Chicago 3,000 gathered and in Philadelphia 5,000 more carried anti-Bush banners. Other marchers massed in more than 100 towns and cities, including Seattle, Miami and Los Angeles... Two marches in Spain – in Madrid and Barcelona – each brought out around 1 million people on Saturday evening, with dozens more gatherings countrywide, taking the total number of protesters towards the 3 million mark... Between 300,000 and 500,000 anti-war protesters marched through some 60 towns across France on Saturday... Berlin's peace march turned out to be five times bigger than expected by police and organisers – and twice as large as the biggest previous demonstration in post-war Germany. By the time Saturday's protest reached its peak, an estimated 500,000 people were packed into the Tiergarten, Berlin's central park... Rome's ancient monuments were draped with peace flags on Saturday and the city swarmed with anti-war campaigners, producing what organisers said was the biggest turnout in Italy's long history of mass popular protest. The crowd included leftwing opposition politicians, film stars, Catholic groups and Iraqi exiles. March campaigners claimed 3 million pacifists "invaded" Rome. Police said the true figure was around 650,000, though it was "difficult to count."[33]

SECTION THREE

WAS IT A FAILURE?

The UK and US Government's response to 15 February 2003

Greg Dyke, *BBC* Chairman 2000–4: I suspect the march scared the Government to death.

Tony Blair, Prime Minister 1997–2006, addressing the Labour Party's spring conference in Glasgow on 15 February 2003: I rejoice that we live in a country where peaceful protest is a natural part of our democratic process. But I ask the marchers to understand this: I do not seek unpopularity as a badge of honour. But sometimes it is the price of leadership and the cost of conviction... As you watch your TV pictures of the march, ponder this: if there are 500,000 on that march, that is still less than the number of people whose deaths Saddam has been responsible for. If there are one million, that is still less than the number of people who died in the wars he started.[1]

Alastair Campbell, Tony Blair's Communications Director, answering a question at the Iraq Inquiry in 2010 about whether the government took account of the "strength of public opinion" shown by the march: The march was getting huge publicity in the build-up. It was clearly going to be an enormous event, and you have got to remember this is a democracy, the Prime Minister was intending to stand for re-election, he knew that this was a deeply unpopular policy with an awful lot of people and not just unpopular like some of the other issues that were unpopular, tuition fees or whatever it might have been; this was deep. I always have a rule of thumb that, if somebody goes on a march, there are probably ten others who thought about it. So there were a lot of people who were opposed. I think, what it definitely – look, there was the political consideration. That was a big protest and he was – he thought about it a lot and he was seized of its significance. But ultimately, I think it just made him think more deeply about the issues.[2]

Charles Clarke, Labour MP 1997–2010 and Education Secretary 2002–4: I remember it being a very large demonstration. As somebody who organised many large demonstrations in my youth, I never thought it was as big as some of those big demonstrations in the early 70s – against the Industrial Relations Bill of the Tories, for example.[i] But you never know about the estimations of numbers on these big demonstrations. It was in any case an enormous demonstration and an enormous expression of a

---

i The author cannot find any evidence that demonstrations against the 1971 Industrial Relations Bill, which proposed to bring in legal restrictions on trade union activity, rivalled the scale of 15 February 2003.

view. I regard demonstrations like that as entirely legitimate, and people are entitled to express their opinions. And they did in a generally restrained and peaceful way. I listened to it, I observed it, and I took it as a statement of opinion. But I didn't take it as necessarily representative of the state of public opinion. It is the opinion of a body of people who feel very strongly on a particular question who want to take the trouble to make their voice as strong as they can – as I think they are entitled to do. In fact, it would be terrible if they weren't able to do that. But I didn't regard it as representative of the nation, necessarily.

David Blunkett, Labour MP 1987–present and Home Secretary from 2001–4: I was never opposed to the march. I spoke as the warm up act for Tony Blair that morning at our Labour Party Conference in Glasgow, and made the point that this demonstration of extremely strongly held views was the strength of our democracy – not its weakness. I went on to say that my own friends and family were deeply divided and (more in hope than anticipation) asked people to treat this as a genuine disagreement – not an issue where people believed that there was bad faith, deception, or even worse, from either camp. In other words, I understood the point of view of the marchers; that they took an entirely contrary view as to how to proceed in the light of the non-compliance with the unanimous UN Resolution of November 7th [2002], and specifically that not agreeing did not mean 'not listening' – it meant not agreeing!

Charles Clarke: It was certainly talked about and discussed. I'm perhaps slightly more hardened to demonstrations in public life through my own political background and experience, than some others. Some other people were more concerned about the demonstration than I was. Did it change things? It made a very, very clear statement that if action was to be taken it needed to be very properly explained.

Condoleezza Rice, US National Security Advisor in 2003, answering a question about whether the Bush Administration was "rattled" by the 15 February 2003 protests across the globe: No. Nothing could be further from the truth. People have a right to protest. People can say what they think. But the fact of the matter is, they're not saying what they think in Baghdad, because that's a regime that cuts people's tongues out if they say what they think.[3]

George Bush, President of the United States 2000–8, 18 February 2003: Two points. One is that democracy is a beautiful thing, and that people are allowed to express their opinion, and I welcome people's right to say what they believe. Secondly, evidently, some in the world don't view Saddam Hussein as a risk to peace. I respectfully disagree... First of all, you know, size of protests – it's like deciding, "Well, I'm going to decide policy based upon a focus group." The role of a leader is to decide policy based upon, in this case, the security of the people.[4]

Tony Blair, 18 February 2003: Of course I understand the concerns of the thousands that marched on Saturday, and of course I should and do listen to those concerns. They have a rightful hatred of the consequences of war... Most of the people who are concerned, who went on the march, are not actually in a position of being against conflict in all circumstances, though obviously some are. When asked indeed, we look at the evidence of public opinion, more than three quarters say they would support war if it has UN support. What people are against is a war they feel is either rushed or unnecessary.[5]

"The atmosphere at the time was enormously tense, emotional and pressurised – dreadful": The 18 March 2003 parliamentary vote, the start of the war and the student protests

Carol Naughton, Campaign for Nuclear Disarmament Chair 2001–3, from 1–2 March 2003 Campaign for Nuclear Disarmament Council Meeting minutes: A big thank you to everybody: 15th February the biggest in history – it was great. Phenomenal to see so many – absolutely fantastic – everyone worked so hard to enable it to happen, stewarding etc. Such a phenomenal kick in the teeth to Tony Blair – "the biggest focus group in the world". It gave everyone a real lift. We have to keep the hope that it is not going to happen and we are going to do everything possible – keep doing whatever you can.[6]

Andrew Murray, Stop the War Coalition Chair 2001–11: For a lot of people, understandably, they went on that march and that was it. They had made their stand and they then got on with the rest of their lives. And were dismayed the Government paid no attention. Of course they all feel vindicated now. But for me the next day I had to get on with something else with Stop the War – we had to think about how we were going to carry this forward, what we were going to do next.

Ian McEwan, Author: I have a friend who is very close to someone who was working with Tony Blair. In early March [2003] there was one night of insomnia where I became convinced that if I just had half an hour with Tony Blair I could talk him out of it. Then the sun came up and I realised this was complete fantasy. Looking back it wasn't a bad plan. I thought what he could do to save face – he had 8,000 troops by then in Kuwait – was to put them in to Afghanistan. So the army wouldn't feel humiliated. You just redeploy as a peacekeeping, 'hearts and minds' operation in Afghanistan.

Alastair Campbell: More than any other debate, specific Parliamentary debate, you just got so many messages from people, not necessarily in the political circle, you had a sense of the country following the debate, as it unfolded. I will never forget – sometimes I used to run to work and sometimes I used to get the 24 bus, and I can remember listening to a conversation of two women on a bus about Resolution 1441 on their way to – they were quite elderly women and they were talking about [that] resolution – and I thought, "People are engaging on this now on a deeper level. It has gone beyond the flim-flam that really represents a lot of what passes for debate in the media today". People were engaged in the debate.[7]

Jeremy Corbyn, Labour MP 1983–present: Within Parliament there was a very intensive lobbying exercise by Blair and his office. The Weapons of Mass Destruction argument, lots of briefings. On the day of the [18 March 2003 parliamentary] vote itself, interestingly the Government whips and ourselves had much the same amount of numbers throughout the day. We had concocted two amendments to the Government's motion, one from [Labour MP] Chris Smith which said the case for war had not been made, an agreed amendment between dissidents in all parties – Liberal Democrats, Labour, some Conservatives and Scottish and Welsh nationalists. And then there was one I put down saying we should not attack Iraq period. That wasn't selected for debate, and I wasn't surprised. We always thought Chris Smith's would be selected and we would coalesce around that one.

Clare Short, Labour MP 1983–10 and International Development Secretary in 2003: They put enormous effort into arm-twisting people. Cherie [Blair] was at it, ringing women MPs, playing the women's rights card, which people in Matrix Chambers [the barristers' where Cherie Blair is a member] really resented. I know he was telling some people he would resign. It was a story in the *Sun*. Just think of the self-indulgence of it? You've got troops on the ground, you've led the country to that point, and then you resign because half of the Labour MPs voted the other way. It was all hype, hype, hype. The atmosphere at the time was enormously tense, emotional and pressurised – dreadful.

Jeremy Corbyn: I have been in Parliament since 1983, and it was never so feverish. Tony Blair opened the debate for the Government and tried to justify on the grounds of removing the threat of WMDs – all very familiar arguments.

He spoke well – he always does, and was clearly convinced himself. His tactic seemed to be to try and invoke a sort of Churchillian 1940 aura. Since the whole building is steeped in military history and the dramas of the Second World War, it was a clever tactic. He was unnerved by [then Leader of the House of Commons] Robin Cook's resignation the night before but emboldened by the non-resignation of Clare Short at that time. The debate in the chamber was passionate and at times memorable, and eagerly followed in the media.[8]

Clare Short: I think if the Tories had been in power like Suez [in 1956], and even if the leadership of the Labour Party had gone along with it, the overwhelming majority of Labour MPs would have voted against it. That is where their heart was, their feeling about the war itself and not complying with the UN – all the traditions of the party. I think the majority of Tories would have been for because of their natural outlook on the world – pro-American, pro-authority, pro-military action. Most Labour MPs went through agonies about whether they should be loyal to their Government; there was a lot of pressure from the Government, a lot of arm twisting. The call to loyalty is a very powerful call... I believed Blair's promises. I knew the vote couldn't be won and that the war was unstoppable, but I believed an internationalised reconstruction and the establishment of a Palestinian state would make the Middle East totally different. I also was stunned by, but believed, the legal advice. I couldn't believe it. I didn't at that stage think what I think now – that the Attorney General was a crony of the Prime Minister and got lent on, and nobody knew about the earlier legal advice...Looking back to it I can see

I was just manipulated. But I was on my own trying to do my best, knowing the vote was unwinnable. If the vote had been very tight and one vote either way could have made a difference, there is no question I would have voted against. But knowing that was not the case, and therefore that the attack was going to happen, and the trouble the Prime Minister was going to [to] give these undertakings to me; I believed him, foolishly.

Greg Dyke: Did she [Clare Short] tell you the story about how she eventually went in and voted for the war and came out and thought Blair would say "Thank you Clare", but he looked straight through her? From that day on she was dead.

George Galloway, Labour MP 1987–2005. Respect MP 2005–10 and 2012–present. Vice President of Stop the War Coalition 2001–present: I think we should not underestimate the importance of the number of Labour MPs who voted against the Government. You must look at this through the prism of the state of knowledge then, rather than now. The fact that 139 Labour MPs voted against the Government before we knew it had all been built on a pack of lies, is not a small thing. The whips were patrolling the corridors, knuckles were being crunched, favours were being promised and careers were threatened. There was a lot of heavy manners. The extraordinary crescendo of war propaganda was still ringing in everyone's ears. Of course I would have been happier if the majority of Labour MPs had voted against the war. Blair would have been dependent on the Tories to take the country to war, and that might have pulled Britain out of the war and brought Blair down. I still think 139 was a pretty big achievement. It was bigger than

I expected it to be. That night is remembered by me, for being the night I ought to have resigned from the Labour Party. Instead of limping on and waiting to be sacked, I should have resigned from the Labour Party that night. But I didn't do it, and I wish now that I had.

Clare Short: I just know Tony Blair just lied and lied and lied... Either he doesn't know the difference between telling the truth and lying, or he made up his mind that he was going to do this, and convinced himself this was the right thing to do, and engaged in deception, thinking it was the right thing to do. That is my conclusion.

Rose Gentle, Founder member, Military Families Against the War: To be honest Gordon [Rose Gentle's son, serving with the Royal Highland Fusiliers, was killed in Iraq on 28 June 2004] really didn't know where Iraq was. He was only a 19-year old boy and he had only done three weeks training. I said to him "Do you know where Iraq is?", and he kind of shrugged his shoulders as if to say "No not really". He was told he was doing peacekeeping...To be honest I don't think Gordon really knew much, just like a lot of the 19-year olds that have been sent to Iraq. I don't think they knew exactly what they were getting put into.[9]

Noam Chomsky, American dissident, 9 March 2003: What's going to happen is not war. The disparity of force is so extraordinary that the term "war" doesn't apply. We wouldn't call it a boxing match if the world champion were in a ring with a kindergarten child.[10]

***Guardian*, 26 April 2003:** On Thursday March 20, 2003 the country awoke to the news that Operation Iraqi Freedom [the invasion] had begun.[11]

Chris Nineham: Stop the War Coalition Chief Steward: After February 15 the big project was to create, threaten, and back up with enough convincing evidence, a day of civil disobedience and hopefully strike action on Day X [the day the war started]. And Day X was impressive. It must have been the biggest day of civil disobedience this country has ever seen. There was the school strikes, there was a number of walk outs from work places. When I say a number I mean hundreds of walk outs from workplaces.

***Guardian*, 26 April 2003:** In the first days of war with Iraq, the country was witness to a new kind of protest. In the most significant child-led campaign for a century, schoolchildren as young as 10 walked out of their classrooms to attend what were, for most, their first political demonstrations. And they weren't simply trotting alongside older activists, or parroting the slogans of their parents. These young people were organising and leading their own protests, leafleting at school gates, organising email networks and expertly working the media.[12]

Emily Churchill, Year 11 student in Birmingham in 2003: In 2003 I had just turned sixteen and I was in Year 11 at Queensbridge School in Mosley in Birmingham. I had just started seeing this guy in a punk band who gave me my first anti-war meeting leaflet and asked me to go to this meeting. It was the first time I had been to a political meeting. I just got stuck in after that… I remember the most active members of the Birmingham Stop the War Coalition group were very keen on school students doing something and they encouraged us to campaign in our schools. It was the first time I had ever been involved in political campaigning. Queensbridge is a normal comprehensive school, quite a rough school. I wasn't particularly cool at school. I remember thinking they were kind of living in fantasy land because they thought that I, a geeky white girl in Year 11, could rally my classmates to protest against the war in Iraq. But we did the petitions anyway in school and the petition was really popular... On 5 March we did a walk out just of Queensbridge School. There were 600 pupils in the whole school, so quite a small school, and 300 of us walked out. We had been encouraged to try by the Stop the War Coalition in Birmingham and I didn't think it would work, but I wanted to do it. It was amazing. The local bus services gave us free buses into town, and more than half the school walked out and we did a peaceful protest in town. Our teachers were really supportive of us, and when we came back to school they gave us the thumbs up.

Yasmin Khan, Stop the War activist, London School of Economics and Political Science 2001–5: I remember anytime we went anywhere we would never actually take the pavement. Even if we were just twenty people walking from LSE to parliament we would do the whole walk down the strand and down Whitehall actually blocking the street with our banner. It was great. "Whose streets? Our streets!" And it's a sign of how the anti-war sentiment rung out with people that we were never really hassled by bus drivers or cabs or the police. I think that was a sign that people generally agreed.

Ruhul Tarafder, London-based community activist: Word got out there was going to be an anti-war demo outside Parliament among all the kids in Tower Hamlets [in East London]. Loads of kids filled up the local park. Everybody wanted to march down to the Houses of Parliament, but I was a little bit concerned because some of these kids were very young. Who is going to bring them all back? Who is going to take responsibility for them? I remember ringing up loads of my friends and saying "We've got a situation here, we've got all these kids up for going to the Houses of Parliament, but we are going to have to manage them and check they are alright and look after them". There were people getting them excited, but I knew these people might not be there later on when you've got to get them home. It was the kids themselves who decided that was what they wanted to do. I remember taking them through the City, through Holborn and all the way to Parliament. I remember the police blocked us on a few occasions and I remember people shouting racial abuse from some of the buildings in the City as we passed. A few scuffles broke out where the police were trying to block people from getting to Parliament. When we got to Parliament – that was probably the best piece of political education for these kids. They were welcomed by everybody. There was a good several hundred kids who had walked from Tower Hamlets to Parliament. Then it was the nightmare of getting them all back. I remember I had to get my credit card and pay for so many kids just to get on the train to get back to Tower Hamlets safely. Some of them had got arrested, so we had to go to Charing Cross police station and get them out.

Emily Churchill: They didn't want us to do the second one [on Day X]. I remember the head teacher calling me and basically she said "Lots of the teachers agree with what you are doing and the protest was great and you've made your point but I don't see why you need to do it again". I remember one teacher at school saying we should just do it anyway. I think the head teacher was worried about the parents. I remember calling the bus service the second time and asking if we could get free buses again, and they said "No way" and put the phone down on me. Someone had obviously spoken to them. So that walkout was school students and sixth form students across Birmingham. It was massive: 4,000 students. It got some bad press because there were a handful of kids throwing stones. One of them unfortunately hit a journalist. I think we just walked around town. We didn't have speakers.

***Guardian*, 26 April 2003:** Over the coming days, the scene was replicated across the UK – 5,000 in Birmingham, 3,000 in Manchester and Edinburgh, 1,000 in Sheffield, 300 in Swansea. Condemned by the police and teaching unions, many of the youngsters who took part were marked down as truants, with a significant number of absences resulting in suspension or expulsion.[13]

Ruhul Tarafder: There were people there from SWP and Stop the War, but it wasn't organised as such. Word got out that there was going to be a protest in the local park. Whether we should block the streets here, or whether to go to Parliament, was debated. It was the kids themselves that wanted to go to Parliament. I remember myself and others saying to them "Are you sure? It's going to be a long walk".

They decided themselves that that was what they wanted to do. It was quite amazing that all of these kids from all of these different schools – some had climbed over school fences – wanted to say the war wasn't in their name.

Asad Rehman: In a lot of places the school walk-outs weren't organised by Stop the War Coalition. They were spontaneous. For example, in east London I remember being on the walk outs from Tower Hamlets. It was done much more on a community level. Of course the SWP people were involved, but they didn't have the power to say "We're going to call that school out." It was not like that at all. Things had a momentum to themselves. Things were spreading in lots of different ways in the community. It was controlled chaos in a sense.

***Guardian*, 24 March 2003:** protesters turned out in much greater number on Saturday [22 March 2003] for the largest demonstration against a war in progress in British history. Police estimated that 200,000 people joined the London rally, while organisers claimed about 400,000, based on comparisons with the February 15 peace march... other protests at RAF Fairford in Gloucestershire, [RAF spy base] Menwith Hill in North Yorkshire, and Manchester and Edinburgh attracted more than 20,000 people.[14]

Reg Keys, Founder member, Military Families Against the War, whose son, Tom Keys, serving with Royal Military Police, died in Iraq on 24 June 2003: I thought Britain was doing the right thing going into Iraq. I supported the war to start with because I believed what my Prime Minister told me. I believed his rhetoric when he said Iraq can launch against British interests within 45 minutes. He left it at that. But what he actually meant was British interests in Cyprus. But he left it at just British interests, which left the average Joe Public to believe the shores of Britain. He said that Iraq had a WMD programme up and running now – that it is clear, detailed and authoritative. He also went on to say that the information, the intelligence, was detailed and authoritative. But at best it was sketchy and untried. This was all spin to make the case for war. And when I look back now, that night of 'shock and awe' when all that hellfire rained down on Baghdad, killing hundreds if not thousands of innocent people I may add, was it nothing short of an act of terrorism by men in suits?[15]

Tony Blair: Our decision to take part in military action against Iraq was undertaken as a last resort. The Iraqi regime's refusal to cooperate in dismantling its weapons of mass destruction left us with no option. While taking military action, we are also taking every possible care to minimise civilian casualties and damage to civilian infrastructure. Throughout this crisis we have acted in full accordance with international law.[16]

The short-term achievements of 15 February 2003

Yasmin Khan: I don't think it's fair or true to see February 15 as anything other than a massive success. It's easy to gloss over achievements as a campaigner, especially a radical campaigner, as you are always on to the next thing, and are always aiming really high. But it's important to step back and reflect on what the outcomes of that day were for the political classes, the media and ordinary people. The fact that you could bring together millions of people onto the streets to campaign against a war that hadn't started yet was a massive success. Most anti-war movements are born after war's start. This was totally unprecedented. This should give us hope that most people don't want unnecessary bloodshed, that they don't believe whatever politicians tell them, that they are willing to stand up for their rights, that for hundreds of thousands of people it was their first ever political demonstration and that the biggest mobilisation in British history was a progressive one. All of those things make me feel positive about the impact of the march.

Mike Marqusee, Press Officer, Stop the War Coalition: At mass demonstrations, the anti-war movement comes together at its broadest and most diverse. They offer the highest degree of visible unity around the most urgent demands. Most importantly, through them, individuals become part of a movement. protesters return home, talk with others about the experience, and in some cases become organisers in their own communities.[17]

Caroline Lucas, Green Party of England and Wales MEP 1999–2010. Green Party of England and Wales MP 2010–present: I think these marches are important in terms of the connections that they give people actually on the marches – the shared solidarity. Lots of people sitting in their own homes and having their own thoughts and views about something, and then coming out and having that wonderful sense of being part of a wider movement that is so much bigger than you ever imagined, and that so many fellow travellers share the same view. And the way that gives you energy to go forward in more political action is a sometimes underrated aspect of demonstrations. In a sense they are about recharging activists themselves, and bringing that activism out to more people, as well as being about the immediate end of what the demonstration is about.

Milan Rai, Activist, Author and Co-Editor of *Peace News*: There is another effect the global anti-war movement had at the time. Before the invasion took place I said that they [the US and UK] were not going to attack the electrical system [in Iraq]. There were others who had been following Iraq for years and they said "Of course they are going to attack the electrical system, they always do". They did in 1991. It's the way you take down a middle-ranking country like Iraq; and they didn't attack the electrical system. In the aftermath of the war the electrical system did get severely damaged. But the invading force didn't attack it. They didn't attack the civilian infrastructure which they did in 1991, when they said it was duel-use and key to the Iraqi military system. They attacked it and it had a devastating effect on the civilian population; this time they didn't. And I think a large part of that was the anti-war movement. The anti-war movement was so strong in conveying its concern for ordinary Iraqi people that it was one of the forces that deterred the US-led forces from attacking the civilian infrastructure, which is very much what they wanted to do as it makes the military's job much easier.

Mike Marqusee: Although it [the march] didn't stop the war, it placed it under a degree of scrutiny that very few wars in British or US history have been, and that has got to have been a good thing.

George Galloway: Perhaps we affected how the war was fought, a little. Perhaps "shock and awe" was not quite as shocking and awful as it would otherwise have been, if there had not been millions on the streets around the world against the war. They might have felt they had more of a blank cheque for how they actually fought the war.

Andrew Murray: I do think the positive side of it is that the whole issue of Iraq, and how it has played out in British politics, has been in the shadow of that demonstration. If two million people hadn't marched, and we hadn't sustained the campaign since, then there is no doubt that Britain could still be occupying Iraq. The fact Gordon Brown is in a hurry to get the troops out of Iraq – in fact is handing over Basra not to Iraqis but to American troops – is a result of that mobilisation of public opinion [the interview took place on 15 April 2009]. So if one looks at it in the longer view, and compares it to the movement against Apartheid, the movement for civil rights in America, the anti-Vietnam war movement, the movement for Women's suffrage – they've all achieved their aims over a longer period. And I think what we can say Stop the War has done is helped foreshorten the war in Iraq.

Long-term achievements of 15 February 2003

Gabriel Carlyle, Peace Activist: A lot of the things that have rumbled on, the fact we are still having an inquiry [the Iraq Inquiry – the interview took place on 26 February 2010] now, are in no small measure a consequence of all that anti-war ferment that happened in the run up to 2003... It has remained a thorn in the flesh, even though nearly all the British soldiers have left… If you compare the invasion of Iraq to Afghanistan in 2001, or the bombing of Yugoslavia in 1999, you can see a huge difference. There were splits inside the establishment, but without the huge anti-war ferment in the country, and the mass mobilisation, I don't think that would be the same. A lot of the achievements of the anti-war movement actually took place after most of the anti-war movement had dropped away. They were legacies of the activism that took place in advance of the invasion.

Lindsey German, Stop the War Coalition Convenor: I don't think you can say that the biggest mobilisation in British history is a failure. If you think about most marches, they don't actually achieve their goal in the sense you march Saturday and by Monday it's all over... If it's a big demonstration nobody would say, or should say, it is a failure – it's part of an ongoing campaign to build these things. I think it was a big success. The problem is you were up against the Prime Minister and cabinet who were determined to go to war, a political system that didn't reflect what most people thought. It was simply an appalling failure of democracy that they voted for the war.

John Rees, Stop the War Coalition National Officer: I understand, especially with people who haven't demonstrated before – and because, unusually, you were able to demonstrate before a war started, and because it was so big and so new to them – they expected it to have that effect. It's almost a sort of pantomime idea of how politics works – that we rush on from one side of the stage waving the Stop the War banner, and the very bad people twirling their moustaches and wearing top hats run off the other side of the stage. That's not a political process. Political processes are deeper and longer than that.

Lindsey German: I do regard these things as something you have to look at over a period of time. If you look at the Suffragettes or the civil rights movement in America, or Vietnam – the biggest marches against Vietnam were years before the war ended. If you think of the 1970s, here there were no marches over Vietnam of any significant size, even in America in the last three or four years of the war, there wasn't. So I think you have to look at [it] as part of a context.

Chris Nineham: In terms of the interpretation of the event, when you actually look at it, it's not surprising one demonstration wasn't enough to derail what is, and was, the central project of US imperialism. The attack on Iraq was something a significant section of the US establishment had been planning and promoting for a long time. So it's not surprising this wasn't enough to stop them. Having said that, I think historically what is remarkable, and what is understated in most of the accounts, is the extent to which that demonstration, and the demonstrations after it – Day X, the protests that followed – demoralised and destabilised the Government. It is quite clear that Blair was massively isolated.

***Guardian*, 18 February 2003:** The rift between Tony Blair and the British public over war against Iraq is today confirmed by an opinion poll... The survey, taken over the weekend, reveals that Mr Blair has sustained significant political damage from the debate over Iraq. His personal rating has dropped through the floor to minus 20 points, the lowest level since the petrol crisis two and a half years ago.[18]

***Guardian*, 11 March 2004:** Of the 5,000 teenagers aged 12 to 18 interviewed for Bliss magazine... on Iraq, 76% thought Britain was wrong to go to war, and 82% "don't trust" Tony Blair.[19]

Bob Crow, Rail, Maritime and Transport Workers (RMT) General Secretary 2002–present: The reality is that everyone knows Blair is a liar, that Bush is a liar. They've got rid of Bush. Blair jumped and is now one of the most hated people in Britain. He has got to look behind his shoulder for the rest of his life in case he gets assassinated.

***Times*, 17 January 2010:** The issue of the war remains highly sensitive among the public. A YouGov poll for the *Sunday Times* this weekend shows that 52% of people believe Blair deliberately misled the country over the war. Almost one in four – 23% – think he should be tried as a war criminal.[20]

Anas Altikriti, Spokesperson, Muslim Association of Britain: Tony Blair and George Bush: the leaders of the two most powerful military nations in the world. They went on a military mission. They won. They achieved their objectives. In any other time of history and circumstance they would have been hailed as Emperors, as victorious. Tony Blair was hoping, according to one insider who then resigned her post, to be paraded through Pall Mall like England winning the World Cup. He had won. What more could he have done? Yet in reality both of them don't even want to hear the word "Iraq" anymore. Wasn't it Tony Blair who once stood up and said "Enough, no more questions about Iraq." Why? This was his ticket out of any other domestic issue, this was his moment of glory. Yet Tony Blair and George Bush will, until the day they die and beyond, they will be associated with something the world opposed. Even the Conservatives, who voted for the war by the way, they themselves now say "We looked at the intelligence we had at the time, we don't want anything to do with the war." It is something that is stained. I think the demonstration of 15 February and the movement as a whole, led to this.

Mark Steel, Comedian, Journalist and former member of the Socialist Workers Party: Although the anti-war movement obviously could be portrayed as a failure because its *raison d'être* was to stop the war on Iraq and it didn't stop the war in Iraq, without question it did change the atmosphere globally. It is now so mainstream to assume the war in Iraq was wrong that you almost look like a complete lunatic if you say anything else. It's just assumed now it was a disaster. Blair knows that somewhere deep down. He can't even launch his shitty little book.[ii] That is his legacy. That is what he will be remembered for. Somewhere deep down he knows that, which is gratifying to some degree.

Ken Livingstone: In a sense, the sheer scale of the march and the fact they ignored it did a huge amount to undermine Blair's credibility. At the following general

---

ii In September 2010 Blair cancelled a book signing in London because of fears about protests. 'Tony Blair cancels book signing amid protest fears', *BBC News*, 6 September, www.bbc.co.uk/news/uk-politics-11197376 [Accessed 20 December 2012]

election [in May 2005] they struggled to beat the Tories by 10 percent. And that was [then Conservative Party leader] Michael Howard for god's sake! If the Tories had had the good sense to have someone like [Conservative MP] Ken Clarke Labour would have lost that election. However much people loathed Tony Blair, they were not going to let Michael Howard in.

***Guardian*, 6 May 2005:** The Labour leadership last night continued to play down the significance of the Iraq war in the election campaign in spite of new evidence that it had been a key issue among floating voters... one of the last polls conducted by the *BBC* and published last night suggests hostility to the war was a bigger issue than has so far been acknowledged. The poll found 23% of people surveyed cited opposition to the war as a reason for being reluctant to vote Labour, while 21% said they did not trust Mr Blair.[21]

Ken Livingstone: I think it [the march] was decisive. It eroded Blair's support so much, that when you got to the horror of the Lebanon invasion [by Israel] in 2006 and Blair wouldn't condemn it, that was the final straw.

John Rees: If you look at this political process, the very least you could say about it [the march] is that it broke the Blair Administration. And it did it in quite an interesting way. Stop the War has always been about the scale but also the stamina of the movement. Because Blair went in very particular circumstances. When the Israeli invasion of Lebanon happened in 2006 he refused to call for a ceasefire. We put 100,000 people on the streets with a week's notice. That was the Saturday. The following Monday six government aides resigned; wrote him a letter saying you've got to say you'll be gone within a year. He said, after the last general election, that he intended to be here now – in 2009-2010 – and within a week he had written the letter saying he would be gone within a year. That's how it happens in Britain most of the time. I think there is pattern in British politics. [Edward] Heath went like this [in 1974] with the Miners, [Margaret] Thatcher went like this [in 1990] over the Poll Tax – there was no doubt in my mind it was the Poll Tax demonstration that did it. They don't like bits of Trafalgar Square on fire. She went immediately after that... It was that that did it. That's the effect it has had.

Salma Yaqoob, Chair of Birmingham Stop the War Coalition in 2003. Birmingham City Councillor 2006–11. Leader of the Respect Party 2005–2012: It [the march] has been so important. For example, creating spaces. The fact that it established these spaces still impacts on politics today. Politicians know now that they are more accountable. The fact that Tony Blair had to leave in circumstances certainly not of his choosing, was because he became so tainted, was because he was associated with ignoring the will of the British people... The march is still affecting politics to this day. Ed Miliband would not have got the Labour Party leadership if he hadn't publicly drawn a line under the Iraq issue. His brother [David Miliband] was still trying to justify it and he lost. So it is still impacting the mainstream political culture. The Tories line now is that they were misled. You will find very few people today who try and justify the war on its own terms. I don't think it's because they have suddenly had an attack of conscience, because these were the same people who were cheerleaders of the war. They didn't come on the marches against the war but they've been forced into adopting more popular positions. It was the same with the American civil rights movement. It's not like the legislators suddenly said "Oh right, Black people deserve the vote". No, pressure built up where it became undeniable and for their own popularity and for their own careers they had to adopt certain stances. I think this is down to the anti-war movement.

Mark Steel: The fact that the next President of America [Barack Obama] was elected [in 2008] having been someone who opposed the war and spoke at demonstrations against the war is extraordinary. A huge change in the way the world is. How different would it have been if [Republican Presidential candidate John] McCain had won the election? You just don't know the impact it had.

Clare Short: I think it underlines this discussion about the state of British politics. An Iraqi man I met told me "Britain is the most free country in the world in that you can read any book, call any meeting, have any demonstration, argue any ideas – but the Government won't take a blind bit of notice". I think it really showed up that deeply inward looking, unresponsive-to-the-views-of-the-public political system that we have. I think there are more and more people reaching that conclusion. The degree of anger about the [2009 parliamentary] expenses scandal is partly because people have reached a point of contempt about the political system – the plank that broke the camel's back. The Iraq War, the size of the demonstration, and the complete unwillingness to take account of that depth and breadth of public opinion has led a lot of people to conclude our political system is deficient, is undemocratic and doesn't listen to the views of people. I agree with them.

George Galloway: We profoundly affected the credibility of the political system in both Britain and the United States. That is a very important gain, because our two systems strutted around as the free world and the world's leading democracies. I think we played a significant part in disabusing a very substantial section the population of both countries of the notion they lived in free and democratic countries. That in fact they were governed by crooks and liars and deceivers. That is still being played out in the expenses scandal and all the other shaking of the foundations of the British political class.

Kate Hudson, Campaign for Nuclear Disarmament Chair 2003–10. General Secretary 2010–present: For me it meant something slightly less tangible – a change in people's attitude towards information and moral judgements about things and what you are prepared to take from the Government. To be more specific, I think there was a massive revulsion towards the Government about the lies, which was damaging towards the political class and Government.

Arundhati Roy, Indian author and activist: The demonstrations and the peace movement really stripped down empire, which was very important. It stripped off the mash. It made it very clear what was going on. And if you look at general public perception of what the U.S. government is about, it's very different today. Not enough people knew what the U.S. government was up to all these years. People who studied it knew. Foreign policy scholars knew. Ex-CIA people knew. But now it's street talk.[22]

***Guardian*, 19 December 2004:** Senior army commanders have expressed fears that the increasingly vocal anti-Iraq war movement is discouraging thousands of young men from considering a career in the armed forces. They blame high-profile campaigns against the war, often led by bereaved parents and supported by celebrities and political figures, for worsening recruitment problems, particularly into the infantry... As well as a shortfall in young men volunteering, army officers have reported a wider reluctance to support a career in the army with parents refusing to sign consent forms for junior soldiers to sign up and, in some cases, local authorities with a strong anti-war sentiment refusing permission for recruitment officers to put up stands at local venues.[23]

Lord Michael Boyce, Chief of the UK Defence Staff 2001–3, 1 September 2011: Suddenly you had a war [the Iraq War] which had quite a lot of negative aspects about it and certainly wasn't a popular war by any definition. And a lot of atmospherics were being s[aid] which made the feeling that what was going on was not a good thing to be doing. You had a strange dichotomy. On the one hand you still probably had the sailor, soldier and airman seen as a good institution, the armed forces being a good institution and highly respected. But on the other hand though they were doing something which was not seen by a lot of people as being popular. And therefore you started to get a lot of negativity into what was going on, particularly reporting out against the government or against defence in general and what we were doing. Then you started getting the stories of how people who now were starting to appear on the streets in uniform for the first time for a very long time and getting a poor reception. Suddenly we had a situation where probably the poison of the virus being spread about how Iraq was not a good war started to be felt by the soldiers and airmen, not probably personally themselves, rather, but rather a reaction against the uniforms which in some way or other represented what the government was doing and which wasn't liked.[24]

Kim Manning-Cooper, Campaign for Nuclear Disarmament Staff Member 2002–3: Even though we didn't stop the war, we had a huge impact in galvanising a lot of people. For example, I think we got young people re-politicised again. For a lot of people I think it was the start of something for them, the start of their political activism. At a time people were de-politicised I think we helped to re-politicise a lot of people.

Madeleine Bunting, *Guardian*, 17 February 2003: This was a day which confounded dozens of assumptions about our age. How much harder it is today than a week ago to speak of the apathy and selfish individualism of consumer society.[25]

Mary Riddell, *Observer*, 16 February 2003: The age of apathy stops here… It is odd to think these are the sloths who could not be prised from their armchairs when elections rolled round and who hit the remote at the first flicker of any *BBC* political coverage that wasn't *Have I Got News For You.* These people, in New Labour's analysis, were the inert of the Earth. And there they are, out in their hundreds of thousands, quoting Hans Blix verbatim.[26]

Madeleine Bunting: Saturday [15 February 2003] proved that the decline of democracy has been overstated. What has changed is the pattern of participation; political parties and turnouts may be declining, but intense episodic political engagement is on the increase.[27]

Kate Hudson: For me one of the most significant things about the demo was that prior to this demonstration the largest demonstration in British history was the CND demonstrations in the early 80s against Cruise and Pershing missiles – 400,000 or 500,000. We all thought we were going to die in a nuclear holocaust. Genuinely. So people went on those demos as a survivalist thing – we have to have a future for our children. A fear driven thing as well. Whereas this wasn't a fear driven thing. It wasn't about us surviving. Nobody believed they were going to hit us with a nuke in 45 minutes! So why was it that two million people were willing to come out and march about Iraq? No one has been there, hardly anyone knows any Iraqis. To be able to mobilise such a large number of people on something that is of no threat to them – why would they do that? I think partly there must be a humanitarian element to it. They wanted to stop people getting killed.

Andrew Murray: I think what we can say Stop the War has done is helped foreshorten the war in Iraq and raised the bar enormously for any such war ever being undertaken in the future. Sometimes, if people ask "What war did you manage to stop?" I say '"The next one."

Mark Steel: In a parallel universe where no one demonstrated against the war in Iraq I personally think it's almost certain they would have bombed Iran. They were itching for it. Bush, Rumsfeld, Perle, Wolfowitz, the guy with the tash, Bolton – all of these people were absolutely clear on this. Full Spectrum Dominance and all these peculiar, sinister sounding phrases they used.

General Wesley Clark, Supreme Allied Commander of NATO during the 1999 Kosovo War: About ten days after 9/11, I went through the Pentagon and I saw Secretary Rumsfeld and Deputy Secretary Wolfowitz. I went downstairs just to say hello to some of the people on the Joint Staff who used to work for me, and one of the generals called me in... He says, "We've made the decision we're going to war with Iraq." This was about the 20th of September... So I came back to see him a few weeks later, and by that time we were bombing in Afghanistan. I said, "Are we still going to war with Iraq?" And he said, "Oh, it's worse than that." He reached over his desk. He picked up a piece of paper. And he said, "I just got this down from upstairs" – meaning the Secretary of Defence's office – "today". And he said, "This is a memo that describes how we're going to take out seven countries in five years, starting with Iraq, and then Syria, Lebanon, Libya, Somalia, Sudan and, finishing off, Iran."[28]

Mark Steel: I think there is no question that they thought they were cashing in the chips for winning the Cold War. The Cold War has ended and American has won – they should be able to rule without any opposition. That was clearly their aim. They spelt it all out in the Project for the

New American Century. But there is no question they were thrown off course by the movement against the war in Iraq. And, of course, they were thrown off course by what happened in Iraq too. So I think all those people who protested contributed to the world being a place where the George W Bush doctrine could not prevail.

Final thoughts on whether the march was a success or failure

Andrew Murray: Was it a failure in its own terms? Yes – you can see that argument. It [the invasion] went ahead. I don't think that was a great surprise to any of us who were centrally involved and around politics and who knew what the real dynamics were. We didn't expect the walls of Jericho to fall at a single trumpet blast. For a lot of people, I think they were quite disillusioned by that experience.

Ken Loach, Film Director: That's how it seems for people who aren't political. They had unrealistic hopes for the march – that suddenly the ruling class will back down: "Oh yes, our long-term economic interests aren't as pressing as we thought, therefore we won't do what we intend because two million people have walked through the streets." It's unrealistic. What did they expect? The ruling class can tolerate demonstrations. If need be they will get the water cannons and CS canisters out. But they didn't need to do that – it was very peaceful and amiable. The ruling class is very happy to allow that as a kind of safety valve. If you are not political you don't see that.

Andrew Murray: The secondarily negative side of this is [that] the idea [that by] demonstrating peacefully you can change things has taken a bit of a knock. I think everyone would have to reflect that if two million people can march and be ignored then demonstrating can only be a part of your political armoury because a government determined enough can simply ignore it.

Mike Marqusee: I would be pretty unhappy if the conclusion people drew was that any form of collective action is futile, rather than what I think is the more logical conclusion, which is that for forms of collective action to be meaningful they have to be sustained, continue for years and involve large numbers of people, and have many forms and expressions.

Noam Chomsky: Consider abolitionism. How long did the struggle go on before the abolitionist movement made any progress? If you give up every time you don't achieve the immediate gain you want, you're just guaranteeing that the worst is going to happen. These are long, hard struggles.[29]

Tony Benn, President, Stop the War Coalition. Labour MP 1963–2001 (with a brief spell in 1983-4 not in Parliament) and former Labour Cabinet Minister: Was the march a failure? That's the argument: we marched and the war went ahead. It did work, it did work. I would give examples – in 1956 I spoke in Trafalgar Square for the first time, against the Suez War, and we were denounced as anti-American and anti-British. And within weeks the Prime Minister had gone and the war had ended. I spoke in Trafalgar Square in 1964 in support of a very well-known terrorist who had just been sentenced to life-imprisonment and denounced in the tabloids. Next time I met him he had a Nobel Peace Prize and was President of South Africa: Nelson Mandela. And when I go to Trafalgar Square I always say "If you want the politics of tomorrow come to Trafalgar Square, if you want the politics of today go to the House of Commons." And it is true: the Suffragettes, the Tolpuddle Martyrs, the Irish, campaigns against Franco – all centred in Trafalgar Square and, less often, Hyde Park. It was the politics of the streets against the politics of the Government. And you have to explain that, because people don't realise to make progress you have to be patient and impatient at the same time. Impatient to get it done but realise it does take a bit of time.

Mark Steel: It's always the case that a process that attempts to mobilise people who feel strongly against injustice, even a process that fails dismally on the face of it, is better than nothing. It's like everything in life, isn't it? If a bully tried to take someone's school dinner money away, and people get up and say "Leave him alone" and cause the bully a bit of a kafuffle, he might take the dinner money but he will think twice about it the next day. It's a fairly standard view of how things work. Just for pragmatic reasons they must have thought "Christ, if we bomb Iran we are going to have all this again and its going to be very difficult. Fuck that for a lark".

Salma Yaqoob: By virtue of their self-interest you will not hear this in the mainstream and on the *BBC*: "Because the anti-war movement did X, Y and Z we are not in this position." We have to remind ourselves we are up against some very powerful interests and the last thing they want to admit is that they have been shaken by the anti-war movement. Don't look for validation from the very people you are opposing. But often we do look for that validation though, don't we? I used to be one of those people who thought if the police made a statement it was true and if the *BBC* reported a fact it was gospel. But having been on all the demos and they reduced the number by a factor of ten to 10,000, even though I was there and witnessed there was something like 100,000. The actual anti-war sentiment was minimised at all times and wasn't reflected in mainstream culture. And then when I saw the big gap when it came to the [18 March 2003] vote in the Houses of Parliament, it was a wake up call for me – that I shouldn't expect validation from these people. This is the political reality. I've seen it with my own eyes. So it's a long hard slog and don't expect it to be otherwise. But are we seeing the fruits of all the work? Most definitely.

The global impact of the march

Brigadier Jeff Mason, Commanding Officer, Commando Logistic Regiment, Royal Marines, Operation Telic, Iraq, January – May 2003: You have all the television screens tuned into *News 24* and there was a big wide TV screen in the main gallery while we were in the administrative area in Kuwait. So clearly everybody could see the major protest in the UK and outside the UK too. And a number of papers were vehemently anti-the-war, and the troops were reading them. That really was the only issue. I got them together to talk them through why we were there, and to put aside any doubt and any issue going on: we had a job to do and we were going to *do* it... certainly, in the build-up to the Iraq war, we in the military had never come across such anti-war feeling at home, and it was difficult to get that across to the soldiers, sailors and marines under my command.[30]

Moazzam Begg, Former prisoner, Guantanamo Bay: I was in solitary confinement at the time I learned about the London anti-war march. I had been there for close to two years. The soldier who told me about it was a Vietnam veteran who'd served two tours of duty as a volunteer during that war. And yet, I believe he did so with the desire to give me hope – hope in Britain. And it did. For the first time in close to three years I actually got a sense, a belief, that people in the UK did care; that I hadn't been abandoned. It stood to reason that if they opposed war they must, by definition, oppose one of the nasty by-products of war: Guantanamo.

Haifa Zangana, Iraqi exile living in the UK: It was advertised by the Ba'ath regime on the TV and in the papers. People knew about it. The regime was looking for any event that might stop the war. They saw it as something that might pressure the British and American Governments to delay.

Hani Shukrallah, Egyptian Journalist: On Thursday, day one of the invasion [of Iraq], thousands of protesters collected in Tahrir Square, in Cairo. "It's like Hyde Park," was the common refrain, expressed in exhilarated tones.[31]

Jo Wilding, Peace Activist and Blogger who travelled to Iraq in 2003: The night of 27–28 March [2003] the bombs [in Baghdad] were so immense that I could see the flashes from inside a room with the curtains drawn and my eyes closed... Akael Zuhair was standing in front of his house opposite the mosque. Shrapnel from one of the missiles hit him. He was 20. The doctor said his condition was critical, with shrapnel wounds to his left shoulder, left chest, right forearm and forehead, possibly lodged in the frontal lobe of his brain. There was no brain-scanning equipment. The doctors were waiting for a skull x-ray to show whether the piercing was superficial or deep. There were no intensive care units either: after 12-and-a-half years of sanctions, most hospitals didn't have enough working units, if any at all, many of the parts being embargoed on the pretext that they had dual military and civilian uses... His dad heard the explosion in the street and said the kids came running in to tell him Akael was hit. "Help us," he said, "because we are attacked in homes and streets and markets. We are not something to be squeezed. We are thank to people in all the world, but especially in America and England. More than a million people in England say no to war. There is not a problem between people. There is a problem with governments."[32]

Malalai Joya, former female Afghan MP and human rights activist: Please understand that for us in Afghanistan, seeing that people all over the world are willing to stand publicly in solidarity with us in our hour of need has great moral value. Demonstrations for peace in the West in fact undermine the message of the fundamentalists that the people of North America and Europe are the enemy of the people in Muslim countries. The demonstrations against the Iraq War – on 15 February 2003, when millions of people in dozens of countries joined the largest protest in human history – did not stop the war happening but they showed people in Arab and Muslim countries that there were a great many peace-loving people who opposed Bush's war. This outpouring for peace helped to remind our people of the distinction between the people and the governments of the West. Never underestimate the importance of the message your actions can send both to your own government and to the people of Afghanistan. Peace movements pose a threat to the war-makers, fundamentalists and terrorists.[33]

What else could have been done to stop the war?

Female Muslim anti-war activist: I was really amazed when the war broke out. In France if the Government still goes ahead with something in the face of a mass movement there are riots. I was in Toulouse in 1995 and there was a huge protest against privatisation of public services, and there was people breaking things on the street – things were really happening. And the movement was nowhere near the size of the anti-war movement in this country. I was extremely surprised on 20 March [2003] because I thought there would be riots and people would be much more angry. And it didn't happen. And the Stop the War Coalition called for another demonstration to march from one point to another point. And I thought "No more". I'm not talking about destroying things, but things like sit-ins and derailing the economic system in this country. I was not about to march like a sheep from one place to another after the war had started.

Symon Hill, Christian peace activist: After the demonstration, the Stop the War Coalition continued to prioritise large marches through central London, finishing with rallies characterised by a seemingly endless series of (often rather repetitive) speeches. Many groups have discovered that a wider mixture of campaigning methods can be more effective, combining smaller-scale and local events with nonviolent direct action, media engagement and political lobbying. Large demonstrations have an important role, but the size of the February march regrettably encouraged an over-reliance on them.

Naomi Klein, *Guardian*, 3 March 2003: Civil disobedience... is exactly the sort of thing the anti-war movement needs to inspire in our countries if we are really going to stop, or at least curtail, the pending devastation of Iraq... For some, this escalation of the war against war seems extreme: there should simply be more weekend marches, bigger next time, so big they are impossible to ignore. Of course there should be more marches but it should also be clear by now that there is no protest too big for politicians to ignore.[34]

Gabriel Carlyle: I think it is fair to say, and it was publicly proclaimed by people close to Stop the War like Mark Steel, that the next step was civil disobedience. There was a big call to actually move to civil disobedience. There had been various things that had been billed as civil disobedience, but there hadn't been any training or people going out getting people to a place where they would feel comfortable doing it. There is a whole range of work that, if you are going to build to that, needed to have started a long, long time before

– at least a year in advance, with people fanning out around the country doing workshops. Whether there was an appetite and enthusiasm for that kind of stuff that far in advance, well that's a good question. I'm not somebody who fetishises civil disobedience – I think it is a question of what is the appropriate tactic at a particular time. But I do think there was a window of opportunity after 15 February where the momentum was clear, where had there been that preparatory work maybe civil disobedience could have been effective.

Andrew Burgin, Press Officer, Stop the War Coalition: That's from the small, direct action groups: "Why didn't we take more direct action?" Well the whole thing was ludicrous. There were groups – and I think Voices UK was one of them – who printed leaflets especially for February 15, but they couldn't hand them out because the coaches were backed up down the street. Voices UK had a plan they were going to have a sit-down in the centre of London on that day. That was going to be their contribution to it. But what would it have achieved? The whole of central London was closed! It was a big sit down. You couldn't get anywhere!... The thing about the small direct action movements – and friends of mine are involved in them – is that if you examine the record of Stop the War, if you actually seriously look at the range of activities it has been engaged in, it has been engaged in far more direct action than any of the direct action groups. In 2002 we had a Halloween day of action where we shut down Brighton, Sheffield, Leeds. We had 5,000 people in Whitehall. There was a massive sit-down. The whole thing about "Why didn't they do direct action?", to be honest we've done massive direct actions. We did banner drops, we closed bridges, we closed motorways. There was a school student's movement – schools were closed. My son's school was closed. I found him down by Parliament. Camden School for Girls closed Whitehall, they marched from Camden all the way down the streets, down to Parliament. These were all direct action. The idea that somehow you have to counterpose mass demonstrations with direct action, as if they are somehow completely different, is completely wrong. They are part and parcel of the same campaign. You have to do both.

George Galloway: There is a place for, and in parallel with the Stop the War Coalition, and indeed it happens all the time, at military bases people nonviolently entering the base and people lying in front of the aeroplanes or even violently smashing the instrument panels. Of course I support all that, and these people are heroic people. But theirs is a different path. If we in the Stop the War movement, with the breadth we had, and the affiliation of such a plural cross section of British society, had got involved with that, we would have been making ourselves smaller. And in making ourselves smaller, I believe we would have been making ourselves less effective.

Clare Solomon, University of London Union President 2010–11: It's a difficult one, isn't it? I don't think you would have had two million people on the march if more radical action was proposed... A demonstration of two million people is a direct action. You are directly taking the streets and preventing things from running. Had they posed it as more than that I wouldn't have gone on it, and I know a lot of other people wouldn't have done.

Andrew Murray: Direct action. Which we supported to a considerable extent. But, in my view, there is no way direct action, in a variety of forms, could have reached critical mass to make the Government back down. Indeed, there might have been negative side effects in that some other elements within the coalition against the war might have peeled off if they felt it was getting immersed in too much illegality and so on. I don't necessarily buy into that argument but it was there in any event – there was a tradition of nonviolent direct action within CND. We encouraged all that as much as we could.

Mike Marqusee: I actually agreed with the SWP and the Communist Party that the emphasis should be on mass, legal, non-violent protests. But I also believed there was room for many other kinds of action. The Stop the War Coalition should be an umbrella for these. Particularly, forms of direct action were attractive to young activists who felt an urgency about this that was absolutely correct. I didn't feel they were contradictory in any way. It was ironic to see people in the SWP, who might have been known to advocate direct action in much less urgent and extreme circumstances, suddenly becoming disciplinarians about it. In particular the movement needed a good debate about it. It isn't an easy question. Which tactics do you condone, which do you reject? You can only have an effective debate that leads to the right resolution if all the different options are meaningfully heard. But that was not favoured by the SWP or a number of the other leaders of the Coalition, who actually feared it. They began labelling people who were saying they wanted a different emphasis as divisive. And that really put my fucking back up. I was in the Labour Party for

20 years, and every time we ever said anything was wrong with the Labour leadership, it would be "You're divisive" or "You're letting the Tories in". It is utterly bankrupt. It is Stalinist, completely Stalinist. It amazed me that people who knew better would come up with this. Ironically, my own conclusion was that I probably veered towards the SWP's position, but I respected and recognised at least the partial truth what other people were saying, and I wanted all of us to be sitting and having an adult debate about it, and I wanted all the tactics to be considered on their merits. I knew from my own experience of the Vietnam War movement – when I was not a leader, I was just an ordinary foot soldier as a teenager – that you need many tactics to make a difference. There are some tactics that are appropriate for a group of ten that are not appropriate for groups of 10,000 and 100,000. The anti-Vietnam War movement boasted a wide array of tactics and was famous for its inventiveness. And I thought that instead of encouraging that, we were discouraging it.

Asad Rehman, Stop the War Coalition Steering Committee member in 2003: This is what led to the fracture between the independents and Stop the War Coalition. Before February 15, there had been some people saying "Let's do other things. Lets have a greater menu of possible actions and strategies" – which I supported absolutely. The Stop the War Coalition is not the anti-war movement. The Stop the War Coalition is part of the antiwar movement. Many other groups were and are doing incredible, brilliant work. The people outside the American airbases and the Voices in the Wilderness people. They all needed to be recognised as being in the anti-war movement. I disagreed with the attempt of some people in Stop the War to say we are the anti-war movement, and to claim the umbrella of everything. What Stop the War should have been doing is creating a space that is non-sectarian and allowing people to come together, and recognising that there are lots of strategies and, most importantly, supporting those multiple strategies. Unfortunately within Stop the War the idea there had to be complete agreement, that you couldn't rock the boat, and there couldn't be alternative voices, started to manifest itself.

Andreas Speck, War Resisters International: My problem was that there was a huge mobilisation by Stop the War Coalition but I always felt they were only focussing on mobilising masses for marching from A to B. They didn't look in to "Yes, but what if that doesn't succeed?" I don't think demonstrations alone will succeed. After the 15 February demonstration, a bit more than a month later, the war started and it collapsed pretty quickly. We were trying a bit to focus on saying "Well, demonstrations are important but we need to make a step to non-violent resistance". This wasn't very welcomed by the Stop the War Coalition. So we were involved in trying to mobilise a bit for blockades of military bases... also because we were saying that military bases in this country are used for the war in Iraq. Planes were taking off from [RAF] Fairford to bomb Iraq, so we could effectively shutdown Fairford if we want to. If of the two million people who were in London on 15 February, if only one percent had gone to Fairford to blockade or to enter the base, they wouldn't have been able to use it.

Tom Harris, Smash EDO activist: The 15 February and demonstrations after it ran alongside demonstrations at military bases – primarily RAF Fairford. At these demonstrations there was an attempt, by Sussex Action for Peace actually, to convince the Stop the War Coalition to give a priority to those actions. The Stop the War Coalition wasn't interested in doing that. They weren't interested in people going to RAF Fairford and taking direct action. They wanted people to march docilely through London and listen to Tony Benn. If two million people had descended on RAF Fairford instead of central London we might have actually affected the events. So going to the root of what was happening rather than engaging in this mass lobbying exercise we would have been far more effective in influencing events. The Stop the War Coalition went as far as to organise demonstrations on the same day as demonstrations at RAF Fairford to deliberately undermine it – there was a demonstration at Fairford a few days before the war and there was a demonstration organised in London by the Stop the War Coalition knowing there was a demonstration at Fairford. They saw direct action as irrelevant and even counterproductive to their aims.

Carol Naughton, 'Strictly confidential – for CND Council Members Only', 19 June 2003: Incidents happened that were actively countering the work that CND was doing such as the office of the [Stop the War] Coalition telling callers that the CND event in Whitehall and the Fairford and Menwith demos were all cancelled when in fact all of these were well and truly going ahead. I have personal experience of this as I received the emails and phoned myself to check it out.[35]

Albert Beale, Militant Pacifist: There is an RAF base at Fairford, which is one of the core places where the killing is run from. 4,000 or 5,000 people went there on March 22 [2003]. There was a network of groups involved. There was a group called the Gloucestershire Weapons Inspectors. They had been having a peace camp at Fairford, on and off. And there were groups like Voices in the Wilderness and ARROW, and people around Peace News. It was very much the NVDA [Non-Violent Direct Action] end of the movement. The pacifist end of the movement who are in to direct action. It was direct action people who were into non-violence. It was all kinds... In the end half the police forces in southern England were there. There were more police [there] than there were of us. There were thousands of police there that day. And all the MoD [Ministry of Defence] police from all over the country were inside that base, along with all the armed Americans. There were contingents from just about every police force in the south of England ringing the outside of the base. From their point of view it made sense. It was real. They had to defend their ability to pursue that war. They had to defend the weapons of war against people who were going to nonviolently stop them. If there hadn't been literally thousands of people defending the base then more of those bombs would have been trashed and more of the planes wouldn't have taken off. So it did have an effect. The ultimate effect was a flea bite, but it did have an effect. It showed the strength of feeling; it showed what you can do. And if people had done that every day the authorities wouldn't have been able to cope. The avowed aim of the event was to blockade and try to invade the base – that was the headline aim. Not everybody who was there would have gone in had the fence been cut, but a lot would have. The authorities had to assume that of the thousands of people there half of us would have got into the base had it been physically possible. And it was probably true. So it adds to the cost of waging war. It adds to the financial, logistical, organisational and political cost to the authorities of waging that war, on a genuine level. For them to have to do what they did to maintain the war effort was something they hadn't had to do before. The whole mentality of that showed me that if it had been pursued and built upon and done bigger then war could be impeded... There are some ways in which putting your own body on the line for your beliefs is actually – in some ways – more meaningful. I wouldn't want to sit down in front of a plane if marching worked, but on the other hand there is something that is more meaningful and valid about that style of activity. If we had all got on the runway and sat in front of the planes, we are not stopping them taking off. They could still run us over and take off. It is confronting the pilots of the planes with the reality of what they are doing when they are a mile up in the sky. In a sense it is about bringing the reality of war home to people. To me it is a very valuable form of action on lots of levels. If waving a banner in Trafalgar Square stopped the war, I probably wouldn't risk death under a plane – I'm not stupid!

Tom Harris: I remember the protest at Fairford being far more effective than what happened on 15 February. For instance during one action [23 February 2003] people pulled the gates of the base open. They had hidden rope inside banners and used it to hook over the fence, and then hundreds of people pulled this rope and pulled down the fence of the airbase and then ran into the base. There were mass trespasses on the runway of the base. In the run-up to the war this could be dealt with, but there was a protest that happened two days after the war broke out. If those protests had continued as those planes were taking off to bomb Iraq we might have saved some lives by stopping those planes from taking off.

Mike Podmore, Stop the War Coalition Steering Committee member in 2003: I think a lot of the mistakes were made following that march. Not necessarily with the next one as I think having a march once the war had begun is fine and the numbers were just about acceptable in terms of being a massive march. But I think it was a big mistake to carry on having marches as the primary and sole activity of Stop the War once the war started. The number of people who came out only dwindled. If the two million people marching on February 15 hadn't had an impact on the British Government and Establishment, then a march of 500,000 or 200,000 or 100,000 or 50,000 – why would they care? I think there was a lot of justified criticism of the Stop the War leadership. It's not to say they shouldn't have done all of those things as a continued opportunity for people who would only feel comfortable doing that. However there was a very significant movement – such as the demos outside airbases – where direct action was being taken. I think that was the natural next step, and should have been actively supported by Stop the War, and put out to members as being something Stop the War supports them to do. But Stop the War didn't support that and didn't promote it. You may hear many different reasons for this, but my personal opinion is that the leadership of Stop the War, which is primarily dominated by the SWP, always saw the Stop the War Coalition as a vehicle for themselves to get national recognition and, ultimately, electable. This has been borne out from their move to Respect and George Galloway, and attempting to become electable on a broader platform. They have failed and turned away from that strategy, but I do firmly believe that was the reason direct action was not supported. It would have gotten them heavy criticism from the Establishment, but if you are going to stop the war, especially with an Establishment hell bent on going to war as Tony Blair was, you have to be willing to step up each time. To take it that one step further. I think it was a real shame they missed that opportunity.

Albert Beale: A) they couldn't control it. B) it's not their style of action. There is also a criticism you sometimes get of direct action groups, that direct action is alienating and middle-class and ordinary people can't do it. Ordinary people who have to cook tea for their family. It's too far ahead of what the masses can do. There are various reasons why they didn't support it. But not only did they not support it, they almost tried to undermine it. They wouldn't publicise it, as far as I can remember. Certainly there were a lot of events like that, that didn't make it on to the Stop the War website. That sort of action tends not to.

Tom Harris: I hadn't been an activist prior to 9/11 but what happened in the anti-war movement seemed to have forgotten everything that had happened in the 90s where the British direct action movement had become prominent. Animal Rights campaigns had been successful in targeting companies involved in vivisection. There had been an effective resistance against the Criminal Justice Act. The anti-road building campaign had been successful. Direct Action had been at the centre of the way people were trying to push for social change. And yet from 2001 onwards the anti-war movement seemed to have been steered towards marching from A to B and then listening to people like Tony Benn and George Galloway. Effectively some kind of mass lobbying exercise. It struck me and many other people involved in the anti-war movement in Brighton as a recipe for failure, which it turned out to be... At the time of the anti-war movement there was a campaign against Genetically Modified foods which was phenomenally successful. Its main tactic was the trashing of crops, which hundreds of people were involved in, which really hampered the development of the GM industry in the UK. So the success of that movement, which happened at the same time as the anti-war movement, has to be juxtaposed with the complete failure of the anti-war movement.

Andrew Murray and Lindsey German: The anti-war movement did not stop the war or British participation in it. This tragic fact cannot be avoided. Of course, this failure is in large measure an indication of the longstanding, overriding determination of the British establishment to remain aligned with the US come what may – a cornerstone of British politics for 60 years... The unions remain the biggest and potentially decisive organisations, not merely for mobilising working people, but for converting the protest into the sort of concrete challenge which would have been required to prevent the government waging war.[36]

Bob Crow: We wouldn't have been able to deliver industrial action. No other union would have been able to either. When the war broke out and the students were demonstrating in the streets, there were people from our union involved in that, but it was purely peaceful protest. We were in no position to push for industrial action.

Andrew Murray: Unfortunately the trade union movement, after 20 years of [first] Thatcherism and [then] neo-Thatcherism under New Labour, was in no state to conduct strike action. There was some on the day the war broke out, and a little bit earlier, but all such actions are illegal. It could have led to the bankruptcies of unions who were seen to support it. So there simply wasn't the spirit, even amongst the most militant union leaders and supporters, who took the view that they were quite willing to support any members who took such action and who may have faced sanctions as a result, but they weren't prepared to initiate it. So I think strike action, which we heartily encouraged from Stop the War's point of view, was not going to work.

Billy Hayes, Communication Workers Union General Secretary 2001–present: There was some talk of railway workers in Scotland.[iii] More recently there was a boycott of arms shipments by South African dock workers. But I don't think you can magic these things up. It was an achievement in itself to get the leading trade union leaders speaking on anti-war platforms. And if, to some degree, you get the membership of the labour movement to fall in behind an anti-war position, it is significant in itself. But I don't think

iii "Train drivers yesterday refused to move a freight train carrying ammunition believed to be destined for British forces being deployed in the Gulf. Railway managers cancelled the Ministry of Defence service after the crewmen, described as 'conscientious objectors' by a supporter, said they opposed Tony Blair's threat to attack Iraq." Kevin Maguire, 'Anti-war train drivers refuse to move arms freight', *Guardian*, 9 January 2003, www.guardian.co.uk/uk/2003/jan/09/politics.military [Accessed 3 April 2012].

you can jump from that to calling industrial action. It is not so much [that] it is illegal, the issue was it didn't go as far as that. In my judgement I couldn't see that happening. I think it was more important to speak on platforms and to get your local branches to affiliate to the Stop the War Coalition, to deepen and strengthen it. There is a great danger, in my view, of a paint by numbers approach thinking "We've done that and that, and now we need to talk about a strike". There certainly wasn't any talk of that, not to any serious extent. The main thing about the anti-war movement was that in a strange sort of way it wasn't a topic of conversation. Being against the Falklands War, which I was a bit, it was a controversial thing. The significant thing about the war in Iraq was that it wasn't massively controversial to be against the war.

Milan Rai: I think a whole bunch of things were missing. In the circles I moved in the most common thing said was "What we need is direct action. Why is Stop the War Coalition channelling everybody into demonstrating?" Personally I thought there was a role for both mass demonstrations and civil disobedience. Another thing people said in the circles I moved in was that we needed to go to where the war machine is, and not always be trudging round in London and city centres. To a certain extent that happened, but there could have been more of that. But really I think the key thing that was missing was political rather than organisational. I think the basic choice in the spring of 2003 was either war now or inspections now. That was the choice. There was a majority against the war now. A lot of those people would have been in favour of war later if it could have been established that weapons of mass destruction were there. But at the time we needed to solidify that anti-war majority and what we really needed was a message from the top to the bottom of the anti-war movement of "Give the inspectors the last change they are asking for". I think that would have had 80+ percent support of the population. That wasn't the message that went out in the anti-war movement, because the Stop the War Coalition at that time was not prepared to focus on supporting the inspectors for a variety of reasons. I think part of it was to do with the fact it was a United Nations initiative and there were lots of people in the anti-war movement whose scepticism of the United Nations tips over into an ideological anti-UN position. People are entitled to have whatever view they like of the UN, but at that point I think what we needed was to solidify the vast majority of people in this country around saying "The inspectors are asking for a final round of inspections. It will take a few months. We should be giving them that opportunity. There is nothing to be lost by doing that." That was not the message that went out. There were other things that went wrong politically. One of them was about what was happening in the UN Security Council. I have a feeling that one of the ways the Government got a lot of unhappy Labour MPs back on board was by distortions about what [French President Jacques] Chirac said at that very last moment about that UN Security Council resolution. There were all these Labour MPs getting all this heat back in their constituency Labour parties, who were saying "You said we were going to have a second resolution – we are not going to have a second resolution." And what the Blair Government said was "There is no point in us having a second resolution because Chirac would never give this to us anyway." That's not what Chirac said.[iv] There were two things about that. One is I think there was some political messaging around the Security Council and around France which was incredibly important. Secondly I don't think we did the lobbying of MPs, which was the critical task after February 15. As soon as we knew there was going to be a vote [in the House of Commons] it should have turned into maximum pressure on MPs. That's what happened in Turkey, where the Government made a tactical error by allowing a free vote. They didn't whip it and the MPs came under unbearable pressure. They had a huge demonstration in the capital and they had constituents ringing up MPs in Parliament on the day of the vote. So there was this massive pressure on MPs. And the MPs gave way. And while they had a majority of MPs vote in favour of the US war proposal, they didn't get the majority they needed to make the deal. As far as I am aware we did not have that strategic focus of getting the MPs to obey the will of the majority of people in this country. There were two factors. For the direct action wing there was not any interest in that, and for the more mainstream folk I don't think Stop the War Coalition led the kind of lobbying effort that could have created the nightmare situation. Maybe we could have done it. If not won the vote, then make sure the majority of Labour MPs were against, which would have been a disaster for Blair. So I think there are a bunch of things we got wrong and looking back on it the anti-war movement would have been better off if we had had a diversity of

iv During the debate in the House of Commons on 18 March 2003 Blair said "The French position is that France will vote no, whatever the circumstances." In fact Chirac had said "My position is that, regardless of the circumstances, France will vote 'no' because she considers *this evening* that there are no grounds for waging war in order to achieve the goal we have set ourselves, i.e. to disarm Iraq." (my emphasis added) 'Full text: Tony Blair's speech', *Guardian*, 18 March 2003, www.guardian.co.uk/politics/2003/mar/18/foreignpolicy.iraq1 [Accessed 8 August 2012].

national coalitions – if the Stop the War Coalition had pursued its kind of politics and there had been another coalition that had been willing to back the inspectors 100 percent and willing to do the detailed lobbying work. Both of those are more reformist in a political sense, but those were the only effective things to do politically at that moment. It was to the disadvantage of people in Iraq that we didn't have another national coalition pushing those political messages and organising people to that end. Leaving aside direct action and going to the war machine ideas, I think these were real strategic errors.

Andrew Murray: Could more have been done? In my view, to sum up, given Blair was utterly determined to go ahead with this war, and had a Parliamentary majority, I don't think anything else could have been done that would have made a difference. The only thing in hindsight that could have been tried, and wasn't tried, was the idea of a more permanent presence in central London to escalate the atmosphere around the Parliamentary votes.

Margaret Jones, Peace Campaigner based in Bristol: I still wonder if we weren't all just a little too polite. Two million people shuffled through London to Hyde Park, trampled on the daffodils and went home. What if even a fifth of that number had sat down and refused to move? What if they'd set up a tent city like they did in Ukraine?[v]

v Between November 2004 and January 2005 hundreds of thousands of people occupied the central square in Kiev to protest electoral fraud in the recent Ukrainian presidential election. The protesters succeeded in getting the election results annulled and another election was run under intense scrutiny from domestic and international observers.

The long-term influence of the march: The Muslim community in Britain

Salma Yaqoob: It is my firm belief that when the Stop the War Coalition is finally put into cold storage and historians look back upon its impact, they will note that one of its achievements was also to create the space for a generation of Muslim youth to grow up with greater confidence and pride in their identity and place in British society.[37]

Abjol Miah, Community activist in Tower Hamlets and Respect parliamentary candidate for Bethnal Green and Bow in 2010 general election: There was a change. Let me talk about the positives first. I think it brought a lot of people together. Myself, I had more exposure working with people outside the Muslim and Bangladeshi framework than I had ever before. It was a fantastic experience. And other community people were exposed to other perspectives, and you may not be comfortable with some things, but it was a great opportunity to meet lots of different people. The whole anti-war movement provided an impetus for re-engaging and re-assessing what the future is for ethnic minorities living in the UK. Also there was a sense of bravery. It was a defining moment for me and everyone I knew. As a British Bangladeshi community we are going out there and we are defiant against Tony Blair. My generation are not trapped. We will say what we want to say. This is the beauty of the freedom that we have in this country. You can't have this in other countries, not even in many Muslim countries. So we were very honoured to be able to participate and express ourselves.

Salma Yaqoob: I know that many Muslims felt, after a long time, really proud to be British. They felt this is Britain. The anti-war movement strengthened a positive Muslim identity. Whereas I think if that hadn't happened British Muslims would have felt more isolated and there would have been more negative consequences of that... that people worked together in the way they did has helped to establish new identities. Identity is never fixed. I think we now have a generation who are more confident as Muslims.

Lindsey German: The role of Muslim women in the movement is astonishing. Every time the movement is on an up, there are always lots of Muslim women involved... When people talk about integration of Muslims or any other people who aren't British nationals, or who don't speak the language, I think our movement has done a huge amount to integrate.

Milan Rai: I'm not in a good position to really judge what the effects were of the anti-war mobilisation on British Muslim communities. My impression is that it did have a significant effect in terms of changing the internal dynamics of the communities, but I don't have a detailed knowledge. My guess would be there was something similar to the way that mining communities had something of a social upheaval due to the mobilisation during the [1984/5] Miners' Strike. You had miners' wives becoming political activists, a political force and in some cases becoming the more active partner in a marriage. That shook up the mining communities. And if you look at what just happened with Salma Yaqoob very nearly winning a seat [at the 2010 General Election] – I think that is a reflection of that upheaval.

Salma Yaqoob: There are these stereotypes that all Muslim women are oppressed, suppressed and depressed. And as with any stereotype there are elements of truth in there. There are genuine issues within the community where there are reactionary practices that have to be challenged. I know when I first took the stage in the anti-war movement it was quite a novel thing for the community to see a Muslim woman take a leadership role. Really it was by default because the Muslim men were afraid to come out. So even though there was this perception of all these radical Muslims, in reality they were all scared! The majority of Muslims were too scared to come out and say anything. I was waiting for someone to do it but didn't see it happen, so that's why I came forward. It wasn't to prove a point as a Muslim woman, it's just that I didn't see anybody else do it. And when I did it even people from my own family said to my husband "How can you let your wife do this? You are going to bring shame on the family." It was quite a new thing – not in Islamic history but in the way Islam had been practiced. A patriarchal interpretation has been dominant. It took a long time to win people's respect and trust, because there was a fear about whether I was going to sell them out. Often Muslims who did come out in public were seen as sell-outs because they often supported the Government line and distanced themselves from the community.

Muhktar Dar, Cultural Activist, Birmingham: Salma Yaqoob, who I think will end up in the Labour Party as a careerist politician, has been a positive role model. For a Muslim woman wearing a hijab to be on TV and to be articulate, she is challenging that male chauvinism within our communities that say women can't get involved in politics. She has been a positive role model for young, Muslim women.

Salma Yaqoob: Initially, getting the support from the movement, that they asked me to speak and wanted to hear what I had to say, meant I had to rise up to the challenge. That was really empowering. That opened doors for other Muslim women. There is always that balance where you don't go so far outside what the community's comfort zone is but you also want to influence and lead. For some, even within the community, wearing a hijab means people will say "Oh gosh, she's one of those". But it gave others a lot of hope, because they could think "Hang on, she is still who she is and she is being heard by all these people – Muslims and non-Muslims." That fed in to being more accepted in the community as well. So on the one hand, whilst you are challenging the status quo and establishment, you still need that validation from them to feel accepted and belonging. It's a double-edged sword. So, when they see me on [*BBC*] *Question Time* and I am on a level with these people and being listened to, they get this boost and this pride. And they can see a Muslim woman doing this and they are not compromising their principles and they are not selling-out. So I think it has made it easier for other people to come forward. We've seen more and more Muslim women organising within the anti-war movement. We normalised something that was previously out of the ordinary for the community. In three years up to 2004 we did more in terms of belonging as citizens and in how women are perceived than had been in the last 30 or 40 years. So now you see more women in mosques, on committees etc. The anti-war movement gave Muslim women a visibility and acceptance that they didn't have before. The certain level of power and influence I now have hasn't been given to me by anybody. It was a long, hard slog. First they think you are mad, nutty and isolated. Slowly it becomes more and more mainstream and before you know it you are being cited as a role model! It's not accidental, I think, that people like Shabana Mahmood and Yasmin Qureshi were given safe Labour seats in the last [2010] election. Muslim women were never approached before. But they saw what was going on here in Birmingham and saw that Muslim women were not just accepted but seen as an asset by the community… I think we changed a lot of things. My election as a City Councillor in 2006 was down to Muslim women getting out and voting. It was a revolution. I'm not saying it was just me, because I know what the barriers are… It was about women coming out for the first time and canvassing, going door knocking. This hadn't been seen before. We had young Muslim women who had never been involved in election politics feeling empowered and fighting for something they believe in.

Fareena Alam, *Observer*, 23 March 2003: There is a new buzz among British Muslims – there are few calls for violent retaliation or slogans of hatred, even from groups of young men. Instead the anger is being channelled into the broader movement of Britons who oppose this war, and which we British Muslims have come to respect and trust. We are re-engaging, mobilising and, by the looks of it, being thoroughly British… the anti-war movement has done more for integration and assimilation of ethnic and religious minorities than any government funded community 'cohesion' programme… Muslims, who have long been isolating themselves at the margins, are now part of the mainstream.[38]

Clare Solomon: After the demonstration, living in a community in Kings Cross [in London] with a high percentage of Muslims, the march had really positive effects on the community. Muslims do feel under attack and continue to feel under attack and it definitely had a positive impact on my [Muslim] husband's family and friends – knowing that other people in the country do want to defend Muslims and are not racist.

George Galloway: The demonstration itself was fantastically beneficial to community relations. There will never be a day when such a kaleidoscope of races and cultures and religions and people of all different class backgrounds will come together in a common cause. It was tremendously important to Muslims in Britain to see that there were so many non-Muslim people who were, as it were, out to defend them, and defend a Muslim country. It was fantastically important for the Left that so many Muslims were on that march because in places like France or Germany there is no connection at all between the Left and the Muslims. No relationship at all. In fact, in France the Left is widely perceived by Muslims to be hostile to them from the standpoint of this kind of ultra-secularism. It was very important for both Muslims and non-Muslims that the march was so big and so plural.

Ken Livingstone, Mayor of London 2000–8: It brought the bulk of the Muslim community into mainstream political activity for the first time. It galvanised them. They went on the march, and then they either voted against Labour or abstained in massive numbers, shown by the defeat of [the incumbent, pro-war Labour MP] Oona King. Very big swings in Muslim areas. Jack Straw had to really bust a gut to get re-elected. He was very worried at the time. It helped forge links between Muslims and people on The Left, which most probably wouldn't have come about otherwise.

Yasmin Khan: There were also many less obvious but very significant impacts of February 15 and the anti-war movement. This includes things like the politicisation of the Muslim community and their linking up with more traditional UK social movements. In certain places, like east London and Birmingham, this even led to them getting more of a formal political voice through Respect. Whatever you think of personalities like Gorgeous George [Galloway] you can't ignore the fact that a section of society, who previously did not have a voice, organised and voted out a pro-war MP.

Abjol Miah: Because Tower Hamlets [in east London] was the strongest anti-war movement branch, Respect got its stronghold here. We managed to say goodbye to Oona King... Labour thought they had such control over our elders and our projects' funding that they thought people would protest but nothing else would happen. They didn't think there would be a political comeback. Well my, and others, intentions were a little bit different. I thought "You've killed over half a million innocent Iraqis, and you've got to pay the consequences." I was instrumental in bringing George [Galloway] into Tower Hamlets. And we used the same knowledge and understanding we used in the anti-war movement build-up in order to galvanise the political support for George. We had to entice other groups in the community by showing them it was in their interest to elect George. Because if George comes in to Tower Hamlets they might get a Bangladeshi MP in the future. So there were incentives thrown in. And I would say 60–70 percent of the Labour manpower was also supporting George at that time. Basically there was a community understanding that George was a fantastic tool to get a few birds with one stone: We would get rid of the pro-war Oona King, we would get an opportunity to get the first British Banglasdeshi member of parliament, and we would get a labour-orientated Bangladeshi in. That energy was pulled together and Oona King was ousted.

Salma Yaqoob: I think we were the first Muslims that people on the Left who would consider themselves supporters of multiculturalism interacted with. So I would say we were not only influenced – and I would say I was influenced – but we also contributed something as well. And this would not have happened without the struggle of the anti-war movement.

Shahed Saleem, Just Peace activist: It's a question mark whether it would have happened anyway, but I think it has opened up the insularity of the Muslim community. To a degree – I think it is still a fairly insular community. Nowadays you have lots of Muslim groups working in a much more diverse way. The idea of interface has grown within Muslim community organisations. It may have happened anyway, but it has certainly been accelerated by the anti-war movement. Also, I think it broke down the idea of the non-Muslim community being a homogenous entity.

In the outside world, as it were, you will find people with a great variety of opinion, beliefs and positions. So you can find people who share your view. It is not 'us' against 'them'. So I think that is very positive.

Anas Altikriti: From a personal perspective, this was exactly the kind of thing I had started campaigning for in the Muslim community 15 years before. It was exactly what I had wanted – for Muslims not to feel Islam was a burden and something they had to relinquish in order to become part of society, but to celebrate it and share with others. It was everything I was taught by my father that Islam was about – about people coming together, agreeing to disagree on various issues, but realising there are some very, very important values and notions and objectives that must be upheld, despite the differences. That manifested itself on that day.

Jenny Pickerill, Co-author of the book *Anti-war activism. New media and protest in the information age*: I do not agree that the relationship between Stop the War Coalition and Muslim Groups such as MAB were wholly positive. There is a superficiality to this view that assumes that Muslim groups were wholly represented by a few token Muslim activists being involved with STWC and that the subsumption of anti-war Muslim activists views under one coalition banner was productive and positive for all involved. Often the interactions were tenuous, transient and fraught with suspicion that groups were more interested in gaining political advantage than necessarily understanding and supporting Muslim concerns. Beyond the temporary interactions of marches, or jointly held meetings, conversations were often not continued. Many non-Muslim anti-war activists had few direct links to Muslims (those that did appear to be the exception), and spoke of their frustration that coalitions had not been built, dialogue had not continued and mutual understanding had not been fostered. In general, interaction between Muslim and non-Muslim anti-war activists has been partial, superficial, at times tokenistic and overall rather temporary.

Ruhul Tarafder: I support the anti-war movement and don't want to be critical because people's objectives were the same, but there were certain things I felt a little bit unhappy about. I was on the [Stop the War Coalition Steering] Committee. They wanted a few token Muslims on the Committee to kind of rubber stamp and agree with everything that was set by the SWP and not to have critical input and not to empower Muslims in terms of the movement. That was something that I felt was problematic.

Mike Marqusee: After February 15, some people in the Coalition seemed to decide that there were certain recognised and exclusive representatives of the "Muslim community". In a way this mirrored, in a positive sense, the pejorative stereotypes of Muslims in the UK. So they assigned a positive value to it, but they still saw it as a homogeneous community. From the beginning I raised this in discussions and so did others. You must speak to Asad Rehman. He played a big role in both [the September 2002 and February 2003] demos. He and I always agreed that the MAB was a welcome constituent in the anti-war coalition for sure – I had no problem working with any MAB people. I enjoyed it. We worked together well – but I didn't think it was for the Coalition, or anybody else, to give them or any other similar organisation an exclusive franchise. I don't think the Muslim community can be represented that way, just like any other community. It is a mistake to see these things as homogeneous, especially the Muslim community where people come from very different countries and different levels of political interest and so forth… I was always keen that we didn't only have Muslims or Asian speakers who were devoutly religious. I was happy to have those voices, but we also needed secular people of Pakistani, Indian and Bangladeshi descent. We particularly needed Black speakers, who represented a Left and anti-imperialist tradition, as well as coming from a particular brand of Islamic discourse. There was an incorrect assessment on the part of some of the leaders of the Coalition that you couldn't do both. I think they were profoundly wrong about that. I think we should have been doing both and needed to do both. Sometimes we did and sometimes we didn't. Particularly after February 15th, because of the huge success of the demo, I felt many on the leaders were turning the particular coalition we put together into a rigid paradigm, with a theory behind it, which to be honest was invented after the fact.

Asad Rehman: From the Black and Muslim perspective, for short-term gain people had defined that the only people to speak from a Muslim perspective were the religious Muslims. Many of us were saying "We are progressives. We are in the religious space, but we don't define ourselves purely in a religious framework. You are also playing this dangerous game of saying the Muslim community is homogeneous, and that people speak for it. No, there are multiple voices and the anti-war movement needs to represent that." And that was one of the many criticisms people made of the SWP: SWP speaker, religious Muslim speaker, MP – the platform it has for every public meeting around the country.

Muhktar Dar: What happened was the Socialist Workers Party isolated the progressive, secular forces in the Muslim community and strengthened the more religious organisations. We had no problem working with people who were religious. But in doing so they [the SWP] strengthened communalism. In Birmingham we had the potential to build a massive, grassroots, diverse Stop the War movement, but by focussing and concentrating on and electing people who were religious it made it look like this struggle was only a struggle for Muslims. It communalised it, so Afro-Caribbean's thought "It's nothing to do with us, it's for Muslims"... there wasn't a large mobilisation of Indians, or Afro-Caribbeans – if you look at the big demonstration there were hardly any Afro-Caribbeans involved – and also hardly any working-class white people, except for some activists and students. Those were the challenges that we faced... How do we engage Afro-Caribbeans so it goes back into their community. In Birmingham the different communities are situated in different parts of the city. The big public meetings took place predominantly in the Muslim communities. Also, as Pakistanis we don't just see ourselves as religious – we have different identities. But increasingly the only way we were seen by progressive, white socialists was through a religious prism. My sister was on one of Birmingham Stop the War Coalition's committees and she challenged this, saying "Excuse me, don't see me as a Muslim; see me as myself, as a Pakistani, as a Black person, as a woman – not purely as a Muslim". That also led to much wider mistakes in society. For example, the arts council I was part of organised a conference in Oldham and they put a person from the Muslim Association of Britain on the platform. In doing so you had someone on the platform saying "This is haram", "This is permissible and this isn't permissible in arts", "You can't have figurative art because it's infidel and heathen". I felt that was a big mistake. So on the one hand you had Islamophobia and on the other hand you began to have Islamomania. Anything Muslim suddenly became flavour of the month. Funding began to be given out on the basis of religion.

Is there any connection between the march and wider anti-war movement and terrorist attacks like 7/7?

Milan Rai: Watching atrocity videos from Chechnya, Palestine and Iraq, however distasteful, was an engagement with reality. Part of their [the four London suicide bombers on 7 July 2005] reason for turning to jihadism may well have been despair at nonviolent attempts to alter this reality. A massive nonviolent movement failed to prevent the Iraq war, and failed to prevent the re-election of the men who had led Britain and the US to war. These young men may also have felt there was no nonviolent movement around them that felt the same anger at the abuses being inflicted on the global Muslim family. They had no movement around them that they saw presenting a convincing picture of how these abuses could be stopped by nonviolent means.[39]

Hussain Osman, one of the failed 21 July 2005 London suicide bombers: I am against war. I've marched in peace rallies and nobody listened to me.[40]

Asad Rehman: Listen to [7/7 suicide bomber] Saddiq Khan's video. He says it very clearly. If you listen to some of the so-called terror suspects, if you look at their background they all say "I went to the anti-war demonstrations, I went to the anti-war meetings, and nothing happened." What the radical Islamists were able to do was say "See these Muslims from the Left, they've said to us we should engage in the political process, lobby our MP, go to public meetings, march on the demonstrations. That's how you make change in a democratic society. But it hasn't worked has it? That path doesn't deliver for us". But it holds weight. For a number of people it's very appealing. There is a powerful narrative that goes along with that, which is "The only thing the government will ever care about is when it suffers the same pain as our people are suffering. Blowing them up will do more to shift them than anything else." People argue the Irish struggle showed that if you hurt them long enough British people will say "Fuck'em. Let's get out". Lebanon showed that. The body bag theory: Send enough body bags home and you can change public opinion. From Madrid they drew the conclusion, wrongly in my opinion, that if you bomb them you can shift public opinion.

Anas Altikriti: One of the things I use in my methods to bring young Muslims away from extremism is to tell them working with society – whether it be politics, the media, social work – it works. It reaps benefits and you get the fruits you want. If you want to go out and kill people, kill yourself, what do you win? You gain further hatred, and you leave behind a legacy of hate, a legacy of corruption. It doesn't work. Violence doesn't work. We live in a society where you can use channels, and they're not perfect but you must use them. That's my message. And unfortunately time and time again, and once again to personalise this, I have been stabbed in the back by governments, by the media and by the so-called intellectuals, because I have been proven wrong. Democracy, politics, engagement – don't work. That's the message the hatemongers want to spread. What the [Islamic extremists] Abu Hamzas and the Anjem Choudarys of this world say when they argue with me is "You can shake the hand of the infidels until the cows come home. Nothing will happen. You will be their servant, and you will do as they wish. You will be no one." That is what they say. I'm trying to disprove them. Now you tell me, who has won the argument? They have won the argument! Unfortunately when you tell this to people who are in office, they fail to understand because they do not want to discuss this link between internal and external policies and security on our streets. It is a link they are too wary of going into. But unfortunately it is there. I have been approached by people who were working with us as organisers for the 15 February march who now turn to me and say "I'm not interested anymore". I hope they have gone in to business, or to do their own stuff, and not something else, but I can't really tell. And it's not just from the Muslim side, it's throughout society. Every single person who was there avidly campaigning against the war, saw what I saw, felt what I felt, came away thinking this has worked for nothing. We have radicalised people way beyond the Muslim community. We have an entire society that has become on the verge of emotional implosion because of the failures of politics and government.

Gabriel Carlyle: I don't recall the exact language in their martyrdom video, but it was fairly explicit. It is not so much the failure of the anti-war movement, but what actually happened.

***BBC News*, 20 July 2010:** The invasion of Iraq "substantially" increased the terrorist threat to the UK, the former head of M15 has said. Giving evidence to the Iraq inquiry, Baroness Manningham-Buller said the action had radicalised "a few among a generation". As a result, she said she was not "surprised" that UK nationals were involved in the 7/7 bombings in London.

Gabriel Carlyle: As someone who isn't a Muslim and has no religious convictions and doesn't have a direct personal contact with religious things, I have been phenomenally angry about this stuff. To the point that if I didn't have my particular brand of politics, I can entirely understand somebody resorting to political violence through sheer rage. I don't find that difficult to understand. I find it very easy to empathise with. I come from somewhere very different politically, that helps insulate me against going down the path of political violence, but I can totally understand people who do.

Mike Marqusee: It is definitely true that the more you reject a community's legal, lawful and nonviolent expressions and aspirations the more some of them are going to turn to illegal and violent responses. That was as true in the American Civil Rights movement as it is now. You can't draw a direct causal link – there have been radical, violent

Islamist groups in very small numbers here for many years. And they continue to be small numbers. I would say the anti-war movement as a whole did more to deter young Muslims from embracing what the newspapers call "radical extremism" than the Government has. We were saying this is the way forward, this is how you achieve justice – through mass action, through democratic action. That you are not alone. That this isn't a Muslim vs. non-Muslim issue. It's right and wrong. It cuts across humanity and decency and justice, which is nothing to do with your ethnic background. To the extent we showed that, it was really beautiful and hugely important, although immeasurable.

Milan Rai: I think the February 15 demonstration was one of the most effective anti-terrorist actions of the last ten years. It was not intended in that way at all, but it convinced a whole bunch of people that Muslim concerns and Muslims as people in the Middle East were of value to large numbers of people in the West.

Hadiya Masieh, former Hizb ut-Tahrir activist: I can only speak from the perspective of being in a small group like HT [Hizb ut-Tahrir]. Deep down it was almost a relief to see people coming out [for the march]. Personally, for ten years it seemed that no one cared, everyone was turning a blind eye to what was going on. In Chechnya and around the world atrocities were being perpetrated and no one cared. You think "They don't care because they hate Islam, they hate Muslims, they demonise Islam and that's why they don't care." That's your mind set. And then you see a million people who obviously feel the war is a problem and it kind of destroys the argument in a way. If no one cares, why are they out there, then? In that sense it [the march] did overthrow some of the arguments of HT – that they [the non-Muslim population] hate Muslims, that they demonise Islam. If so, then why is everyone out there?

Milan Rai: I think it helped to counteract, in a small way, the massive political blow that was dealt by the invasion. And if you want to stop people trying to blow up civilians on the tube I think things like the February 15 demonstration are one of the most effective ways of doing that. But it has to be at a higher level so those people who have those concerns actually have an effect, that it actually can protect Iraq or Iran. So if you really want to have an effect you have to stop some of this stuff happening. But nevertheless I think it had a significant impact, and one that shouldn't be discounted.

Moazzam Begg: The Stop the War movement has become a buffer between people who may want to carry out acts of violence on innocent Westerners, and the government itself that does carry out acts of violence against people in the Middle East. I had a conversation with the only self-described member of Al-Qaida I've met, in Guantanamo. He said that people in the West are not innocent because they vote in their leaders and therefore must share part of the blame. I explained that most people vote on domestic issues like the health service and roads. I said you'll probably find a great number of them don't support the war, but when you strike you don't discriminate. Then he started thinking about it a little bit. The Stop the War movement is a buffer which helps prevent terrorism in a way that the government would never conceive; when they see people demonstrating against the war it helps to pacify some of the radical elements who would otherwise have said, "They're all the same – go and bomb the whole lot of them."[41]

Mark Steel: There is no doubt in my mind that the jihadist, Islamic wing of Islam was put completely on the defensive by the fact the vast majority of Muslims wanted to side with non-Muslims in opposing the war. If you were an Islamist... Islam will rule everything and all that, then you clearly would have been put on the defensive. For example, down in Croydon 150 people from the local mosque all came to a meeting at the Labour Club organised by the Left. This did happen. I remember watching two or three Muslims come down and yell at all the other Muslims: "What are you doing with these people, they are not Muslim?", and everyone else was like "Fuck off – they are organising an anti-war meeting". Why would they want to be like them, bumbling around like the blokes in [the 2010 film] Four Lions? I think this dynamic was played out all over the country.

Abjol Miah: Some people say the anti-war movement radicalised Muslims politically. But if it wasn't for the anti-war movement I think the Muslim youth would have been radicalised physically more. I don't know if you know about the history of the [1990s] Bosnian conflict? Before 9/11 the whole political reality for Muslims in the UK was totally different. To give one example, at the time of the Bosnian War it was normal and accepted that if anyone could go over and defend the Muslim community they would. It was normal. The Christians went over to defend the Serbian community. At that time international law didn't define who is a military combatant and who is not. It was only after

9/11 that things started changing. So many people, Muslims from the UK, went and participated in the frontline in Bosnia. The Jihadi type of philosophy was accepted. What the anti-war movement did was show people that wasn't the only option. That there are other ways people could exercise their rights. So if you've got a grievance then politically you can take a stance and join a coalition with other people – be part of a collective force. That option was very important. I don't think the anti-war movement consciously realised that they did this but from my perspective it was a positive contribution. Without the anti-war movement you could have had more people physically radicalised than ever before.

Mark Steel: As the movement went down over the next few years Muslim anger certainly increased. People want to feel they are doing something. If you feel you are organising a mass anti-war meeting you feel you are doing something effective. But once the marches decline and the movement has gone down, that's when angry people are much more likely to say "That's a waste of time. Another bloody march. Another lot of placards. I know what we could do that would be effective – blow something up." I think it's fairly obvious that that was the case. Historically, it has always been the case when movements die down. When the movement of '68 started to go in to decline, young dynamic people who were still angry about the issues started to form the Red Brigades,[vi] the Baader-Meinhof Gang[vii] and all that sort of thing. Who knows? I don't know what would have

vi The Red Brigades were an Italian Marxist-Leninist terrorist group active in the 1970s and 1980s.

vii The Baader-Meinof Gang, or Red Army Faction, was a German Marxist-Leninist terrorist group active from the 1970s–1990s.

happened. Maybe those blokes from Leeds would have strapped explosives to themselves and gone on the underground anyway. But that was four years later and I think there was no doubt that the growth of that crazy, Islamist terrorist movement was curtailed in this country by the size of the anti-war movement.

The long-term influence of the march: The environmental direct action movement

Caroline Lucas: I think the march probably made people think more creatively about how they do peaceful protest. Marches still have a role, but it has become so easy for the police to contain marches, for the media to ignore them, for their political impact to be minimised… I think that is one of the things that has given birth to much more creative ways of demonstrating, like Climate Rush or Plane Stupid – the whole sense of playing with the ideas of protest and how to surprise people.

Joss Garman, Founder member, Plane Stupid: We're the Iraq generation. You'd be hard pressed to find somebody involved in the climate direct action movement who wasn't influenced in their politics and their choice of tactics by the whole Iraq debacle. Almost every activist you meet in any of the groups like Plane Stupid and the Climate Camp were all part of the anti-war movement.

Richard George, Founder member, Plane Stupid: It's difficult to overestimate the failure of the mass march on my activism. It brought about a genuinely life-changing revelation that politicians will not listen to public opinion until it is forced upon them in an unavoidable manner. Further, it underlined the problems of disparate-but-mass movements; the focus is always on forming this consensus which invariably means defusing any radicalism so that everyone can sign up. But what's the point of getting mass support if what you're asking for is trite or ineffectual?

Joss Garman: Certainly 2003 and the outbreak of the Iraq war was probably the defining moment of my political awakening as it was for my whole generation. That time I'll not forget, as it was instrumental in shaping the way I think about politics.

Tamsin Omond, Founder member, Climate Rush: It was the first demonstration I went on. And I think it was the first demonstration for a lot of people – and potentially the last! I was there with a group of friends from boarding school… We snuck out and it seemed quite naughty. I remember it being really exciting and empowering and very hopeful – youthful and vibrant. More people than I have ever been in a crowd with. Just very exciting. Then there was the declaration of war. I've had this conversation so many times with so many people – about how they went on that march and it made them feel there was no role for protest, that marching didn't work. That is why people, of my generation especially, are turning to direct action and saying if two million people marching doesn't have an impact then we need to start doing things that will have an impact.

Joss Garman: It made me wake up to the level of disconnect between the political establishment and everybody else – and how little power we have even in huge numbers in terms of influencing our government. The weakness of Labour backbenchers, and supposedly progressive MPs, in failing to stand up to the Party's leadership has definitely affected my politics and increased by scepticism about party politics and the entire British political process. The events of that time also strengthened my support for direct action as a tactic of activism, because I still think a greater scale of direct action could have potentially stopped British involvement in the war, and in retrospect I think the anti-war movement was poorly led, in that it could have been more effective and more imaginative had it not relied pretty much solely on A to B marches and speeches from Tony Benn.

Richard George: My frustration with how 15 February turned out led directly to my falling in with people who took direct action... There were hundreds of people out there, all frustrated, all eager for change... We were so angry, partly because we felt lied to by Government, but also because we felt betrayed by the organisations which had stepped up to mobilise. There was such a sense that we either did what they wanted – mass, pointless marches followed by even larger marches – or we did nothing at all... Out of this depression emerged a cohesive network of direct activists. When we started Plane Stupid we were coming out of this morass where we knew what didn't work – mass demos – but also that, to be effective, action needs to have a focus. There was no point, we realised, in doing one-off actions. The companies would take it in their stride, calmly ignoring you, and the media weren't interested because you weren't a recognisable group. So when we brought Plane Stupid together, we were really explicit that we wanted to pick one target and stick with it for the duration. We also wanted to build up relationships with the media, which benefited us at least as much as them.

Tamsin Omond: In terms of PR and amplifying our message, and getting photos in the next day's newspapers – you can achieve that way more often by doing clever, creative actions. If those two million people had turned to direct action then there wouldn't have been a war.

Joss Garman: I think we're a generation who are pretty cynical and who won't take political action unless we're pretty sure it will be effective. I think we have to be far more sophisticated, creative and targeted to capture attention... for our generation we face a series of crises that will directly impact upon us – the economic crash and the debt we'll be paying off for the rest of our lives through our taxes, the ecological crash that is beginning to happen now, the unemployment and housing crises, the health crises – it's difficult to see how young people will be able to continue as usual without ultimately waking up and being extremely angry and/or scared.

Richard George: If nothing else, the failure of the anti-war movement showed us that it is not enough to be right; you have to be right and hit them where it hurts. The million plus people on the streets had right on their side, but the way they expressed it was always doomed to fail, because it caused no pain to those making the decision to go to war.

The long-term influence of the march: The 2010/11 student protests, UK Uncut and Occupy London

Salma Yaqoob: The period we are in now [the interview took place on 14 December 2010], reminds me a little of the start of the anti-war movement... The politicians are doing the same thing again. "We are being sensible, we are doing the morally right thing, there is no choice, there is no alternative and you guys are pie in the sky and naïve because the money just isn't there." And we are saying "Hang on, that's a load of rubbish. What you are doing is ideological and politically driven." This is the biggest question for the next decade. And in the same way the anti-war movement had to go against the mainstream press and find a space, find a voice for what we thought was obvious, humanitarian and right, is what people are having to do in the anti-cuts movement now. It is the most vulnerable in society who will pay a price for what the irresponsible financial elite has done. And their analysis is a lie today, just like it was in 2003: "We've got no choice because Saddam Hussein is going to blow us up in 45 minutes." It's a total distraction. And they know it. And they have a compliant press, just like they did in 2003. It's the same people who were the cheerleaders of the war, surprise, surprise, who are now the cheerleaders of the cuts. The Murdochs of this world, the multinationals. It's the same interests at play. There is a political consistency there.

Clive Bloom, Professor Emeritus, Middlesex University: I think the march revitalised middle-class activism... And I think that radicalism now is very evident in the student riots and the student protests of 2010/11.

Clare Solomon: I was brought up in a military home. My Dad was in the military police. I went to military schools and I was interested in the army myself and perhaps in joining one of the forces. I was also interested in joining the police at one point because my Dad was a Police Officer. When I went on the big demo I was thirty and I had never been involved in anything political at all before. In fact you could say I came from the opposite side of the political spectrum. I used to vote Liberal Democrats perhaps, before the war. I was pro-business. I was pro-capitalism. I used to have my own business – a number of restaurants in the Russell Square area, one in Russell Square and one in Kings Cross. It was in my café I was introduced to the Stop the War Coalition. The Camden Stop the War Coalition group used to have their planning meetings in my café in Kings Cross, and I used to vaguely listen in on the meetings as I was serving them food and tea and coffee and became interested in what they were saying... So when Camden Stop the War Coalition had these meetings it resonated with me and I decided to go on the demonstration... A lot of the school children that left school on the day [the Iraq] war broke out are now seven years older and at university and are still anti-war and definitely they have been involved in the current wave of [student] protests and occupations we have seen in the last couple of months over the education proposals [the interview took place on 9 February 2011].

Salma Yaqoob: The students will have been on the anti-war marches or had family who went on the marches. Maybe some of them will think they have to be a bit more in your face because they ignored the marches. But in a way

I think it's about them being affected directly. The anti-war marches were marching for other people. So there was anger but it wasn't as personal. And also there was an acute awareness that any violent incident would be used against the movement. Because terrorism was such an issue people were hyper, hyper sensitive as organizers that we could not allow violence. It was a different dynamic. We were under a huge amount of pressure to make sure it was not only peaceful but seen to be peaceful. But with the student issue, almost because their citizenship is not in question, it's a different pressure. It's like with a family – if you have an argument you can say more things because it's family. But with other people you tend to have more restraint. I think because the student's sense of belonging in this country is not under question they can go further.

Clive Bloom: I don't think anybody would say "Oh yes that's definitely the case", but I think the march can certainly be noted as a starting point for that type of protest. I think the students probably wouldn't have been on the streets if we hadn't had Tony Blair and that business beforehand. I think they would have been more acquiescent. So I think the defeat produced the protests today.

Tim Gee, author of *Counter Power: Making change happen*: I think it was a profound and important learning experience for a lot of people, and especially for my generation. We were just coming into politics and our first experience was of a Government lying to a country in order to kill first 3,000 people [in Afghanistan], and what has turned out to be 100,000 people [in Iraq] by some estimates. The idea that governments would do that for any reason, but especially in pursuit of selfish economic oil interests, I think created a great sense of distrust in politicians.

Tony Smith, UK Uncut: I guess if I was to give my biography I'd start by saying I was at a secondary school just up the road from here [the interview took place in Kentish Town, London], Acland Burghley School. At the sixth form there. That's where I was in 2003. I'm 24 now. I was 17/18 at that time. The anti-war movement in general, and that march being the pinnacle of it, played a big role in my political education. It was at a time in life when I was starting to engage more fully with those issues, starting to think about the world around me… I was in a group of friends who started it [UK Uncut] as a direct response to the Coalition Government's planned spending cuts. So on the day that the Comprehensive Spending Review [20 October 2010] was announced by George Osborne there was a march organised to Downing Street. I think it was organised by a Camden Branch of the NUT and Unite or something like that. A trade union march. And we marched to Downing Street and stood outside Downing Street shouting a bit. It was really fantastic that people were doing something but I came away from that feeling quite disempowered. I went to the pub afterwards with a group of friends and we spoke about how the political landscape in this country has changed. The next five years would be characterised by this assault on the welfare state by the government. We would be losing lots of services. It was a very ideological assault. And we were laughing about whether we were going to spend the next five years of our lives going on a march every month, listening to Tony Benn speak and then going to the pub and then going home and feeling depressed – often talking about, and referring back to, our experiences of the marches organised by Stop the War Coalition. From there we started to think about how things could be done different. We realised that nobody else was really organising at that moment. So there was a need to get this battle started early. We knew the trade unions were talking about organising a big action for March of the following year [2011], but that was months down the line. We thought we needed to do something now. And we talked about bringing in the tactics we had learnt in things like Climate Camp, and bringing them into the political mainstream... Around that time an article had been written by Johann Hari in the *Independent* and he cited the fact Vodafone had avoided £6 billion worth of tax. This fitted really nicely, or you could say horribly, with the £7 billion which the Government were planning to cut from the welfare bill.

Sam Baker, UK Uncut, *Guardian*, 1 November 2010: On Wednesday morning, after a few days' planning, I met a few friends and 60-odd strangers outside the Ritz hotel in London, listened to a quick briefing and then made the short walk up to Oxford Street where together we occupied and shut down Vodafone's flagship store... the 65 protesters who gathered on Wednesday did not know each other, did not belong to the same organisation and had not had a planning meeting. We called the action after a conversation in a pub, a few speculative emails and a decision to issue a mysterious call-out on twitter... the next day, three Vodafone stores were forced to close in Leeds. And then on Saturday – just three days after the first action – Vodafone stores were shut down for the day in Edinburgh, Glasgow,

Leicester, Portsmouth, Hastings, Brixton, Worthing, Brighton, Bristol, Birmingham, York, Liverpool, Manchester and Oxford, along with another five in central London.[42]

David Wearing, Co-Editor, *New Left Project*: The struggle seems to be waged more as a guerrilla war. Rather than having the big set piece marches like we did during the Stop the War movement, we've now got disruptive tactics like student occupations, the occupation of shops on the high street for companies that aren't paying their taxes properly. It seems to be people are being a bit more intelligent about how to disrupt the machinations of power and get their message on the political agenda.[43]

Ellie Mae O'Hagan, UK Uncut: I do think that is a huge difference and I would probably say that was intentional. When UK Uncut formed, one of the first statements given to the press was that we can't simply march to Whitehall and hear Tony Benn speak this time. Don't get me wrong, I love Tony Benn, I think he is amazing, but I think a lot of people felt disillusioned by that form of protest.[44]

Sam Baker: The fight against the cuts will be the fight of our generation. And it is a fight that is winnable as long as we're willing to get creative tactically. The anti-cuts movement is still in its infancy. The [SWP-influenced anti-cuts group] Coalition of Resistance hasn't even had its first meeting yet, but already we worry that the movement is beginning to resemble the anti-war campaigns of the early 2000s. Characterised by large, unwieldy, centralised organisations, the anti-war movement became complacent, overly reliant on rallies and petitions. We can't spend the next five years marching on Whitehall to hear Tony Benn speak – it's uninspiring, disempowering and largely ineffective. Tools such as Twitter, Facebook and blogs ignite the potential of bypassing these hierarchies and mass rallies in favour of a more decentralised, democratised, spontaneous model of protest. In these ways, this model most resembles the UK's climate movement – especially groups such as Climate Camp and Plane Stupid, which have consistently proven themselves to be the most creative and confrontational of leftwing activist organisations.[45]

Tony Smith: These were tactics we brought from the environmental movement. The idea of direct action as a protest philosophy is, rather than demonstrating and showing your displeasure at something – showing your anger at something – you are directly doing something about it. The best examples are taken from the environmental movement. So groups opposed to there being a third runway at Heathrow went and camped on the site of where the runway would be built. So they were physically putting themselves in the way of that happening. Similarly trying to occupy or shutdown power stations. The concept is that you are directly stopping something from happening, you are not lobbying the Government. You are directly trying to do something. That's what we tried to do with our early actions against Vodafone. We had this message that if the Government weren't going to make them pay then we were. They owed this money to the public purse but were refusing to pay it. We weren't going to let them get away with it. We called this campaign "The Big Society Revenue and Customs." If the tax people aren't going to chase them then we are. We started shutting down their shops on that basis. So it's different from marching, in the sense that when you go on a march you are showing your collective strength and you are showing your displeasure at something. As opposed to direct action, where you are actually trying to stop it yourselves.

***Guardian*, 2 April 2011:** They dressed in black, masked their faces and flew red and black flags as if they were a revolutionary army, but anarchists who smashed up shops, banks and hotels during last Saturday's [26 March 2011] anti-cuts protests in London have dismissed government allegations they are "mindless thugs"... Unmasked and talking to the Guardian... All of them said the failure of the peaceful anti-Iraq war march to overturn government policy was formative in their decision to turn to violence.[46]

Tony Smith: I think it is tempting to look at protest in very black and white terms: we set out to stop the war, we didn't stop the war and therefore we failed. But I think there are many more immeasurable things that came out of it. Part of it is movement building. A lot of the people have gone on to other things such as UK Uncut, the Occupy movement.

Naomi Colvin, Supporter of Occupy London: Occupy London came together [on 15 October 2011] for many reasons, not least in reaction to the financial crisis, but immediately in response to what was going on with Occupy Wall Street in New York, in solidarity with them. It's part of the grassroots, democratic movement which started in Tunisia and Egypt at the beginning of last year, before it spread to southern Europe, Wisconsin, then New York and elsewhere. It's a genuinely popular movement and probably the first time since that Iraq march where you have people who don't really see themselves as particularly political coming together for a political purpose. Occupy is not a single issue campaign. It's about a whole raft of political and economic issues that have their ultimate cause in elite capture and a popular disconnect from political activity. That's why we talk about participation rather than policy prescriptions, process as well as protest. Once people feel that they are rightfully part of the discussion and able to take part in it on the same level as anyone else, the substantive proposals should follow naturally from that – and whether they emerge under the 'Occupy' umbrella isn't important. Occupy is just the catalyst... If you think how old the younger generation of people who are involved in Occupy were in 2003 – and a lot of these people came up through UK Uncut – the antiwar movement was a really formative experience for them. It's an event that colours everything else. That the government didn't listen means people of that generation are more naturally skeptical of what governments claim... Occupy isn't "run" really. That's not a reaction to how the SWP do things. It's a natural consequence of what has happened in the past ten years with electronic communication and social networking. The way things come together through social media is that there is a huge rush of people who come together for a relatively short period of time, cooperating for a specific purpose. It's about treating people as autonomous individuals. It's not "Please sign up", "Please join our organization". It's "This is what we are doing. This is what we stand for. If this sounds like you, then you're part of it too – come and join us". I don't think you can run a successful campaign now where you ask people to sign up and become members and toe your line. Any contemporary movement is about autonomous individuals coming together for a particular purpose. You harness that energy and then it dissipates. That's the way these things work and, yes, it means it is more difficult to maintain some sort of long-term organization. I'm not sure Occupy London will exist as long as Stop the War Coalition has existed, but in the short space of time that it has been very active, I suspect it's done as much, if not more, to change the national conversation.

"Probably the anti-war movement's best asset and, in some respects, its greatest liability": The Socialist Workers Party and the Stop the War Coalition

Carol Naughton: People say Socialist Workers Party dominated the Stop the War Coalition. Certainly a lot of the leadership of Stop the War were Socialist Workers Party.

Shahed Saleem: I think they were – Lindsey [German], John [Rees] and Chris [Nineham] were SWP. Andrew Murray, who was from the unions, and Andrew Burgin – I'm not sure he was SWP, but they all seemed to know each other quite well. I think it was effectively run by the SWP.

Andrew Burgin: My opinion has always been that it is precisely the opposite. In many campaigns what far-left organisations do is set up front organisations to work with others but ultimately they control the front. Presumably it is not just far-left organisations. Any political organisation would do this. Liberty, the NCCL, was the creation of the Communist Party in the 1930s. The Communist Party had all sorts of fronts that it would work through – the Spanish

Civil War, or civil liberties with the NCCL. And the SWP have done that throughout their history – for example, the Anti-Nazi League was a creation of the SWP. But it was a good creation of the SWP. It had a certain breadth within it. People like Peter Hain and others were quite involved in it and it actually did what it said on the tin – it opposed the Nazis at a time when they were growing in the 1970s. But it was ultimately the creation of, and organ of, the SWP. They dominated it. Stop the War was never that. The SWP were important in its beginning and its continuation and were always central to it, but they never controlled it in the way they controlled the ANL, or any of their front organisations. There was much more of a balance within Stop the War of other political forces, whether they were from the trade unions, or from MPs of the Labour Party like George Galloway and Jeremy Corbyn, political organisations like the Communist Party and campaigning organisations like CND, and their relationship with the Muslim community. For the SWP, in a sense, it was their most successful creation, but not their creation. It was both. I would never want to negate their importance and centrality to Stop the War, but they never sought to narrow it. It was a very broad movement.

Chris Nineham: At one level it's factually incorrect. The organising committees of Stop the War, the weekly meeting of people who organise stuff, there are three SWP members, some Communist Party members, some Labour Party people, and non-aligned, like CND. The SWP are in a small minority. Just at that level it's incorrect. It doesn't match up to the reality of the situation. We had all sorts of people in the officers' groups at different times. Definitely the SWP has always been outweighed by anyone else. And normally outweighed by people who are broadly supportive of Labour actually, let alone all the independents and other people.

James O'Nions, Stop the War Coalition Steering Committee Member in 2003: They were quite clearly a dominant force. They had allies – the small bit of the Communist Party that was left, for example. The Convenor of Stop the War Coalition – Lindsey German – at the time was a central committee member of the SWP, John Rees was a leadership figure within Stop the War Coalition, and another SWP central committee member. There were one or two other SWP central committee members on the Stop the War committee.

Gabriel Carlyle: I don't have a spy cam in the Stop the War office, but as an outsider it was clear to me it was dominated by the SWP. They certainly weren't the only force but they were the dominant force. They brought all of the resources. I would put it this way: the SWP were probably the anti-war movement's best asset and, in some respects, its greatest liability as well. There were huge plus points to this. Whatever political differences I may have with them, they were organised and got things done... If I'm honest I would have to say that if it had been up to the traditional peace movement to organise the response, they might have had a candlelit vigil with 200 people. That's being slightly facetious – more would have happened than that. But you wouldn't have had the same mass mobilisation.

Mike Marqusee: First of all I want to begin by praising them [the SWP]. We needed their resources and capacity for coordinating people and their network of activists across the country to get the thing off the ground. I think that was a huge contribution and I will never begrudge that. But earlier on they were less certain, I would say less arrogant, about this coalition, and therefore more willing to listen than they subsequently became. I used to have fierce arguments with people who used to say to me "What are you doing with them? They are dominating. It is better if we all go off and protest on our own". First, unity in the anti-war movement was absolutely fucking essential. It was utterly naïve and irresponsible to think otherwise. We had to get the maximum number of people involved on the simplest possible programme. That was a moral responsibility. I think those who put their resentment and mistrust of the SWP ahead of that were wrong.

George Galloway: You are speaking to the man in the country who likes the SWP least. If the SWP has a bigger enemy in Britain than me, I couldn't imagine who it would be. In fact the efforts of leading members of the SWP in the Stop the War Coalition was not only fundamental to the success of the movement, and its vibrancy and so on, I'd go so far to say they were indispensable. People like Lindsey German as the convenor [of Stop the War Coalition] – we couldn't have done it without her. The SWP approach, or at least the leaders of the SWP who were leaders of the Stop the War Coalition then, played a blinder. They were always the people who wanted to be broadest, to be most accommodating, to be resisting ultra-left and fissiparous tendencies. You know – people who wanted to turn the Stop the War movement into some kind of Marxist-Leninist insurrection. A general strike, or block all the roads in the run up to Christmas [2002]. On all of these things the SWP did not take the ultra-left line. In fact they were decisive in defeating it.

Mike Marqusee: The SWP by and large will not engage in critical examination of their own history or current analysis and practice. When events embarrass them, the error is buried in silence. There is a fear of looking harsh realities or awkward questions in the face and a reluctance to spend time addressing them.[47]

Damon Albarn, Musician: I've got a problem with them [the Socialist Workers Party] because they just turn up for everything. I'm sure there are people amongst their group who are consistent in their beliefs, but I have to say I feel they are in danger of spreading themselves a little thin, in the sense they seem to turn up to any kind of agitation. I don't think it is credible once you do that. You just become absorbed in the process of agitation, as opposed to meditating on problems, which is different.

Yasmin Khan: The SWP did dominate the Stop the War Coalition and it is only fair to say that they put a hell of a lot into it and played a very important and much valued role in building STWC – for this, I congratulate them. But their centralised style of working, their power and control obsession, and hierarchies and aggressiveness, also played a part in the downfall of the movement. I'm sure they think this is justified as a style of working but its not the kind of movement I believe will bring about proper social change. Ultimately they bottled it on the big questions of taking more direct action on the day war broke out, and they totally sidelined the direct action movement as well as taking credit for a Coalition which was a movement of people, not just SWP hacks.

Albert Beale: Within what I would call the real peace movement, if CND get a phone call from a journalist about conscientious objectors they will put them on to the PPU [Peace Pledge Union]. If the PPU get a phone call about the arms trade they will put them on to CAAT. All the groups are very non-sectarian and all know one and other and don't try to step on each other's toes. Everybody accepts their own limitations. But groups run by the Socialist Workers Party don't behave like that. Their [Stop the War Coalition] website over the years has miraculously avoided listing actions that aren't their style of action. For example some of Gabriel [Carlyle]'s Voices in the Wilderness gang had been doing direct action and civil disobedience, but somehow it didn't get on to their listings. It is not that what they are doing is bad, it's that they are doing it in a way that pisses everybody else off. It's not fully honest. They use the fact they have the strength and the party and that degree of discipline and organisation behind them to step on other people in a way that they don't have to. But that's their way of doing things.

Carol Naughton, 'Strictly Confidential – For CND Council Members Only', 19 June 2003: It is always difficult working with different organisations to plan events and there were problems presented by all sides. However CND and MAB were able to compromise when needed to, to resolve disputes and to 'give in' with good grace... Problems stemmed to some extent from the different cultural background of the Coalition to both CND and MAB. The Coalition did not seem to understand or accept the culture of working in partnership once we had agreement to go ahead with joint events. For example, decisions were taken by the Coalition with no reference to either CND or MAB… Press releases and advance publicity was a problem as posters, leaflets and press releases were distributed with only the Coalition's name on them. This was particularly irritating when, the day after a joint meeting at which we agreed a common understanding of what 'joint' and 'collaborative' meant, i.e. everything going out to have all three organisations on it, a press release was sent out by the Coalition without CND or MAB on it… I was on the end of some very unpleasant, aggressive and abusive phone calls from the Coalition… I was lied to and misled by Coalition leadership and found them to be duplicitous and manipulative in trying to get my agreement when I had given them a decision that they disliked.[48]

Asad Rehman: If you have the numbers it is easier to bully people. And they [the Socialist Workers Party] had the numbers – Lindsey [German], John Rees, Chris Nineham. Bit by bit they had driven everyone who was independent out of the Stop the War office. When the Stop the War office was set up there were a number of independent people helping. By the end it was full of SWP full-timers. There were two reasons for this. One, they were the only people to whom you could say "You are working in that office", and they would go and work in the office 9–5 every day. Second, whenever a post came up they would recruit an SWP person. All the non-SWP people in the office felt they were being shoved out. So slowly the Independents were pushed out.

Mike Podmore: Obviously the SWP – in terms of John Rees, Lindsey German and Andrew Murray, who wasn't

SWP but very sympathetic – were the coordinators of Stop the War. So they made the day to day decisions. So that was sown up. But they also had this Steering Group which met monthly which was made up of representatives from different organisations – MAB, CND, Worker's Power etc. A whole range of organisations. Ostensibly this is where decisions would be made. But the SWP – and this is one of their great, great strengths, but also one of their weaknesses in terms of keeping people on board – orchestrated those meetings completely. So they would have a position or a decision that they wanted to make, and they would have [happen] what they wanted to happen. And they would have SWP members who were also the representatives from other organisations on the Steering Group, such as Globalise Resistance with Chris Nineham... If anyone had a dissenting view they would be argued or shouted down. And because people only met once a month, and they were from different organisations so they didn't know each other, unless they got together to pre-meet and discuss the issue, there wouldn't be any kind of coordinated response to that approach. I actively pushed for the issues to be sent out before the meeting to allow people to meet and discuss before the meeting, but the Stop the War coordinators actively fought this. Even to have an email list for the Steering Group, and this is the amazing thing – they never had, never allowed us to have, an email group for the Steering Group. Because with this, of course, people would be able to discuss the issues before they actually got to the meeting. Certainly when I was there that didn't happen.

Ruhul Tarafdar: I went to some of the [Steering Committee] meetings, and there were some things I wasn't in agreement with, and then I never received any more invites. I was never fussed to say "Why am I not being invited?" As long as you agreed with everything it was alright, but as soon as you had some reservations about particular things it suddenly became a problem. I felt there were elements within the SWP that were trying to get political mileage out of Muslims. At one time it was with black communities – deaths in custody, for example – and now it was with the Muslims. So while I very much welcomed people championing the Muslim cause, I had reservations about whether it was for genuine reasons.

James O'Nions: In 2004 I was involved in setting up something called Iraq Occupation Focus, which was a modest attempt to get a little bit beyond the simple slogans Stop the War were using, and to look at the real situation in Iraq... I went along to a couple of the Stop the War Steering Committee meetings as a representative of Iraq Occupation Focus, who were affiliated to Stop the War. I found these Steering Committee meetings were not about everybody having a discussion with everybody. Instead each session was run a bit like any Socialist Workers Party conference. You had a member of the SWP central committee give a spiel about what we should think about a certain thing, and then there would be a discussion. But there was no common attempt to find a solution. Rather the solution had already been agreed, and the session was about the officers of the Stop the War Coalition winning over everyone else to what they wanted and trying to get people to mobilise around it. That is how the SWP operate basically. It was operating in a similar way that it does with its own cadre. After a couple of times I went back and said somebody else should go to these as I found them too frustrating, and somebody else from Iraq Occupation Focus went. I didn't think there was any point in us being there to be honest.

Shahed Saleem, November 2003: For the anti-war movement to remain meaningful means that it has to be opened up and handed over to a more diverse array of groups.[49]

Mike Marqusee: Here I go back to my experiences in the Vietnam War movement and the civil rights movement. In both those cases there was a plethora of national and local and international organisations. There was never a single dominant organising group. Of course they fought like cats and dogs very often, but they often collaborated as well. And they changed – constantly. Every six months or so you had new leaders and constituencies getting involved. That really is the sign of a healthy movement. And the sign of an unhealthy movement is one which has the same leaders for eight years... I've got to be careful what I say here because I don't want to exaggerate it, but on the other hand the record should be clear. They [the Socialist Workers Party members] used methods to isolate, exclude or discredit people who were questioning their leadership that are not acceptable, including smearing people, misrepresenting them and whispering things about them that weren't true. There was a fear of what they considered to be mavericks or loose cannons. What is an anti-war movement without mavericks and loose cannons? I mean please. The anti-Vietnam War movement wouldn't have got anywhere if it had excluded those people because they were doing the whole show from the beginning.

Mukhtar Dar: On the big demonstration [15 February 2003] Birmingham had a huge contingent – one of the largest in the country. But then problems began to arise in the sense Birmingham Stop the War Coalition wasn't very democratically run. The Socialist Workers Party more or less rigged the meetings. For example, as Artists Against the War it had been agreed that we would create the banner. This sounds like a trivial point but it's symptomatic of the wider issues. So we had designed a banner which said 'Birmingham Stop the War Coalition' in a number of different languages. And part of the process of designing and making the banner is involving new people – you have discussions and you politicise people. At that time I wasn't part of any political organisation and I felt I should play my part because I felt this was an unjust war. I was concerned about civil liberties, the racist backlash, Islamophobia and obviously I wanted to make sure the war didn't take place. So it had been agreed that we would design and make this banner. And then when we went to the next meeting we were told that a banner had already been done. And essentially this was indicative of how the SWP dominated and controlled, and didn't really want to broaden the movement.

Tom Harris: Sussex Action for Peace, an anti-war group in Brighton which was fairly independent of the Stop the War Coalition: we were affiliated to Stop the War Coalition and then cancelled our affiliation... In Brighton 100 people were regularly turning up to meetings, of which maybe ten were from the SWP. The vast majority weren't from any party at all. But the activists from the SWP were pushing a particular line that was coming from the Party hierarchy. This was happening in anti-war groups all around the country. A

Party line was being pushed. And the Party line was aimed at furthering the ends of their political party – gaining more participation in the Party, selling more papers, and attempting to get people to join the Respect Party. The zenith of resistance against the war as far as the SWP was concerned was joining the Respect Party, which struck me, and a lot of people, as the final insult really, and ended my participation in the anti-war group in Brighton. Sussex Action for Peace gradually imploded. It kept going maybe until 2007, but because of splits between the SWP and other people in the group they eventually split into two groups: the SWP-led Brighton Stop the War Coalition and Sussex Action for Peace. The latter eventually folded. Brighton Stop the War Coalition may exist as a website but not really any more than that.

Mukhtar Dar: The SWP were ruthless... When the [Birmingham Stop the War Coalition] committee was to be re-elected they had shipped in people from Walsall and lots of other places, so the elections were rigged. So here we were exposing how undemocratic the war was and yet in the Stop the War Coalition lots of undemocratic practices were taking place. Elections were rigged and decisions were made secretly... Birmingham Stop the War Coalition is now over. It's finished.

Gabriel Carlyle: I have lots of friends and colleagues who like to kick the SWP and bitch about Stop the War, but I'm not particularly interested in doing that. I think one has to give them all due credit for the remarkable things they did, at the same time one has to recognise it had weaknesses as well. I think for all of us, the primary focus of our criticism should be our own activity. I'm very conscious of my own activities at the time, and opportunities we [the traditional peace movement] missed. Whatever other people were doing, I've never really thought I managed to make an adequate response. There are some people who step up to the plate and meet the challenge of the times. I don't think we did. We tried, and we worked hard, but there were lots of other things we could have done. Although we were much less significant than Stop the War in terms of our actions and activities, I think my primary focus of criticism should be the things that I was involved in and that I could do something about. I couldn't have much of an impact on the decisions and policies of Stop the War, whatever I may think about them in retrospect. It really goes back to the systemic problems within the traditional peace movement. When 9/11 came along there suddenly lots of people interested in foreign policy, who knew that something was wrong and wanted solutions. And there was a window to engage with people about a whole bunch of important issues, and the traditional peace movement was in no sense prepared for that, or able to step in and do anything. And we still haven't learned from that experience. Should there be another period where you can engage with people over these issues and make big shifts, I don't think the traditional peace movement would be able to do any better than after 9/11. I think the traditional peace movement's primary criticism should lay in its own camp rather than being critical of other people, which is always very easy.

Final reflections on trying "To steer the course of our country with our own hands"

Tony Benn: I think it [the Stop the War Coalition] has been the most powerful political movement of my life because it really has helped to change opinion in Britain and America against the war.[50]

Bruce Kent, Campaign for Nuclear Disarmament Vice-President in 2003. CND Chair 1987–1990: Nothing has hit the button like February 15. Nothing. I've never been involved in a march of that size. During the cruise missiles days with CND we used to get 300,000 in Hyde Park, but there was vastly more than 300,000 on February 15. People talk of a million. It was a unique affair. It hit parts of the country that had never got anywhere near public protest before.

Kim Manning-Cooper: I often think now that if social networking, Twitter, Facebook and all the rest of it had been available to us from 2001 to 2003 who knows how many people we could have got involved. Maybe we could have increased it. Now social networking shows you how quickly you can get a message out to a large number of people. Who knows what we could have done.

Mike Marqusee: It grew much more quickly to mass size than the Vietnam movement. We had mass demonstrations before the attack on Iraq. Of course the invasion and war against Vietnam by US forces began by stealth, and had already been going on a large scale for two and a half years before we started to put together demos in five figures, nevermind six. So in a way, and this makes me sound like a really dreadful old fogey, but it was really impressive to see so many people come out so quickly. It was probably a legacy of the Vietnam War protests; even people too young to remember any of it were aware there have been terrible military adventures in our recent past that resulted in utter human disasters, and that people did protest against it. Whereas at the start of the Vietnam War we felt, in our naiveté, that we were very much starting from scratch.

Ken Loach: The big march had massive support across the country – far bigger than the Miners [during the 1984-5 Miners' Strike]. The Miners had huge public support but I think this was the biggest I'd ever known. But it dissipated a lot more quickly. The Miners' support was not quite as broadly based but it was sustained for much longer – for a year. The Miners' support had a more political base in that it was pro-trade union and anti-capitalist. It had a deeper political base. Whereas the anti-war movement went from people who were political all the way to people who weren't political at all, who just knew this was a con and that we would be killing mothers and babies. You don't need to be very political for that – it's just a humanitarian response. So I think that was the difference.

Emily Churchill: I feel it is important not to glorify those "heady days" of marches and walkouts too much, because although it was exhilarating to try to steer the course of our country with our own hands, we must remember that, where it was most important, we didn't succeed.[51]

Tom Harris: Since 2003 Stop the War haven't stopped doing this theatrical march from A to B, listen to Tony Benn thing. They are still doing it, even to this day! It strikes me as a bizarre ritual.

Shahedah Vawda, Just Peace activist: The Stop the War Coalition – does it still exist? I still get the emails, but how much influence and sway does it have? I think it is quite sad. They had a good coalition but I don't think it is sustainable. I do follow things but I don't really see them having much impact on the political landscape – on this election [2010 General Election] for example. Some people are cruel and say it was a "one trick pony" and a one-party issue. What saddens me is that we had a real opportunity to make an impact and have someone in Parliament that represents us, and we really bumbled it in a sense.

Asad Rehman: The SWP will want to keep it going in one shape or another. From the SWP's point of view the tactic of having popular fronts, from the Anti-Nazi League onwards – all of them have failed, apart from Stop the War. So Stop the War allows them to speak with the greatest number of people they have ever done, and allows them access to people. They went from being pariahs and "stupid Trots", to suddenly being able to ring up trade union general secretaries and ask them to appear on a platform, ring up Bianca Jaggar. In short, it gave them a veneer of respectability, and I would say they will be very loath to hand that over. I've always wondered what will happen when the wars in Iraq and Afghanistan end. Will they then switch to saying there is another war somewhere else. Whilst I'm fully supportive about the issue of Palestine, I've always wondered if that is used to keep the momentum going in the Muslim community, in the sense of opening more fronts for the anti-war movement… It's not going away. They will keep it alive in one way or another.

Jenny Pickerill: I believe that the relationship between STWC and the British Muslim community has been gradually eroding since the mid-2000's. Gradually the STWC has become less of a coalition and tended to return to its socialist roots which define a certain way of organising and campaigning that potentially exclude some of the more interesting and diverse Muslim activist groups. I do not think that they will continue to have a close relationship.

Jeremy Corbyn: Great days. Although it's not over yet you know. Afghanistan is not the same. Yet. It is unpopular with the public, so given time I think there will be very big protests about Afghanistan.

Gabriel Carlyle: The peace movement didn't come into existence on 11 September 2001. And the more traditional part of the peace movement are still knocking about in their distinctive fashion... My sense is that it is not a healthy time for the peace movement and anti-war movement [the interview took place on 26 February 2010]. Most of the activist energy is clearly elsewhere – climate change, for example. What happened with all the students who were involved in the anti-war protests? Just on the narrow issue of Afghanistan, my sense is that Stop the War have only been working and focussing on Afghanistan for maybe a year to 18 months. And even then it seems difficult to get anyone fired up about Afghanistan here in the UK. I guess it is the glass half full, half empty thing. You can look around and see people doing lots of different positive things – the Gaza boats and march, the new anti-arms trade groups that are springing up around the country, the student occupations that happened around the attack on Gaza.[viii] But we should be in a different place, with more people involved and engaged with these issues. And we are not, and I think that is quite telling.

***Peace News*, editorial, July–August 2011:** One question that perplexes us is why there is so little resistance to the wars Britain is currently fighting. Do we in Britain find it somehow easier to struggle against other people's crimes (such as Israel's brutality towards the Palestinians) than against our own crimes in Afghanistan and Libya? We are not suggesting that there is too much solidarity with people in Palestine, there is far too little. What puzzles us is why there seems to be so little energy for opposing Britain's wars.[52]

Noam Chomsky: The real question people have, I think, is, "What can I do to bring about an end to these problems that will be quick and easy?" I went on a demonstration, and nothing changed. Fifteen million people marched in the streets on February 15, 2003, and still Bush went to war; it's hopeless. But that's not the way things work. If you want to make changes in the world, you're going to have to be there day after day doing the boring, straightforward work of getting a couple of people interested in an issue, building a

---

viii Since 2008 the Free Gaza Movement has attempted to challenge the Israeli-Egyptian blockade of Gaza by sending ships to Gaza with humanitarian aid on board. In January 2009 students occupied more than twenty universities across the UK in protest at Israel's attack on Gaza in December 2008–January 2009.

slightly bigger organization, carrying out the next move, experiencing frustration, and finally getting somewhere. That's how the world changes. That's how you get rid of slavery, that's how you get women's rights, that's how you get the vote, that's how you get protection for working people. Every gain you can point to came from that kind of effort – not from people going to one demonstration and dropping out when nothing happens, or voting once every four years and then going home.[53]

Symon Hill: I was struck by the role of religious groups in the campaign. Muslims had mobilised each other in huge numbers to oppose the invasion. A significant number of Christian churches, Christian groups and individual Christians were also actively opposed. But the level of Christian involvement was rather feeble compared to the Muslim activism. As a Christian, I became frustrated by the unwillingness of many Christian leaders and churches to adopt a firmly anti-war position. Christians had been mobilised a few years previously for the Jubilee 2000 protests but the same level of passion and commitment was not there for the anti-war movement. As I marched on 15 February 2003, I remember thinking about the number of Christians in Britain, and reflecting on what could be achieved if they could be mobilised for anti-war and other campaigns.

Lindsey German: The role of women in the movement is, in itself, a really interesting story, if you think how prominent women are – me and Kate [Hudson] are kind of the leading people in Stop the War and CND. But loads of other people as well at the local and national level.

Ghada Razuki: What stood out for me most is that the women did all the work, and the blokes took a lot of the glory. Kate Hudson's brilliant, and she gets to speak, but doesn't get much credit for what she does. In the main, if you look at the way the office was run, it was women who were doing all the work. But that's par for the course in life for women.

Phillip Steele, Freelance writer of children's non-fiction and peace activist based in Bangor: The march was not the main thing. The main thing was the discussion, the analysis, the wider campaigns on human rights and international law, the coming together of global opinion against neo-conservatism, the growing commitment and understanding of thousands of ordinary people who had never previously been engaged in political protest. However the march did provide a great assembly of people of goodwill, which still endures – people who return to local demos still identify themselves as having been on the bus to London in February 2003.

Ghada Razuki: For me Stop the War was never about the people who ran it, it was about the people out there who came on the demos. Without them we would be nothing. And we should remember that.

George Galloway: To people who say "You failed", I say this: Even if I had been marching alone, I would still have marched. Because when my children grow up and ask me "What did you do when all this as going on?", I can tell them what I did – that every breath I had I used it to stop this disaster. As a religious believer, on the Last Day this will be to my credit – that I can say I tried my very best to stop this cataclysm. So even if we failed and nobody listened, it was still right to do what we did. At least no one can say that we could have done something and didn't. We took to the streets. In my case I travelled thousands of miles over the country, from 9/11 till now. I have travelled tens of thousands of miles and spoken thousands of times. I'm proud of what we did, even though we failed.

***New York Times*, 17 February 2003:** The huge antiwar demonstrations around the world this weekend are reminders that there may still be two superpowers on the planet: the United States and world public opinion.[54]

Map of the march route published in the *Guardian* on 13 February 2003

Threat of war

Capital awaits as hundreds of thousands p

Saturday's demonstration London

- Organisers are anticipating more than 500,000 people will attend – some estimate as many as 1m
- There are more than 1,000 coaches bringing people to the event
- Two fully-booked trains are coming, one from Manchester, one from Liverpool
- Six coaches arrived from Devon at last year's London demonstration. This time they are sending 37
- 81 coaches are coming from Manchester, 20 from York and 10 from Stroud
- There are 200+ coaches due from Birmingham and 60 from Bristol

List of speakers

1-2pm
Caroline Lucas MEP, Jack Heyman (ILWU), Shaheeda (Just Peace), Paul Mackney (Natfhe), Mark Serwotka (PCS), Salma Yacoob (SWC), Adrian Mitchell (poet), Bob Crow (RMT)

2.00-2.15pm
Mark Seddon (Tribune)/ Michael Foot, Ruth Winters (FBU)

2.15-2.30pm
Jill Evans MEP, Bruce Kent (CND)

2.30-2.45pm
Tariq Ali (writer), Bishop of Aston, Imran Khan (lawyer)

2.45-3.05pm
Mick Rix (Aslef), Alice Mahon MP, Ben Bella (Algerian politician)

3.05-3.20pm
Tony Woodley (TGWU), Charles Kennedy MP, Jeremy Corbyn MP

3.20-3.35pm
Billy Hayes (CWU), Tony Benn

3.35-3.50pm
Mo Mowlam MP, George Galloway MP

3.50-4.05pm
Lindsey German (SWC), Harold Pinter

4.05-4.20pm
Bianca Jagger, Ken Livingstone, Jesse Jackson

4.30-5.00pm
Damon Albarn, Ms Dynamite

SWC Stop the war coalition, MAB Muslim association of Britain, CND Campaign for nuclear disarmament

Information

Tubes

- Avoid using Embankment tube, which is likely to close
- There are **no** Central or Waterloo & City line services
- There are **no services** on the Circle, Hammersmith & City or Metropolitan lines between Baker street station and Liverpool street station
- LU asks that marchers do NOT arrange to meet friends at station entrances before the march, as this will cause overcrowding and increase the likelihood of stations being shut
- Recommended stations for the return journey
Bond street for northbound Jubilee line and **Westminster** for southbound Jubilee line.
Green park for northbound Victoria line and **Victoria** for southbound Victoria line
Green park for eastbound Piccadilly line and
Knightsbridge for the westbound Piccadilly line

Coaches

After the demonstration, coaches will pick up on both sides of Park Lane W1 adjacent to Hyde Park. The demonstration will disperse at around 5.30-6pm

Contact information

www.stopwar.org.uk
tel: 07951 235 915 or
020 7053 2153/4/5/6
www.unitedforpeace.org

www.liftshare.com
have set up a car sharing database for the use of people wishing to share transport to and from London on Friday 14 and Saturday 15

www.railtrack.co.uk
www.londontransport.co.uk/tfl/
www.thetube.com
National rail enquiries
08457484950

Euston
REGENT'S PARK
St George's Square
Warren Street
Marylebone Rd
Regents Park
Gt Portland St
Portland Pl
Tottenham
Goodge Street
Paddington
Baker St
Tottenham Court
Oxford Street
Oxford Circus
Marble Arch
Bond Street
Piccadilly Circus
Park Lane
HYDE PARK
Piccadilly
Green Park
Pall Mall
Hyde Park Corner
GREEN PARK
The Mall
ST JAMES'S PARK
Birdcage
Victoria

Map key

Route A

A People travelling from the south and west, and those from London, are asked to go to the Embankment

Route B

B Those travelling from the north (M1/A1) are advised to go to start B (set-down Woburn Place)

The two marches will join at Piccadilly

Coach drop off point

Tube station

Closed tube station

Mainline rail station

Entering Hyde park

Lancaster Gate
Black Lion Gate
Kensington Church St
Kensington Palace
Round pond
Kensington Gardens
Palace Gate

10 million join wor

re to descend on Hyde Park

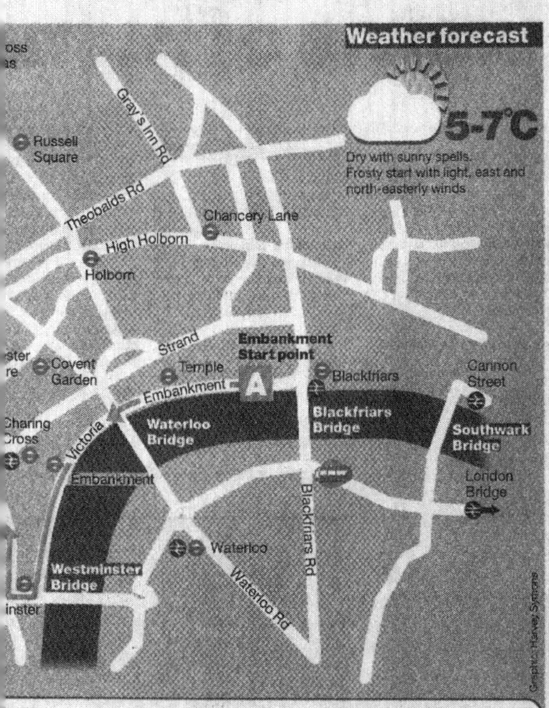

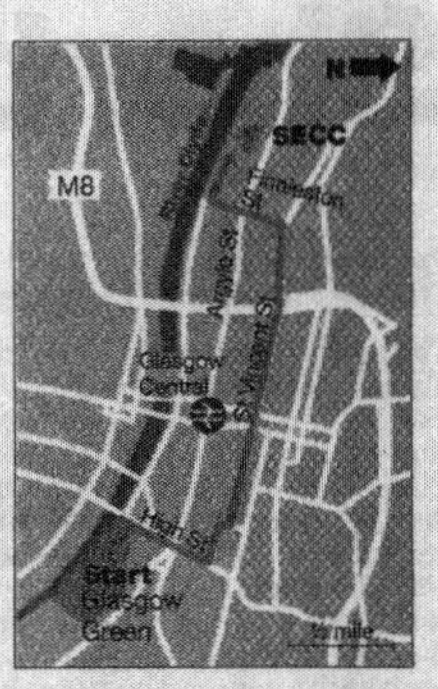

Stop the War Coalition is a collection of anti-war groups and individuals formed on September 21, 2001 at a public meeting of 2,000 people. In autumn 2002, the coalition's London march attracted 75,000-100,000 people

The Muslim Association of Britain was established in 1997. Involved in pro-Palestinian campaigning, it organises talks, and publishes newsletters, booklets and pamphlets

The Campaign for Nuclear Disarmament held its first public meeting in February 1958. Much reduced in membership since its heyday in the cold war 1980s, CND still campaigns non-violently to rid the world of nuclear weapons

Details of Glasgow march

Assemble
10am Glasgow Green, march off at 11am to arrive at 1.30pm at Scottish Exhibition and Conference Centre (SECC)

Labour party spring rally
This is taking place at the SECC. Tony Blair is to speak at 2pm and this is the focus for the demonstration and speeches

Speakers
John Swinney MSP, Tommy Sheridan MSP, Lord Provost Alex Mosson, Bill Spiers (STUC), Rev Alan Macdonald (Church of Scotland), Wael Shawish (Scottish Campaign for Palestinian Rights). There will also be speakers from the Muslim Association of Britain, Globalise Resistance and the Scottish Green party

Transport and access
All footbridges over the Expressway and the River Clyde to the SECC will be closed. Pedestrian access to the SECC will only be from Finnieston Street. Nearest train station Exhibition Centre/Finnieston (500 m) — access from SECC via underpass. Frequent trains between here and Argyle Street station.

protest rallies

TIMELINE

11 September 2001	Terrorist attacks on the United States.
20 September 2001	Meeting at Friends Meeting House in London establishes the Stop the War Coalition (STWC).
7 October 2001	US/NATO bombing and invasion of Afghanistan begins.
13 October 2001	Campaign for Nuclear Disarmament (CND)-organised march in London against the war in Afghanistan.
29 January 2002	President Bush delivers his State of the Union address calling Iraq, Iran and North Korea an "axis of evil".
13 April 2002	Muslim Association of Britain (MAB)-organised march in London against the Israeli attack on Jenin.
6-7 April 2002	Tony Blair travels to Crawford, Texas for a summit with President Bush.
23 July 2002	Top secret meeting on Iraq at Downing Street, minuted in the so-called 'Downing Street Memo'.

24 September 2002	UK Government publishes the 'Iraq's Weapons of Mass Destruction: The assessment of the British Government' report – aka the "September Dossier".
28 September 2002	STWC and MAB-organised march in London under the banners "Don't attack Iraq" and "Freedom for Palestine".
8 November 2002	UN Security Council passes Resolution 1441 giving Iraq "a final opportunity to comply with its disarmament obligations".
27 November 2002	UN weapons inspectors arrive in Iraq.
3 February 2003	UK Government publishes what becomes known as the "Dodgy Dossier", quickly found to be plagiarised from a postgraduate student's thesis.
5 February 2003	US Secretary of State Colin Powell presents the UN Security Council with supposedly compelling evidence about Iraq's weapons of mass destruction.
11 February 2003	Tanks and soldiers are deployed at Heathrow airport because of concern about a possible terrorist attack, says the UK Government.
15 February 2003	STWC, MAB and CND-organised march in London against the attack on Iraq – the largest protest in British history.

18 March 2003	House of Commons votes to support the British involvement in the invasion.
20 March 2003	Bombing of Iraq begins. Nationwide demonstrations against the war.
22 March 2003	STWC, MAB and CND-organised march in London opposing the war on Iraq – the largest wartime protest in British history. Thousands protest at RAF Fairford.
1 May 2003	Standing in front of a banner that reads "Mission Accomplished", President Bush declares the end of major combat operations in Iraq.
18 December 2011	US combat troops complete their withdrawal from Iraq.

SPEAKERS AT THE RALLY IN HYDE PARK ON 15 FEBRUARY 2003

Below is a list of people (and their affiliations in 2003), in approximate chronological order, who spoke from the platform at the rally in Hyde Park on 15 February 2003.

Adrian Mitchell, Poet
Shahedah Vawda, Just Peace
Mark Serwotka, PCS
Aisha Awan, Federation of Student Islamic Societies
Sabah Jawad, Iraqi Democrats Against War and Sanctions
Paul Mackney, NATHFE
Caroline Lucas MEP, Green Party
Jack Hayman, International Longshore Workers' Union
Bob Crow, RMT
Mark Seddon, Editor of *Tribune* and member of the Labour Party's National Executive Committee
Michael Foot, Former leader of the Labour Party
Dilwa Hah, Islamic Forum of Europe
Bruce Kent, CND
Salma Yaqoob, Birmingham STWC

Jill Evans MEP, Plaid Cymru
Ismail Patel, Friends of Al-Asqa
Tariq Ali, Author and political campaigner
John Aston, Bishop of Birmingham
Tony Woodley, TGWU
Alice Mahon MP, Labour Party
Imran Khan, Civil Rights attorney
Ahmed Ben Bella, Former President of Algeria
Keith Sonnet, UNISON
Mo Mowlam, Former Labour Party MP and cabinet minister
Azzam Tamini, MAB
Tony Benn, Former Labour Party MP and cabinet minister
Charles Kennedy MP, Leader of the Liberal Democrats
Jeremy Corbyn MP, Labour Party
Billy Hayes, CWU
George Galloway MP, Labour Party
Harold Pinter, Author and political campaigner
Michael Maseeh, MAB
Lindsey German, STWC
Mick Rix, ASLEF
Bianca Jaggar, Human Rights activist
Ken Livingstone, Mayor of London
Jesse Jackson, US Civil Rights leader and former candidate for the Democratic presidential nomination

The rally was jointly chaired by Andrew Murray (STWC), Anas Altikriti (MAB) and Carol Naughton (CND).

NB As there is no official record of the rally the list above has been compiled from a variety of incomplete sources (television footage, audio recordings and the list printed in the *Guardian* on 13 February 2003) and therefore may be incomplete.

INTERVIEWS

Original interviews:

All interviews were conducted in person unless otherwise stated.

Al-Adhami, Mundher. Iraqi exile living in UK. 1 May 2010.

Al-Ali, Nadje. Academic and activist. Founding member of ACT Together: Women's action for Iraq. 5 May 2010.

Al-Chalabi, Munir. Iraqi political and oil analyst living in the UK. 31 May 2010 email interview.

Albarn, Damon. Musician. Member of Blur, Gorrilaz and The Good, the Bad & the Queen. 1 March 2010.

Ali, Tariq. Author and political campaigner. 7 February 2011.

Altikriti, Anas. Spokesperson for the Muslim Association of Britain in 2003. President of the Muslim Association of Britain 2004-5. 9 February 2010.

Beale, Albert. Militant Pacifist. 27 February 2010.

Beech, Liz. Activist involved in Occupy London. 25 September 2012.

Begg, Moazzam. Former prisoner, Guantanamo Bay. Coordinator, Cage Prisoners. 2 December 2009 email interview.

Benn, Tony. President, Stop the War Coalition. Labour MP 1963-2001 (with a brief spell in 1983-4 not in Parliament) and former Labour Cabinet Minister. 6 January 2009.

Bloom, Clive. Professor Emeritus of Middlesex University and author of *Violent London: 2000 years of riots, rebels and revolts*. 18 July 2011.

Blunkett, David. Labour MP 1987-present. Home Secretary from 2001–4. 10 August 2009 email interview.

Brown, Carmel. Stop the War Coalition Press Officer in 2003. 9 May 2009.

Burgin, Andrew. Stop the War Coalition Press Officer in 2003. 21 March 2009.

Campbell, Menzies. Liberal Democrat MP 1987-present. Liberal Democrat Foreign Affairs spokesperson in 2003. 21 May 2012.

Carlyle, Gabriel. Peace Activist. 26 February 2010.

Churchill, Emily. Year 11 student in Birmingham in 2003. 16 February 2011.

Clarke, Charles. Labour MP 1997–2010. Education Secretary 2002–4. 20 March 2010.

Colvin, Naomi. Supporter of Occupy London. 18 February 2012.

Corbyn, Jeremy. Labour MP 1983–present. Stop the War Coalition Chair from 2011–present. 14 May 2009.

Crow, Bob. Rail, Maritime and Transport Workers (RMT) General Secretary 2002–present. 2 November 2009.

Dar, Mukhtar. Cultural Activist, Birmingham. 11 December 2010.

Dyke, Greg. BBC Chairman 2000–4. 6 December 2010.

Evans, Maya. Peace activist. 17 January 2010.

Female activist, Leeds Earth First! 31 May 2010 email interview.

Female Muslim anti-war activist. 14 May 2010.

Flett, Keith. Historian. 24 November 2009 email interview.

Former senior *Mirror* executive. 27 January 2012.

Francis, Ger. Respect Party member and agent to Salma Yaqoob. 14 December 2010.

Galloway, George. Labour MP 1987–2005. Respect MP 2005–10 and 2012–present. Vice President of Stop the War Coalition 2001–present. 6 October 2009.

Garman, Joss. Climate activist. 30 April 2010 email interview.

Gee, Tim. Author of *Counter Power: Making change happen*. 8 January 2012 in-person interview and 26 September 2012 email interview.

George, Richard. Founder member, Plane Stupid. 10 February 2010 email interview.

German, Lindsey. Stop the War Coalition Convenor and member of the Socialist Workers Party until 2010. 5 March 2009.

Goldsmith MP, Zac. Editor of the *Ecologist* 1998–2007. Conservative MP 2010–present. 14 October 2009 email interview.

Graham, James. Member of the Liberal Democrat Federal Executive 2003–5. 18 June 2012.

Griffin, Ben. Served in Iraq with the Special Air Service between 2003 and 2005. Currently the coordinator for Veterans for Peace UK. 9 May 2012.

Gun, Katharine. Employee at GCHQ in 2003 who leaked top secret memos relating to UN negotiations about Iraq. 5 March 2010 email interview.

Harris, Tom. Smash EDO activist. 3 September 2010.

Hayes, Billy. Communications Workers' Union General Secretary 2001–present. 8 December 2009.

Hill, Symon. Christian peace activist. Associate Director of Ekklesia (Christian thinktank) and former media co-ordinator of the Campaign Against Arms Trade. 2 August 2010 email interview.

Hudson, Kate. Campaign for Nuclear Disarmament Chair 2003-10. General Secretary 2010–present. 19 May 2009.

Ibrahim, Salih. Iraqi living in Britain in self-imposed exile. 9 July 2010 email interview.

Ippy. Editor of *Peace News* 1999–2007. 19 November 2012.

Iraqi living in UK in 2003. 26 January 2010 email interview.

Jones, Margaret. Peace campaigner based in Bristol. 6 March 2010 email interview.

Kember, Norman. Member of the Baptist Peace Fellowship who was held hostage in Iraq in 2005-6. 13 July 2009 email interview.

Kent, Bruce. Campaign for Nuclear Disarmament Vice-President in 2003. CND Chair 1987–1990. 7 July 2009.

Khan, Yasmin. Stop the War activist at London School of Economics and Political Science, 2001–5. 5 January 2010 and 28 April 2010 email interview.

Khan, Zainab. Iraqi woman living in UK. 1 March 2010 email interview.

Kilroy, Alice. Stop the War Coalition Finance Officer in 2003. 23 June 2009 email interview.

Livingstone, Ken. Mayor of London 2000-8. Labour MP 1987-2001. 29 July 2009.

Loach, Ken. Film Director. 27 May 2010.

Lucas, Caroline. Green Party of England and Wales MEP 1999–2010. Green Party of England Wales MP 2010–present. 10 October 2009.

McCarthy, Donnachadh. Deputy Chair of the Liberal Democrat Federal Executive in 2003. 6 June 2012.

McEwan, Ian. Author. His 2005 novel *Saturday* was set on 15 February 2003. 3 March 2010.

McLaughlin, Steven. Royal Green Jacket in 2003 and author of *Squaddie: A soldier's story*. 22 April 2010 email interview.

Mackney, Paul. National Association of Teachers in Further and Higher Education (now UCU) General Secretary 1997–2005. 22 August 2009.

Mahdi, Kamil. Iraqi academic living in the UK. 28 July 2010 email interview.

Majid, Kamal. Iraqi academic living in the UK. 30 October 2010.
Manning-Cooper, Kim. Campaign for Nuclear Disarmament staff member 2002–3. 20 July 2010.

Marqusee, Mike. Stop the War Coalition Press Officer in 2003. 23 November 2009.

Marsh, Kevin. *BBC Today* programme Editor 2002–6. 8 September 2010.

Masieh, Hadiya. Former member of Hizb ut-Tahrir. 15 December 2011.

Miah, Abjol. Community activist in Tower Hamlets and Respect parliamentary candidate for Bethnal Green and Bow in 2010 general election. 8 October 2010.

Murray, Andrew. Stop the War Coalition Chair 2001-11. Member of the Communist Party. 15 April 2009.

Myers, Tony. Campaign for Nuclear Disarmament Campaigns Officer 1995-2003. 4 December 2010.

Naughton, Carol. Campaign for Nuclear Disarmament Chair 2001-3. 2 December 2009.

Nineham, Chris. Stop the War Coalition National Officer and Chief Steward. Member of the Socialist Workers Party until 2010. 16 April 2009.

Offord, Peter. Founder member of Norwich Stop the War Coalition and President since 2009. 30 and 31 January 2011 email interview.

O'Nions, James. Stop the War Coalition Steering Committee member in 2003. 30 December 2009.

Omond, Tamsin. Co-founder, Climate Rush. 20 October 2009.

Phillips, Richard. Researcher into anti-war movements and Islamophobia, University of Liverpool. 22 October 2010.

Pickerill, Jenny. Co-author of the book *Anti-war activism. New media and protest in the information age*. 9 November 2010 email interview.

Podmore, Mike. Stop the War Coalition Steering Group member in 2003. 19 January 2010.

Rai, Milan. Activist, Author and Co-Editor of *Peace News*. 17 May 2010.

Razuki, Ghada. Stop the War Coalition Officer Manager in 2003. 21 May 2009.

Ramadani, Sami. Iraqi political exile and a Senior Lecturer in Sociology at London Metropolitan University. 9 March 2009 email interview.

Rees, John. Stop the War Coalition National Officer. Member of the Socialist Workers Party until 2010. 5 March 2009.

Rehman, Asad. Stop the War Coalition Steering Committee member in 2003. 28 January 2010.

Royal Parks spokesperson. 23 November 2009 email interview.

Sacranie, Iqbal. Muslim Council of Britain Secretary-General 1997–9 and 2001–4. 21 March 2012.

Saleem. Shahed. Just Peace activist. 27 April 2010.

Shemeld, John. Coordinator of Nottingham Stop the War Coalition. 20 January 2011 email interview.

Short, Clare. Labour MP 1983-2010. International Development Secretary in 2003. 16 June 2009.

Sian. Feminist anti-militarist involved in direct action and civil disobedience at military bases and nuclear establishments since the 1980s. 19 November 2012.

Siddiqqui, Ghayasuddin. Leader of the Muslim Parliament since 1996 and former executive committee member of the Stop the War Coalition. 2 August 2010.

Smith, Tony. UK Uncut. 1 February 2012.

Smithson, Marie. Norwich Stop the War Coalition Steering Committee member. 30 January 2011 email interview.

Solomon, Clare. University of London Union President 2010-11. 9 February 2011.

Steel, Mark. Comedian, Journalist and former member of the Socialist Workers Party. 5 November 2010.

Steele, Philip. Freelance writer of children's non-fiction and peace activist based in Bangor, Wales. 11 June 2010 email interview.

Tarafder, Ruhul. London-based community activist. 26 April 2010.

Tonge, Jenny. Liberal Democrat MP 1997-2005. Liberal Democrat spokesperson for International Development in 2003. 24 April 2012.

Vawda, Shahedah. Just Peace activist. 27 April 2010.

Wade, Chris. Press Officer for Trinity Mirror in 2003. 22 September 2009 email interview.

Wallis, Sean. Stop the War Coalition Web Manager in 2003. 12 June 2009 email interview.

Weston, William. Chief Executive, Royal Parks 2000-5. 14 December 2009 email interview.

Wilding, Jo. Peace Activist and Blogger who travelled to Iraq in 2003. 14 May 2010 email interview.

Wyatt, Vic. Norwich Stop the War Coalition Treasurer 2001-9. 30 January 2011 email interview.

Yaqoob, Salma. Chair of Birmingham Stop the War Coalition in 2003. Birmingham City Councillor 2006-11. Leader of the Respect Party 2005-12. 14 December 2010.

Zangana, Haifa. Iraqi exile living in UK. 1 May 2010.

Imperial War Museum sound archive interviews:

Benn, Tony. President, Stop the War Coalition. Labour MP 1963–2001 (with a brief spell in 1983-4 not in Parliament) and former Labour Cabinet Minister. 2008. Reference 31686.

Gentle, Rose. Founder member, Military Families Against the War. 2009. Reference 32723.

Gentleman, David. Artist who created the Stop the War Coalition's most famous 'branding' and images. 2008. Reference 31507.

German, Lindsey. Stop the War Coalition Convenor and member of the Socialist Workers Party until 2010. 2009. Reference 32727.

Hudson, Kate. Campaign for Nuclear Disarmament Chair 2003-10. General Secretary 2010-present. 2009. Reference 32734.

Kent, Bruce. Campaign for Nuclear Disarmament Vice-President in 2003. CND Chair 1987-1990. 2008. Reference 31555.

Keys, Reg. Founder member, Military Families Against the War. 2009. Reference 32736.

Shevlane, Maggie. Advanced Skills Teacher, Kent. 2009. Reference 32737.

Speck, Andreas. War Resisters International. 2009. Reference 32726.

Letters and emails to the author from people on the march:

I collected these letters and emails by writing to a number of local newspapers in the UK explaining that I was writing a book on the 15 February 2003 anti-war march and asking those that had any memories of the day to write to me. Once in contact I usually sent a small number of questions to them to answer. Unfortunately I was only able to use a few of these testimonies in the book, however I am grateful to everyone who took the time to write to me as all the memories I collected greatly enhanced my understanding of the day.

Boothman, Liz. 28 August 2010 email.

Bulsara, Cyrus. 14 September 2010 email.

Chisnell, Ian. 23 August 2010 email.

Cox, Johanna. 13 September email.

Dennis, Jan. 27 August 2010 email.

Edmundson, Steve. 14 September 2010 email.

Howard, Nick. 18 September 2010 letter.

Hill, John. 10 September 2010 letter.

McFarlane, Peter. 1 September 2010 letter.

Owens, Pauline. 25 August 2010 letter.

Perraton, Jean. 13 September 2010 email.

Robinson, Dael. 6 September 2010 email.

Schicker, Patrick. 25 August and 4 September 2010 email.

Sweeney, Simon. 2 and 5 September 2010 email.

Tarelli, Laura. 28 August 2010 email.

Westmoreland, Roger. 4 and 5 September 2010 email.

Whittall, Vance. 23 September 2010 email.

Wiseman, Michael. 26 October 2010 letter.

Wootton, Nigel. 2 October 2010 email.

Yousef, Adam. 8 November 2010 email.

GROUPS AND ORGANISATIONS MENTIONED IN THE BOOK

1990 Trust is a UK human rights and race equality charitable organisation. www.1990trust.org.uk.

Active Resistance to the Roots of War (ARROW) was a nonviolent direct action affinity group set up in 1990 to oppose the first Gulf War. ARROW was active until 2003.

Campaign Against Arms Trade (CAAT) was founded in 1974 and works to end the international arms trade using nonviolent methods. www.caat.org.uk.

Campaign for Nuclear Disarmament (CND) campaigns nonviolently to rid the world of nuclear weapons. It was founded in 1958. The Campaign for Nuclear Disarmament worked with Stop the War Coalition and the Muslim Association of Britain to organise the 15 February 2003 anti-war demonstration in London. www.cnd.org.uk.

Climate Camp are periodical gatherings held in the UK since 2006 which draw attention to the issue of climate change and act as a base for people taking direct action against major carbon emitters. www.climatecamp.org.uk.

Climate Rush is a nonviolent direct action group that takes creative action to raise awareness of climate change. Climate Rush was set up in 2008. www.climaterush.co.uk.

Globalise Resistance is an anti-capitalist activist group set up after the emergence of what is known as the worldwide anti-globalisation movement. Many see Globalise Resistance as a Socialist Workers Party front group. www.resist.org.uk.

Gloucester Weapons Inspectors is an informal group of people who take nonviolent direct action to highlight the issue of Weapons of Mass Destruction in the UK. The group was formed in 2002.

Hizb ut-Tahrir (HT), according to its website, is "a global Islamic political organisation established in 1953". www.hizb.org.uk.

Iraq Occupation Focus was a group set up in 2004 by a group of activists in the anti-war movement which campaigned to end the occupation of Iraq through media work and action. www.iraqoccupationfocus.org.uk.

Just Peace was a Muslim group set up in 2001 to promote the involvement of Muslims in the broader anti-war movement.

Media Workers Against the War was set up by John Pilger and Paul Foot in 1990 to campaign against the first Gulf War. Since 2001 it has been campaigning for better media coverage of the "war on terror". www.mwaw.net.

Military Families Against the War (MFAW) was an organisation of families of servicemen, set up in 2004 to campaign for British troops to be withdrawn from Iraq.

Muslim Association of Britain (MAB) was founded in 1997 to serve society through the promotion of Islam. The Muslim Association of Britain worked with the Stop the War Coalition and the Campaign for Nuclear Disarmament to organise the 15 February 2003 anti-war demonstration in London. www.mabonline.net.

Muslim Council of Britain (MCB) is a nationwide Muslim umbrella body with 500 affiliated organisations, mosques and schools nationwide. The Muslim Council of Britain was formed in 1997. www.mcb.org.uk.

Muslim Parliament works "towards creating an informed, caring and morally upright Muslim community ready to engage with its environment at all levels." The Muslim Parliament was founded in 1992. www.muslimparliament.org.uk.

Newham Monitoring Project is a grassroots organisation that was formed in the London borough of Newham in 1980 "to monitor both racist attacks and the statutory response to them in order to campaign effectively around the resultant issues for justice and change." www.nmp.org.uk.

Occupy Movement is an international protest movement primarily directed at economics and social inequality. Occupy London was established close to the London Stock Exchange on 15 October 2011. www.occupylsx.org.

Palestine Solidarity Campaign was founded in 1982 and promotes peace and justice for the Palestinian people. www.palestinecampaign.org.

Peace News is a monthly newspaper that focuses on nonviolent direct action. Peace News was first published in 1936. www.peacenews.info.

Peace Pledge Union (PPU) is a pacifist organisation established in 1934. www.ppu.org.uk.

Plane Stupid is a network of grassroots groups across the UK that takes nonviolent direct action against airport expansion. Plane Stupid was set up in 2005. www.planestupid.com.

Respect is a socialist party that was established in 2004. www.respectparty.org.

Smash EDO is a direct action group based in Brighton that opposes the work of the EDO Corporation's arms factory in Brighton. Smash EDO was set up in 2004. www.smashedo.org.uk.

Socialist Alliance was a left-wing electoral alliance active in England between 1992 and 2005.

Socialist Workers Party (SWP) is a far-left party that was established as the SWP in 1977, although it has roots going back to 1950. www.swp.org.uk.

Stop the War Coalition (STW/STWC) is an umbrella anti-war organisation that was founded in 2001. Stop the War Coalition worked with the Muslim Association of Britain and the Campaign for Nuclear Disarmament to organise the 15 February 2003 anti-war demonstration in London. www.stopwar.org.uk.

Sussex Action for Peace was a Brighton-based peace group established in 2001.

UK Uncut is a grassroots organisation established in 2010 to protest against tax avoidance and to raise awareness about public service cuts. www.ukuncut.org.uk.

Voices in the Wilderness/Voices UK was active from 1998 to 2008. Initially campaigning against UN sanctions on Iraq, from 2001 onwards it was actively opposed to the invasion and then occupation of Iraq. www.voicesnetuxo.co.uk.

War Resisters International is an international anti-war organisation that was set up in 1921. www.wri-irg.org.

Workers Revolutionary Party is a far-left group in the UK. www.wrp.org.uk.

NOTES

Prologue

1 'Sean Gittins in conversation with Dan Hind, Ellie Mae O'Hagan, Richard Thomas, and David Wearing', *Resonance 104.4 FM*, 2011, www.archive.org/details/SeanGittinsInConversationWithDanHindEllieMaeOhaganRichardThomas [Accessed 7 November 2011].
2 Michael Goldfarb, 'Political marching: What's at risk?', *BBC News*, 27 November 2010, www.bbc.co.uk/news/world-11849259 [Accessed 7 November 2011].
3 Milan Rai, *Regime unchanged. Why the war on Iraq changed nothing* (London: Pluto Press, 2003), p. xix.
4 Tony Blair, *A journey* (London: Hutchinson, 2010), p. 424.
5 Cherie Blair, *Speaking for myself. The autobiography* (London: Little, Brown, 2008), p. 350.
6 Andrew Rawnsley, *The end of the party. The rise and fall of New Labour* (London: Viking, 2010), p. 147.
7 Mark Thomas, *The night war broke out* (Laughing Stock Productions, 2004).
8 'Blair: I was ready to quit over Iraq', *Guardian*, 18 April 2003, www.guardian.co.uk/world/2003/apr/18/iraq.iraq [Accessed 1 August 2012].
9 Chris Mullin, *A view from the foothills. The diaries of Chris Mullin* (London: Profile Books, 2009), p. 385-6.
10 Suzanne Goldenberg, 'Blair refused three offers to stay out of Iraq', *Guardian*, 19 April 2004, www.guardian.co.uk/world/2004/apr/19/politics.iraq [Accessed 1 August 2012].
11 Colin Brown and Francis Elliott, 'Blair stands firm after Wobbly Tuesday', *Sunday Telegraph*, 16 March 2003, www.telegraph.co.uk/news/worldnews/middleeast/iraq/1424775/Blair-stands-firm-after-Wobbly-Tuesday.html [Accessed 1 August 2012].
12 Chris McLaughlin, 'Duff Hoon to go', *Sunday Mirror*, 16 March 2003, p. 6.

13 Brown and Elliott.

14 Ewen MacAskill and Michael White, 'Blair to defy anti-war protesters', *Guardian*, 17 February 2003, www.guardian.co.uk/uk/2003/feb/17/antiwar.foreignpolicy [Accessed 1 August 2012].

15 Seamus Milne, *The enemy within. The secret war against the miners* (London: Verso, 2004), p. 19.

16 Johann Hari, 'Protest works. Just look at the proof', *Independent*, 29 October 2010, www.independent.co.uk/opinion/commentators/johann-hari/johann-hari-protest-works-just-look-at-the-proof-2119310.html [Accessed 1 August 2012].

17 'The footnotes for: Understanding Power. The Indispensable Chomsky edited by Peter R. Mitchell and John Schoeffel', Chapter One Footnotes – 41, www.understandingpower.com/allchaps.pdf [Accessed 1 August 2012].

Introduction

1 Alastair Campbell and Richard Stott, *The Blair years. Extracts from the Alastair Campbell Diaries* (Hutchinson: London, 2007), p. 667. See also Tony Blair, *A journey* (Hutchinson: London, 2010), p. 424.

2 Blair, p. 414.

3 For a readable review of protests in Britain since 1800 see Ian Hernon, *Riot! Civil insurrection from Peterloo to the present day* (Pluto Press: London, 2006).

4 Alan Travis and Ian Black, 'Blair's popularity plummets', *Guardian*, 18 February 2003, www.guardian.co.uk/uk/2003/feb/18/politics.iraq [Accessed 7 November 2011].

5 Andrew Murray, 'We didn't stop that war, but may have stopped the next', *Guardian*, 15 February 2008, www.guardian.co.uk/commentisfree/2008/feb/13/antiwar.iraq [Accessed 5 November 2011].

6 'Millions join global anti-war protests', *BBC News*, 17 February 2003, http://news.bbc.co.uk/1/hi/world/europe/2765215.stm [Accessed 5 November 2011]. John Vidal, '10 million join world protest rallies', *Guardian*, 13 February 2003, www.guardian.co.uk/uk/2003/feb/13/politics.world [Accessed 5 November 2011].

7 Madeleine Bunting, 'We are the people', *Guardian*, 17 February 2003, http://www.guardian.co.uk/politics/2003/feb/17/voterapathy.antiwar [Accessed 5 November 2011].

8 Ellie Mae O'Hagan in 'Sean Gittins in conversation with Dan Hind, Ellie Mae O'Hagan, Richard Thomas, and David Wearing', *Resonance 104.4 FM*, 2011, www.archive.org/details/SeanGittinsInConversationWithDanHind EllieMaeOhaganRichardThomas [Accessed 7 November 2011].

9 Joel Roberts, 'Plans for Iraq attack began on 9/11', *CBS News*, 10 September 2009, www.cbsnews.com/stories/2002/09/04/september11/main520830.shtml [Accessed 5 November 2011].

10 'Letter to President Clinton on Iraq', *Project for the New American Century*, 26 January 1998, www.newamericancentury.org/iraqclintonletter.htm [Accessed 5 November 2011].
11 Julian Borger, 'Bush decided to remove Saddam 'on day one'', *Guardian*, 12 January 2004, www.guardian.co.uk/world/2004/jan/12/usa.books [Accessed 7 November 2011].
12 'Full text: State of the Union address', *BBC News*, 30 January 2002, http://news.bbc.co.uk/1/hi/world/americas/1790537.stm [Accessed 5 November 2011].
13 Lisa O'Carroll, 'Tony Blair knew immediately that 9/11 terror attacks 'changed everything'', *Guardian*, 10 September 2011, www.guardian.co.uk/world/2011/sep/10/tony-blair-knew-9-11-changed-everything [Accessed 5 November 2011].
14 'David Manning Memo – 14 March 2002', *The Downing Street Memo(s)*, http://downingstreetmemo.com/manningtext.html [Accessed 5 November 2011].
15 'Christopher Meyer letter – 18 March 2002', *Downing Street Memo(s)*, http://downingstreetmemo.com/meyertext.html [Accessed 5 November 2011].
16 Richard Norton-Taylor, 'Iraq inquiry: Blair told Bush he was willing to join, 11 months before war', *Guardian*, 30 November 2009, www.guardian.co.uk/uk/2009/nov/30/iraq-inquiry-david-manning [Accessed 5 November 2011].
17 'Cabinet Office paper text – 22 July 2002', *Downing Street Memo(s)*, http://downingstreetmemo.com/cabinetofficetext.html [Accessed 5 November 2011].
18 'Downing Street memo – 23 July 2002', *Downing Street Memo(s)*, http://downingstreetmemo.com/memos.html [Accessed 5 November 2011].
19 Mark Curtis, 'Psychological warfare against the public: Iraq and beyond' in David Miller, *Tell me lies. Propaganda and media distortion in the attack on Iraq* (Pluto Press: London, 2004), p. 70.
20 'The future strategic context for defence', Ministry of Defence, www.mod.uk/issues/strategic_context. Gary Younge and Giles Tremlett, 'UK 'nervous of public opinion'', *Guardian*, 15 March 2003, www.guardian.co.uk/world/2003/mar/15/foreignpolicy.politics [Accessed 5 November 2011].
21 Benedict Brogan, 'Attack on Iraq rejected by 2 in 3 voters', *Telegraph*, 12 August 2002 www.telegraph.co.uk/news/worldnews/middleeast/iraq/1404191/Attack-on-Iraq-rejected-by-2-in-3-voters.html [Accessed 5 November 2011]. An August 2002 *Guardian*/ICM poll found similar results: 52 percent of respondents said Bush's policy towards Iraq was wrong and 52 percent said Blair should not support American policy on Iraq. Alan

Travis and Nicolas Watt, 'Blair faces defeat on Iraq', *Guardian,* 28 August 2002, www.guardian.co.uk/politics/2002/aug/28/uk.iraq1 [Accessed 5 November 2011].

22 'Full text of Tony Blair's foreword to the dossier on Iraq', *The Guardian,* 24 September 2002, www.guardian.co.uk/world/2002/sep/24/iraq.speeches [Accessed 5 November 2011].

23 Richard Norton-Taylor, 'Iraq dossier drawn up to make case for war – intelligence officer', *Guardian,* 13 May 2011, www.guardian.co.uk/world/2011/may/12/iraq-dossier-case-for-war [Accessed 5 November 2011].

24 'Archbishop condemns US stance on Iraq', *BBC News,* 30 September 2002, http://news.bbc.co.uk/1/hi/uk/2288810.stm [Accessed 5 November 2011].

25 Alan Travis and Suzanne Goldenberg, 'Support for attack on Iraq falls to new low', *Guardian,* 5 November 2002, www.guardian.co.uk/politics/2002/nov/05/uk.iraq [Accessed 5 November 2011].

26 'Christopher Meyer letter – 18 March 2002'.

27 'Cabinet Office paper text – 22 July 2002'.

28 'Security Council meeting 4644', *UN Democracy,* 8 November 2002, www.undemocracy.com/securitycouncil/meeting_4644 [Accessed 15 November 2011].

29 Tony Blair, Iraq Inquiry, 21 January 2011, transcript of morning session, page 62 http://www.iraqinquiry.org.uk/transcripts/oralevidence-bydate/110121.aspx [Accessed 1 August 2012].

30 Campbell and Stott, p. 657.

31 'Iraq must do more, UN told', *BBC News,* 27 January 2003, http://news.bbc.co.uk/1/hi/world/americas/2698741.stm [Accessed 5 November 2011]. Richard Norton-Taylor, 'Blair-Bush deal before Iraq war revealed in secret memo', *Guardian,* 3 February 2006, www.guardian.co.uk/world/2006/feb/03/iraq.usa [Accessed 5 November 2011].

32 'Mandela condemns US stance on Iraq', *BBC News,* 30 January 2003, http://news.bbc.co.uk/1/hi/uk_politics/2770955.stm [Accessed 7 November 2011].

33 Simon Jenkins, 'There is no reason for Britain to go to war', *Times,* 1 January 2003, p. 16.

34 'Straw says dossier was 'embarrassing'', *BBC News,* 24 June 2003, http://news.bbc.co.uk/1/hi/uk_politics/3015272.stm [Accessed 5 November 2011]. For an insight into the immediate fallout of the 'dodgy dossier' see Colin Brown and Julian Coman, 'How not to win a propaganda war', *Telegraph,* 9 February 2003, www.telegraph.co.uk/news/worldnews/middleeast/iraq/1421543/How-not-to-win-a-propaganda-war.html [Accessed 9 January 2012].

35 'Transcript of Blair's Iraq interview', *BBC News,* 6 February 2003,

http://news.bbc.co.uk/1/hi/programmes/newsnight/2732979.stm [Accessed 7 November 2011].

36 ''Dodgy dossier' mocked in Sundays', *BBC News*, 9 February 2003, http://news.bbc.co.uk/1/hi/uk/2741737.stm [Accessed 5 November 2011].

37 Nick Hopkins, Richard Norton-Taylor and Michael White, 'UK on missile terror alert', *Guardian*, 12 February 2003, www.guardian.co.uk/uk/2003/feb/12/terrorism.world1 [Accessed 5 November 2011].

38 10 July 2003 letter published in the *Financial Times* in 'Peace Dossier', *The Bertrand Russell Peace Foundation*, 2003, No. 8, www.spokesmanbooks.com/Spokesman/PDF/79doss.pdf [Accessed 5 November 2003].

39 'Powell presents US case to Security Council of Iraq's failure to disarm', *UN News Service*, 5 February 2003, www.un.org/apps/news/storyAr.asp?NewsID=6079&Cr=iraq&Cr1=inspect [Accessed 5 November 2011].

40 'The *BBC*'s Jeremy Paxman on Iraq – 'We were hoodwinked'', *Media Lens*, 6 November 2009, www.medialens.org/alerts/09/091106_the_bbcs_jeremy.php [Accessed 5 November 2011].

41 'Powell briefing: key points', *BBC News*, 6 February 2003, http://news.bbc.co.uk/1/hi/world/middle_east/2728545.stm [Accessed 5 November 2011].

42 'Full text of Benn interview with Saddam', *BBC News*, 4 February 2003, http://news.bbc.co.uk/1/hi/2726831.stm [Accessed 5 November 2011].

43 'YouGov survey results. The propaganda war – part II', YouGov, 11 February 2003, www.yougov.co.uk/extranets/ygarchives/content/pdf/YOU020101110.pdf [Accessed 9 January 2012].

44 'Polls find Europeans oppose Iraq war', *BBC News*, 11 February 2003, http://news.bbc.co.uk/1/hi/world/europe/2747175.stm [Accessed 7 November 2011].

45 'Banned weapons unaccounted for', *BBC News*, 14 February 2003, http://news.bbc.co.uk/1/hi/world/middle_east/2759653.stm [Accessed 5 November 2011].

46 Justine Jordan, 'A life in writing', *Guardian Review*, 14 May 2011, www.guardian.co.uk/books/2011/may/14/china-mieville-life-writing-genre [Accessed 7 November 2011].

47 Andrew Roberts, *A history of the English-speaking peoples since 1900* (Orion: London, 2006), p. 622–5.

48 Andrew Marr, *A history of modern Britain* (Macmillan: London, 2007), p. 629.

49 Marr, p. 182–3.

50 David Marquand, *Britain since 1918: The strange career of British democracy* (Weidendfield & Nicolson: London, 2008), p. 391.

51 John Clark and Cathy Ross, *London. The Illustrated History* (Allen Lane: London, 2008).
52 Clive Bloom, *Violent London. 2000 years of riots, rebels and revolt* (Palgrave Macmillan: London, 2010), p. xvii-xxii.
53 Eric Hobsbawn, *On history* (Abacus: London, 1999), p. 267.
54 Noam Chomsky, *American power and the New Mandarins* (New York: Pantheon Books, 1969), p. 74.
55 Simon Jenkins, 'Britain has long been a poor venue for protest – tomorrow wont change that', *Guardian*, 25 March 2011, www.guardian.co.uk/commentisfree/2011/mar/24/protest-trafalgar-square-tahrir-square [Accessed 7 November 2011].
56 '(1857) Frederick Douglass, "If There Is No Struggle, There Is No Progress"', *BlackPast.org*, www.blackpast.org/?q=1857-frederick-douglass-if-there-no-struggle-there-no-progress [Accessed 15 April 2012].
57 David Grossman, *BBC Newsnight*, 17 February 2003 in 'Media Lens Alert: Civil Disobedience', *Media Lens*, 26 February 2003, www.medialens.org/alerts/03/030226_Civil_Disobedience.html [Accessed 5 November 2011].
58 Ian Hernon, 'A riot of their own', *Tribune*, 17 December 2010, www.tribunemagazine.co.uk/2010/12/a-riot-of-their-own/ [Accessed 7 November 2011].
59 Michael Goldfarb, 'Political marching: What's at risk?', *BBC News*, 27 November 2010, www.bbc.co.uk/news/world-11849259 [Accessed 7 November 2011].
60 Murray.
61 Peter R. Mitchell and John Schoeffel, *Understanding Power. The Indispensable Chomsky* (The New Press: New York, 2002), p.188–9.
62 Howard Zinn, *The Zinn reader. Writings on disobedience and democracy* (Seven Stories Press: New York, 1997), p. 542.
63 Robert Perks and Alistair Thomson, *The Oral History Reader* (Routledge: London, 1998), p. ix.
64 'This Much I Know: Niall Ferguson', *Observer Magazine*, 18 January 2009, p. 10. Quoted in Ann Day, 'Book review. Doing oral history: A practical guide by Donald A. Ritchie', *Oral History*, Autumn 2004, p. 101.
65 Paul Thomson, 'The voice of the past. Oral History' in Perks and Thomson, p. 28.
66 Peter Manso, *Mailer. His Life and Times* (Penguin Books: London, 1986). Jonathon Green, *Days in the Life. Voices from the English Underground 1961–1971* (Pimilco: London, 1998). Peter Grafton, *You, you & you! The people out of step with World War II* (Pluto Press: London, 1981). Legs McNeil and Jennifer Osborne, *The Other Hollywood. The uncensored oral history of the porn film industry* (10 Regan Books: New York, 2005).

67 Alessandro Portelli, 'What makes oral history different' in Perks and Thomson, 1998, p. 67.
68 Perks and Thomson, 1998, p. ix.
69 Anthony Seldon and Joanna Pappworth, *By word of mouth. Elite oral history* (Meuthuen: London, 1983), p. 6.
70 Studs Terkel with Tony Parker, 'Interviewing an interviewer' in Robert Perks and Alistair Thomson, *The Oral History Reader* (Routledge: Oxon, 2008), pp 123–7.
71 Eric Hobsbawn, p. 273.
72 E.H. Carr, *What is History?* (Palgrave: Basingstoke, 2001), p. 6.
73 Alessandro Portelli, 'What makes oral history different' in Perks and Thomson, 1998, p. 72.
74 'Howard Zinn: "To Be Neutral, To Be Passive In A Situation Is To Collaborate With Whatever Is Going On"', *Democracy Now*, 27 April 2005, www.democracynow.org/2005/4/27/howard_zinn_to_be_neutral_to [Accessed 3 April 2012].

Section I

1 Andrew Murray and Lindsey German, *Stop the War. The story of Britain's biggest mass movement* (London: Bookmarks, 2005), p. 4.
2 Mike Bygrave, 'Where did all the protesters go?', *Observer*, 14 July 2002, www.guardian.co.uk/world/2002/jul/14/globalisation [Accessed 1 August 2012].
3 Hilary Wainwright, 'Challenging US power', *Red Pepper*, November 2001, p. 5.
4 Andy Beckett, 'Kabul fell in five weeks. The Islamic world has not erupted. So did the left get it all wrong – and does it matter?', the *Guardian*, G2, 17 January 2002, www.guardian.co.uk/world/2002/jan/17/socialsciences.terrorism [Accessed 1 August 2012].
5 Kevin Gillan, Jenny Pickerill and Frank Webster, *Anti-War Activism. New Media and Protest in the Information Age* (Basingstoke: Palgrave Macmillan, 2008), p. 14.
6 Gillan, Pickerill and Webster, p. 2.
7 Gillan, Pickerill and Webster, p. 3.
8 Murray and German, p. 6.
9 Salma Yaqoob, 'Global and local echoes of the anti-war movement: a British Muslim perspective', *International Socialism*, 2003, Issue 100, pp. 39-63.
10 Kate Hudson, Sound Archive, *Imperial War Museum*, 32734, Reel 1.
11 Hudson, Reel 1.
12 Yaqoob.
13 Robert Lambert and Jonathan Githens-Mazer, *Islamophobia and Anti-Muslim Hate Crime: UK case studies 2010. An introduction to a ten year Europe-wide research project, 2011*, European Muslim Research Centre, University of

Exeter, p. 101.
14 Yaqoob.
15 Nick Cohen, 'The Left's unholy alliance with religious bigotry', *Observer*, 23 February 2003, www.guardian.co.uk/politics/2003/feb/23/politicalcolumnists.antiwar [Accessed 1 August 2012].
16 'DON'T STOP THE WAR Except through Islamic Politics', Hizb ut-Tahrir, Britain, 22 January 2003, www.ummah.com/forum/showthread.php?12840-DON-T-STOP-THE-WAR-Except-through-Islamic-Politics [Accessed 1 August 2012].
17 'Iraq's weapons of mass destruction: The assessment of the British Government', *BBC News*, 24 September 2002, http://news.bbc.co.uk/nol/shared/spl/hi/middle_east/02/uk_dossier_on_iraq/html/full_dossier.stm [Accessed 1 August 2012].
18 Greg Dyke, *Inside story* (London: HarperCollins, 2004), p. 316.
19 Chris Ames, 'Memo reveals intelligence chief's bid to fuel fears of Iraqi WMDs', *Observer*, 26 June 2011, www.guardian.co.uk/uk/2011/jun/26/intelligence-chief-iraqi-wmds [Accessed 1 August 2012].
20 Murray and German, p. 81.
21 Murray and German, p. 81–2.
22 Steve Platt and John Pilger, 'Beyond the dross', *Red Pepper*, July 2010, www.redpepper.org.uk/beyond-the-dross/ [Accessed 1 August 2012].
23 Piers Morgan, *The Insider. The private diaries of a scandalous decade* (London: Ebury Press, 2005), p. 303–4.
24 Morgan, p. 304.
25 Murray and German, p. 94.
26 Hudson, Reel 1.
27 Peter Ford, 'Minutes of CND National Council – 1–2 December 2001', pp. 1–2. CND archive, London School of Economics and Political Science.
28 27 April 2005 letter in Kate Hudson, *CND – now more than ever. The story of a peace movement* (London: Vision Paperbacks, 2005), p. 244.
29 Murray and German, p. 55.
30 'Statement on Iraq adopted by the TUC General Council 26 February 2003', attached to letter to the author, 10 February 2010.
31 Lindsey German, Sound Archive, *Imperial War Museum*, 2009, Reel 2, 32727.
32 Murray and German, p. 109.
33 Jamie Wilson, 'Keep off the grass: minister bans Hyde Park war protest', *Guardian*, 29 January 2003, www.guardian.co.uk/uk/2003/jan/29/politics.antiwar1 [Accessed 1 August 2012].
34 Mark Steel, *What's going on?* (London: Simon & Schuster, 2008), p. 65.
35 Laura Peak, 'Allow rally or face a riot, says MP', *Times*, 30 January 2003, p. 19.
36 'March and Rally Saturday 15th February 2003', Public Order Branch, New

Scotland Yard, 3 February 2003, access via a 26 February 2010 Freedom of Information Request.

37 'Stop the war rally on 15 February – statement from Tessa Jowell, Secretary of State for Culture, Media and Sport', *Royal Parks*, 4 February 2003.

38 Letter to author, 10 February 2010.

39 'UN 'should lead against Iraq'', *BBC News*, 25 September 2002, http://news.bbc.co.uk/1/hi/uk_politics/2280053.stm [Accessed 25 August 2012].

40 'Resolution of the Federal Executive of the Liberal Democrats, passed on 21/1/03', *Marching for Peace London, 15 February 2003*, www.theliberati.net/stopwar/index.htm [Accessed 28/9/1x.htm [Accessed 28/9/12].

41 'Lib Dems on the march', *Guardian*, 7 February 2003, www.guardian.co.uk/world/2003/feb/07/iraq.guardianletters1 [Accessed 25 August 2012].

42 'Kennedy's moment', *Guardian*, 8 February 2003, www.guardian.co.uk/politics/2003/feb/08/foreignpolicy.liberaldemocrats [Accessed 1 August 2012].

43 'BBC Breakfast with Frost interview: Charles Kennedy, MP Liberal Democrats Leader February 9th, 2003', *BBC News*, http://news.bbc.co.uk/1/hi/programmes/breakfast_with_frost/2742565.stm [Accessed 1 August 2012].

44 Nick Hopkins, Richard Norton-Taylor and Michael White, 'UK on missile terror alert', *Guardian*, 12 February 2003, p. 1.

45 Blunkett, p. 447.

46 'What if a dirty bomb hit London?', *BBC News*, 14 February 2003, http://news.bbc.co.uk/1/hi/uk/2708635.stm [Accessed 1 August 2012].

47 Sir Rodric Braithwaite, Letter to the *Financial Times*, 10 July 2003 in The Bertrand Russell Peace Foundation, 'Peace Dossier', 2003, Number 8.

48 Ian Mayes, 'Leading lights', *Guardian*, 20 October 2001, www.guardian.co.uk/books/2001/oct/20/books.guardianreview1 [Accessed 1 August 2012].

49 Julia Day, 'Murdoch backs 'courageous' Blair over Iraq', *Guardian*, 11 February 2003, www.guardian.co.uk/media/2003/feb/11/iraqandthemedia.news [Accessed 1 August 2012].

50 Murray and German, p. 111.

51 Alastair Campbell, Iraq Inquiry, 12 January 2011, transcript of afternoon session, p. 46–8 http://www.iraqinquiry.org.uk/transcripts/oralevidence-bydate/100112.aspx [Accessed 1 August 2012].

52 Charles Stuart, *The Reith Diaries* (London: Collins, 1975), p. 96.

53 'Dyke's letter to Blair', *BBC News*, 1 February 2004, http://news.bbc.co.uk/1/hi/uk_politics/3448797.stm [Accessed 1

August 2012].

54 Jason Deans, '*BBC* bans stars from anti-war march', *Guardian*, 11 February 2003, www.guardian.co.uk/media/2003/feb/11/broadcasting.antiwar [Accessed 1 August 2012].

55 Tony Blair, Iraq Inquiry, 21 January 2011, transcript of morning session, p. 62 www.iraqinquiry.org.uk/transcripts/oralevidence-bydate/110121.aspx [Accessed 1 August 2012].

56 Murray and German, p. 155.

57 Murray and German, p. 261.

58 Nick Hopkins, 'Met cancels police leave', *Guardian*, 14 February 2003, www.guardian.co.uk/uk/2003/feb/14/terrorism.antiwar [Accessed 1 August 2012].

59 Murray and German, p. 158.

Section 2

1 Alastair Campbell and Richard Stott, *The Blair years. Extracts from the Alastair Campbell diaries* (London: Hutchinson, 2007), p. 667.

2 Andrew Murray and Lindsey German, *Stop the War. The story of Britain's biggest mass movement* (London: Bookmarks, 2005), p. 155.

3 'Where were you on 15 February 2003', *Stop the War Coalition*, 10 January 2008, Address unknown [Accessed 8 January 2009].

4 Andrew Norfolk, 'Cities and Dales head south to join peace chorus', *Times*, 15 February 2003, p. 21.

5 Sue Townsend, *Adrian Mole & the Weapons of Mass Destruction* (London: Penguin Books, 2007). First published 2004, p. 246.

6 Ian McEwan, *Saturday* (London: Vintage, 2006), first published 2005, pp. 69–70.

7 Email to author, 3 October 2011.

8 Tony Benn, *More time for politics. Diaries 2001–2007* (London: Hutchinson, 2007), p. 99.

9 Maggie Shevlane, Sound Archive, Imperial War Museum. 2009, 32737.

10 David Gentleman, Sound Archive, Imperial War Museum, 2008, 31507.

11 Gentleman.

12 Johann Hari, 'The case for war: we must fight to end the Iraqi's suffering', *Independent*, 15 February 2003, www.iraqfoundation.org/news/2003/bfeb/20_case.html [Accessed 1 August 2012].

13 McEwan, p. 73.

14 'Iraq: war is not the way', *Guardian*, 5 September 2002, www.guardian.co.uk/theguardian/2002/sep/05/guardianletters1 [Accessed 1 August 2012]

15 'Stop the War march – February 15th 2003'. Audio recording made by John Gardner with Steve Ruby.

16 Euan Ferguson, 'One million. And still they came', *Observer*, 16 February 2003, www.guardian.co.uk/uk/2003/feb/16/voterapathy.iraq [Accessed 4 January 2013]
17 Ferguson.
18 Campbell and Stott, p. 667.
19 David Aaronovitch, 'Dear marcher, please answer a few questions', *Guardian*, 18 February 2003, www.guardian.co.uk/politics/2003/feb/18/voterapathy.comment [Accessed 1 August 2012].
20 Hari.
21 Christopher Hitchens, 'I wanted it to rain on their parade', *Daily Mirror*, 18 February 2003, p. 6.
22 Hari.
23 Aaronovitch.
24 Hari.
25 George Galloway, *I'm not the only one* (London: Penguin Books, 2005). First published 2004, p. 11.
26 John Vidal, 'They stood up to be counted – and found nobody could agree on totals', *Guardian*, 17 February 2003, www.guardian.co.uk/uk/2003/feb/17/politics.antiwar1 [Accessed 1 August 2012].
27 Royal Parks background note to Parliamentary Question from Dr Lewis MP, February 2003, accessed via a 26 February 2010 Freedom of Information request.
28 Alan Travis and Ian Black, 'Blair's popularity plummets', *Guardian*, 18 February 2003, www.guardian.co.uk/uk/2003/feb/18/politics.iraq [Accessed 1 August 2003].
29 Murray and German, p. 163.
30 'Millions worldwide rally for peace', *Guardian*, 17 February 2003, p. 6.
31 'John Vidal, '10 million join world protests', *Guardian*, 13 February 2003, www.guardian.co.uk/uk/2003/feb/13/politics.world [Accessed 1 August 2012].
32 'Millions join global anti-war protests', *BBC News*, 17 February 2003, http://news.bbc.co.uk/1/hi/world/europe/2765215.stm [Accessed 1 August 2012].
33 'Millions worldwide rally for peace'.

Section 3

1 'Blair speech – key quotes', *BBC News*, 15 February 2003, http://news.bbc.co.uk/1/hi/2765763.stm [Accessed 1 August 2012].
2 Alastair Campbell, Iraq Inquiry, 12 January 2010, transcript of afternoon session, p. 51-2, http://www.iraqinquiry.org.uk/transcripts/oralevidence-bydate/100112.aspx [Accessed 1 August 2012].

3 'Transcript: Condoleezza Rice on *Fox News Sunday*', *Fox News*, 16 February 2003, www.foxnews.com/printer_friendly_story/0,3566,78723,00.html [Accessed 9 August 2012].
4 'Analysis: President Bush discounts impact of anti-war protest marches around the world', *NPR*, 18 February 2003, www.npr.org/programs/atc/transcripts/2003/feb/030218.gonyea.html [Accessed 1 August 2012].
5 'PM press conference 18 February transcript', *Number10.gov.uk*, 19 February 2003, http://webarchive.nationalarchives.gov.uk/20061004051823/number10.gov.uk/page3006 [Accessed 1 August 2012].
6 'CND National Council. Minutes of meeting held on 1st & 2nd March 2003', p. 1. CND archive, London School of Economics and Political Science.
7 Alastair Campbell, Iraq Inquiry, 12 January 2010, transcript of afternoon session, p. 50–1, www.iraqinquiry.org.uk/transcripts/oralevidence-bydate/100112.aspx [Accessed 1 August 2012].
8 Andrew Murray and Lindsey German, *Stop the war. The story of Britain's biggest mass movement* (London: Bookmarks, 2005), p. 205.
9 Rose Gentle, Sound Archive, *Imperial War Museum*, 2009, 32723.
10 'Action not speculation. Noam Chomsky interviewed by Cynthia Peters', *ZNet*, 9 March 2003, www.zcommunications.org/action-not-speculation-by-noam-chomsky [Accessed 1 August 2012].
11 Libby Brooks, 'Kid power', *Guardian*, 26 April 2003, www.guardian.co.uk/politics/2003/apr/26/schools.antiwar [Accessed 1 August 2012].
12 Brooks.
13 Brooks.
14 John Vidal and Tania Branigan, 'UK sees biggest wartime protest', *Guardian*, 24 March 2003, www.guardian.co.uk/uk/2003/mar/24/iraq.iraq [Accessed 1 August 2012].
15 Reg Keys, Sound Archive, *Imperial War Museum*, 2009, 32736.
16 Letter to Steve Sinnott, Deputy General Secretary, National Union of Teachers, 8 April 2003, copied to Stop the War Coalition.
17 Mike Marqusee, 'Demos make a difference', 1 February 2003, www.mikemarqusee.com/?p=43 [Accessed 1 August 2012].
18 Alan Travis and Ian Black, 'Blair's popularity plummets', *Guardian*, 18 February 2003, www.guardian.co.uk/uk/2003/feb/18/politics.iraq [Accessed 1 August 2012].
19 Rebecca Allison, 'Teenagers react against 'anything goes' society', *Guardian*, 11 March 2004, www.guardian.co.uk/uk/2004/mar/11/britishidentity.rebeccaallison, [Accessed 1 August 2012].
20 Michael Smith, 'Revealed: Jack Straw's secret warning to Tony Blair on Iraq', *Times*, 17 January 2010, www.commondreams.org/headline/2010/01/17-4 [Accessed 1 August 2012]. Two other polls at the time produced similar results. Glen Owen, 'Chilcot war inquiry: we STILL think Blair lied, says 8

out of 10', *Mail Online*, 31 January 2010, www.dailymail.co.uk/news/article-1247394/Chilcot-war-Inquiry-We-STILL-think-Blair-lied-say-8-10.html [Accessed 1 August 2012]. 'Poll Digest – Political – Chilcot inquiry poll for The Independent', ComRes, 3 February 2010, www.comres.co.uk/poll/344/chilcot-inquiry-poll-for-the-independent.htm [Accessed 1 August 2012].

21 Ewen MacAskill, 'Poll shows war factor was key issue for many', *Guardian*, 6 May 2005, www.guardian.co.uk/politics/2005/may/06/uk.iraq1 [Accessed 1 August 2012].

22 Arundhati Roy, *The chequebook and the cruise-missile* (London: Harper Perennial, 2004) p. 153.

23 Lorna Martin, 'Army blames Iraq for drop in recruits', *Guardian*, 19 December 2004, www.guardian.co.uk/uk/2004/dec/19/military.antiwar [Accessed 1 August 2012].

24 'Upswing in public view of military', *BBC Today Programme*, 1 September 2011.

25 Madeleine Bunting, 'We are the people', *Guardian*, 17 February 2003, www.guardian.co.uk/politics/2003/feb/17/voterapathy.antiwar [Accessed 1 August 2012].

26 Mary Riddell, 'The great unheard finally speak out', *Observer*, 16 February 2003, www.guardian.co.uk/politics/2003/feb/16/voterapathy.iraq [Accessed 1 August 2012].

27 Bunting.

28 'Gen. Wesley Clark weighs presidential bid: "I think about it everyday"', *Democracy Now*, 2 March 2007, www.democracynow.org/2007/3/2/gen_wesley_clark_weighs_presidential_bid [Accessed 1 August 2012].

29 Noam Chomsky, *Imperial ambitions. Conversations with Noam Chomsky on the post-9/11 world* (London: Penguin Books, 2005), p. 16.

30 Lyn Smith, *Voices against war. A century of protest* (London: Mainstream, 2009), pp. 280–5.

31 Hani Shukrallah, 'We are all Iraqis now', *Guardian*, 27 March 2003, www.guardian.co.uk/world/2003/mar/27/iraq.features11 [Accessed 1 August 2012].

32 Jo Wilding, Don't shoot the clowns. T*aking a circus to the children of Iraq* (London: New Internationalist, 2006), pp. 50-1.

33 Malalai Joya, *Raising my voice. The extraordinary story of the Afghan woman who dares to speak out* (London: Rider, 2009), p. 264.

34 Naomi Klein, 'Civil disobedience may be the only way to stop the war against Iraq', *Guardian*, 3 March 2003, www.guardian.co.uk/politics/2003/mar/03/iraq.antiwar [Accessed 1 August 2012].

35 Carol Naughton, 'Strictly Confidential – For CND Council Members Only. Response to London Region CND's proposal', 19 June 2003, CND archive, London School of Economics and Political Science.

36 Murray and German, p. 200.
37 Murray and German, p. 60.
48 Fareena Alam, 'How war has brought hope to Muslims', *Observer*, 23 March 2003, www.guardian.co.uk/politics/2003/mar/23/race.iraq [Accessed 1 August 2012].
49 Milan Rai, 7/7. *The London bombings, Islam and the Iraq War* (London: Pluto Press, 2006), p. 160.
40 'Bomb suspect: 'No al Qaeda links', *CNN World*, 1 August 2005, http://edition.cnn.com/2005/WORLD/europe/07/31/london.tube/index.html [Accessed 1 August 2012].
41 Patrick Ward, 'Operation end your freedom', *Socialist Review*, July/August 2008, p. 20.
42 Sam Baker, 'Vodafone protest shows tweets can get people on the street', *Guardian*, 1 November 2010, www.guardian.co.uk/commentisfree/2010/nov/01/vodafone-protest-social-media [Accessed 1 August 2012].
43 'Sean Gittens in conversation with Dan Hind, Ellie Mae O'Hagan, Richard Thomas and David Wearing', *Resonance 104.4 FM*, 2011, www.archive.org/details/SeanGittinsInConversationWithDanHindEllieMaeOhaganRichardThomas [Accessed 7 November 2011].
44 Gittens.
45 Baker.
46 Robert Booth and Marc Vallee, 'Inside the 'black bloc' – the masked militants who say they've hit a nerve', *Guardian*, 2 April 2011, www.guardian.co.uk/society/2011/apr/01/anarchists-anti-cuts-march [Accessed 1 August 2012].
47 Mike Marqusee, 'The Socialist Workers Party and the Stop the War Coalition', *What Next?*, www.whatnextjournal.co.uk/Pages/Back/Wnext26/Marqusee.html [Accessed 1 August 2012].
48 Carol Naughton, 'Strictly Confidential – For CND Council Members Only. Response to London Region CND's proposal', 19 June 2003, CND archive, London School of Economics and Political Science.
49 Natasha Grzincic, 'What now for Stop the War?', *Red Pepper*, November 2003, www.redpepper.org.uk/What-now-for-Stop-the-War/ [Accessed 1 August 2012].
50 Smith, p. 274.
51 Murray and German, p. 187.
52 'Energy crisis', *Peace News*, July–August 2011, p. 14.
53 Chomsky, pp. 90–1.
54 Patrick E. Tyler, 'Threats and responses: News analysis; A new power in the streets', *New York Times*, 17 February 2003, www.nytimes.com/2003/02/17/world/threats-and-responses-news-analysis-a-new-power-in-the-streets.html?pagewanted=all&src=pm [Accessed 1 August 2012].

BIBLIOGRAPHY

Books:

Al-Ali, Nadje and Pratt, Nicola, *What kind of liberation? Women and the occupation of Iraq* (Berkley: University of California Press, 2009).

Ali, Tariq, *Bush in Babylon. The recolonisation of Iraq* (London: Verso, 2003).

Ali, Tariq, *Rough music. Blair/Bombs/Baghdad/London/Terror* (London: Verso, 2005).

Anthony, Andrew, *The fallout. How a guilty liberal lost his innocence* (London: Vintage, 2007).

Begg, Moazzam, *Enemy combatant. A British Muslim's journey to Guantanamo and back* (London: The Free Press, 2006).

Benn, Tony, *More time for politics. Diaries 2001–2007* (London: Hutchinson, 2007).

Bennett, Alan, *Untold stories* (London: Faber & Faber, 2005).

Blair, Cherie, *Speaking for myself. The autobiography* (London: Little, Brown, 2008).

Blair, Tony, *A journey* (London: Hutchinson, 2010).

Bloom, Clive, *Violent London. 2000 years of riots, rebels and revolt* (London: Palgrave MacMillan, 2010).

Blunkett, David, *The Blunkett tapes. My life in the bear pit* (London: Bloomsbury, 2006).

Cable, Vince, *Free radical. A memoir* (London: Atlantic Books, 2009).

Campbell, Alastair and Stott, Richard, *The Blair years. Extracts from the Alastair Campbell diaries* (London: Hutchinson, 2007).
Campbell, Menzies, *Menzies Campbell: My autobiography* (London: Hodder & Stoughton, 2008).
Carr, E.H., *What is history?* (Basingstoke: Palgrave, 2001).
Chomsky, Noam, *Imperial ambitions: Conversations with Noam Chomsky on the post-9/11 world* (London: Penguin Books, 2006).
Cohen, Nick, *What's left? How Liberals lost their way* (London: Fourth Estate, 2007).
Cook, Robin, *The point of departure* (London: Simon & Schuster, 2003).
Dyke, Greg, *Inside story* (London: Harper Collins, 2004).
Flynn, Paul, *The unusual suspect* (London: Biteback, 2010).
Fraser, Antonia, *Must you go? My life with Harold Pinter* (London: Weidenfeld & Nicolson, 2010).
Galloway, George, *I'm not the only one* (London: Penguin Books, 2005).
Gillan, Kevin, Pickerill, Jenny and Webster, Frank, *Anti-war activism. New media and protest in the information age* (Basingstoke: Palgrave Macmillan, 2008).
Hernon, Ian, *Riot! Civil insurrection from Peterloo to the present day* (London: Pluto Press, 2006).
Hobsbawn, Eric, *On history* (London: Abacus, 1999).
Hudson, Kate, *CND – now more than ever. The story of a peace movement* (London: Vision paperbacks, 2005).
Hurst, Greg, *Charles Kennedy: A tragic flaw* (London: Politico's Publishing, 2006).
Jeffreys, Kevin, *Politics of the people. A history of British democracy since 1918* (London: Atlantic Books, 2007).
Joya, Malalai, *Raising my voice. The extraordinary story of the Afghan women who dares to speak out* (London: Rider, 2009).
Kampfner, John, *Blair's wars* (London: Free Press, 2004).
Khan, Saddiq, *Fairness not favours. How to reconnect with British Muslims. Fabian Ideas* 624 (London: Fabian Society, 2008).

Kilfoyle, Peter, *Labour pains. How the party I love lost its soul* (London: Biteback, 2010).

Lambert, Robert and Githens-Mazer, Jonathan, *Islamophobia and anti-Muslim hate crime: UK case studies 2010. An introduction to a ten year Europe-wide research project* (University of Exeter: European Muslim Research Centre, 2011).

Marquand, David, *Britain since 1918. The strange career of British democracy* (London: Weidenfeld & Nicolson, 2008).

Marr, Andrew, *A history of modern Britain* (London: Macmillan, 2007).

McEwan, Ian, *Saturday* (London: Vintage, 2006).

Milne, Seamus, *The enemy within. The secret war against the miners* (London: Verso, 2010).

Morgan, Piers, *The insider. The private diaries of a scandalous decade* (London: Ebury Press, 2005).

Mullin, Chris, *A view from the foothills. The diaries of Chris Mullin* (London: Profile Books, 2009).

Murray, Andrew and German, Lindsey, *Stop the war. The story of Britain's biggest mass movement* (London: Bookmarks, 2005).

O'Farrell, John, *An utterly exasperated history of modern Britain or 60 years of making the same stupid mistakes as always* (London: Transworld, 2009).

Omond, Tamsin, *Rush! The making of a climate activist* (London: Marion Boyars, 2009).

Perks, Robert and Thomson, Alistair, *The oral history reader* (London: Routledge, 1998).

Perks, Robert and Thomson, Alistair, *The oral history reader* (London: Routledge, 2008).

Prescott, John, *Prezza. My story* (London: Headline Review, 2008).

Rai, Milan, *Regime unchanged. Why the war on Iraq changed nothing* (London: Pluto Press, 2003).

Rai, Milan, *7/7. The London bombings, Islam and the Iraq war* (London: Pluto Press, 2006).

Rawnsley, Andrew, *The end of the party. The rise and fall of New Labour* (London: Viking, 2010).
Roberts, Andrew, *A history of the English-speaking peoples since 1900* (London: Orion, 2006).
Roy, Arundhati, *The chequebook and the cruise-missile* (London: Harper Perennial, 2004).
Seldon, Anthony, *Blair unbound* (London: Pocket Books, 2008).
Seldon, Anthony and Pappworth, Joanna, *By word of mouth. Elite oral history* (London: Meuthen & Co Ltd, 1983).
Short, Clare, *An honourable deception. New Labour, Iraq and the misuse of power* (London: The Free Press, 2004).
Smith, Lyn, *Voices against war. A century of protest* (Edinburgh: Mainstream publishing, 2009).
Steel, Mark, *What's going on?* (London: Simon & Schuster, 2008).
Stuart, Charles, *The Reith diaries* (London: Collins, 1975).
Stevens, John, *Not for the faint-hearted. My life fighting crime* (London: Weidenfeld & Nicolson, 2005).
Townsend, Sue, *Adrian Mole and the weapons of mass destruction* (London: Penguin, 2007).
Van Der Zee, Bibi, *The protestor's handbook* (London: Guardian Books, 2010).
Wells, Tom, *The war within. America's battle over Vietnam* (London: University of California Press, 1994).
Wilson, A.N., *Our times. The age of Elizabeth II* (London: Hutchinson, 2008).
Woodward, Bob, *Plan of attack* (London: Simon & Schuster, 2004).
Wyndham Goldie, Grace, *Facing the nation. Television and politics 1936–1976* (London: The Bodley Head, 1977).

Newspaper articles:

Aaronovitch, David, 'War or peace – blood will still be spilled', *Guardian*, 11 February 2003.

Aaronovitch, David, 'Dear marcher, please answer a few questions', *Guardian*, 18 February 2003.
Aaronovitch, David, 'The real reasons so many are marching', *Guardian*, 25 March 2003.
Bunting, Madeleine, 'We are the people', *Guardian*, 17 February 2003.
Cohen, Nick, 'The Left isn't listening', *Observer*, 16 February 2003.
Cohen, Nick, 'The Left's unholy alliance with religious bigotry', *Observer*, 23 February 2003.
Cohen, Nick, 'The lesson the left has never learnt', *New Statesman*, 21 July 2003.
Hari, Johann, 'The case for war: We must fight to end the Iraqis' suffering', *Independent*, 15 February 2003.
Jenkins, Simon, 'Britain has long been a poor venue for protest – tomorrow won't change this', *Guardian*, 25 March 2011.
Hitchens, Christopher, 'I wanted it to rain on their parade', *Daily Mirror*, 18 February 2003.
Monbiot, George, 'Too much of a good thing', *Guardian*, 18 February 2003.
Steel, Mark, 'Diary', *New Statesman*, 17 February 2003.

Journal articles:

Perks, Rob, 'Corporations are people too!: Business and corporate oral history in Britain', *Oral History*, Spring 2010, pp. 36–54.
Phillips, Richard, 'Standing together: the Muslim Association of Britain and the anti-war movement', *Race & Class*, 2008, Vol. 50(2), pp. 101–113.
Rafeek, Neil, Bertie, Angela and Young, Hilary, 'Scotland and 'the coalition for justice not war' march, Glasgow, 15 February 2003', *Oral History*, Autumn 2004, pp. 73–85.
Yaqoob, Salma, 'Global and local echoes of the anti-war movement: a British Muslim perspective', *International Socialism*, October 2004, Issue 100.

Ward, Patrick, 'Operation end your freedom', *Socialist Review*, July/August 2008, pp, 18-20.

Audio and video:

'British anti-war rally Feb, 15 2003', *C-Span video library*, www.c-spanvideo.org/program/175139–1 [Accessed 24 September 2012].

'Stop the War march – February 15th 2003'. Audio recording of the march and rally made by John Gardner with Steve Ruby.

Thomas, Mark, *The night war broke out* (Laughing Stock Productions, 2004).

Newspapers consulted at the British Library Newspaper Reading Room:

Daily Mail

Daily Mirror

Daily Telegraph

Guardian

Independent

Independent on Sunday

Morning Star

Observer

News of the World

Sun

Sunday Mail

Sunday Mirror

Sunday Telegraph

Sunday Times

Times

INDEX OF TESTIMONIES